PUBLISHING CONTRACTS AND THE POST NEGOTIATION SPACE

Many writers dream of having their work published by a respected publishing house but don't always understand publishing contract terms – what they mean for the contracting parties and how they inform book-publishing practice. In turn, publishers struggle to satisfy authors' creative expectations against the industry's commercial demands. This book challenges our perceptions of these author–publisher power imbalances by recasting the publishing contract as a cultural artefact capable of adapting to the industry's changing landscape. Based on a three-year study of publishing negotiations, Katherine Day reveals how relational contract theory provides possibilities for future negotiations in what she describes as a 'post negotiation space'.

Drawing on the disciplines of cultural studies, law, publishing studies and cultural sociology, this book reveals a unique perspective from publishing professionals and authors within the post negotiation space, presenting the editor as a fundamental agent in the formation and application of publishing's contractual terms.

Katherine Day is an academic and book editor with over fifteen years of experience in the publishing industry. Her research interests include publishing and editorial practice, book audiences and reception, and publishing contracts.

PUBLISHING CONTRACTS AND THE POST NEGOTIATION SPACE

Lifting the Lid on Publishing's Black Box of Aspirations, Laws and Money

Katherine Day

Routledge
Taylor & Francis Group
LONDON AND NEW YORK

Designed cover image: © Getty

First published 2023
by Routledge
4 Park Square, Milton Park, Abingdon, Oxon OX14 4RN

and by Routledge
605 Third Avenue, New York, NY 10158

Routledge is an imprint of the Taylor & Francis Group, an informa business

British Library Cataloguing-in-Publication Data
A catalogue record for this book is available from the British Library

Library of Congress Cataloging-in-Publication Data
A catalog record has been requested for this book

ISBN: 9781032373539 (hbk)
ISBN: 9781032373522 (pbk)
ISBN: 9781003336570 (ebk)

DOI: 10.4324/9781003336570

Typeset in Bembo
by Apex CoVantage, LLC

CONTENTS

FIGURES

1

INTRODUCTION

Picture this scene from the office of nineteenth-century Boston publisher Roberts Brothers: Louisa May Alcott sits on one side of a large, official-looking desk, opposite Thomas Niles, a gruff, hard-nosed businessman, reader and publisher, who edits authors' manuscripts before their eyes, striking his swordlike quill through careful, heart-rendered prose. Alcott's offering this time is *Little Women* – a book that would become an American classic, as well as a cherished and popular read to the modern day. Neither Niles nor Alcott knows this at the time, and in an attempt to minimise the economic risk of taking on board a relatively new and untested novelist (Alcott had only since published short stories), Niles challenges Alcott's unconventional ending, in which the story's point-of-view character, Jo March, remains unmarried – a 'literary spinster' (Myerson & Shealy 1995, xxvii). Niles is resolute, claiming readers will want a romantic ending in which Jo finds success *and* love. Alcott concedes, though with a plan to put her own twist on that finale. During negotiations about the contract's terms, Niles suggests a 5 per cent royalty and full copyright of the work; Alcott bargains up to a 6.6 per cent royalty and retains ownership of the work but licenses rights to the publisher. The rest, as they say, is history.

This is the ending of the 2019 movie *Little Women*, the negotiation (portrayed as a meta-narrative of Alcott's experience through Jo March) within the screenplay of the novel. The real-life ending, according to some scholars (Madison 1974; Elbert 1987) and Alcott's correspondence (Myerson & Shealy 1995), conveys a different picture: Niles was, by account, generous to his authors, offering cash bonuses on top of royalties to successful novelists 'in his eagerness to retain their goodwill' (Madison 1974, 38). It had also been Niles' idea for Alcott to write a book that would appeal to young female readers. Alcott had not been enamoured with the suggestion but reluctantly acquiesced. Despite finding the first draft of *Little Women* 'dull', positive feedback from a number of readers was enough for Niles to make an offer. Unlike the movie's rendition of events, Niles in fact encouraged Alcott to retain copyright, for which the author was grateful some seventeen years later when she wrote of Niles that he was an 'honest publisher' (Madison 1974, 37). The success of *Little Women* took them both by surprise, and Niles was particularly generous in his cash bonuses to Alcott, whom he considered his 'greatest find' (Madison 1974, 38).

DOI:10.4324/9781003336570-1

The movie version of this negotiation is a fiction and a fantasy. It renders the author proactive in their negotiation of the contract's terms and the publisher tyrannical in their approach to the author's rights as sole creator and owner of the work – seemingly without reason. The portrayal of the publisher, in particular, is a narrative that has been perpetuated, especially in recent times, with larger publishing conglomerates having more money and power to dictate the terms of author contracts. It's more likely that the publisher would not be so heavy-handed in their dealings with authors who could potentially be their 'greatest find', and the author would be unlikely to challenge the publisher (not without an agent, anyway) or know enough about the terms of the contract to understand what, exactly, they were negotiating. We know this to be the case with the real story between Alcott and Niles, and it is still so in the present day for many writers. As exciting as it is to witness an author fighting for their rights so decisively, and to depict the publisher as a convenient and colourful villain, the truth is much more complex and nuanced.

Publishing contract negotiations in fact provide two very different narratives: one is an official record of the contract's terms; the other is an ongoing conversation about what is possible in getting the book made, and what might change in the process. The latter is precarious and involves human interactions separate to the written document. It is a relationship of trust in an industry that uniquely combines culture and commerce and has evolved in a way not normally associated with standard business practices. Publishing, therefore, cannot be studied in the same way as other businesses; the contracts that bind the parties to publishing transactions also cannot be explored utilising standard analytical tools only, or by reference to legal contract theory alone. Understanding how contracts work in commercial book publishing requires a close relationship with the field itself and a deep understanding of how the players within it operate. While this book focuses on publishing contracts specifically, the research outcomes and discussions can be applied to many creative industries that are subject to the same challenges as publishing. These might be the fine arts, dramatic arts, music and design industries, where market demands are dynamic and changeable, and where relationships underpin the agreements that form the contract's terms. For this book, however, the focus is publishing, and the contents provide a distinct perspective on publishing contract negotiations because they combine objective analysis of the official document alongside learned experience of the industry. One cannot be studied without the other, but publishing studies' scholarly research to date focuses on the author–publisher relationship alone, without consideration of the legal foundation upon which it operates; for legal studies, the contract is viewed separately to its relational complexities.

As a book editor, a lecturer in publishing studies and a communications law graduate, I am in a rare position to be able to combine close analysis of the legal terms of publishing agreements and existing research around publishing negotiations, within a framework of knowledge from actual practice. In doing so I have discovered that editors and publishers facilitate the negotiations that this study explores, and do so flexibly. These negotiations are not confined to conversations around the craft of writing, as most previous research on author–editor relationships dictates; this research reveals how these negotiations focus on authors' livelihoods and the expression of the work within the publishing industry more broadly, and how those who work in publishing facilitate opportunities for authors as opposed to obstructing them via rigid legal frameworks. That is not to say that the facilitation is uncomplicated. Each book presents its own set of opportunities and challenges, and I have found that the most effective way to explain how the process transpires is through my own editorial lens.

My study, therefore, is decidedly autoethnographic, informed by my personal perspective of publishing agreements and negotiations alongside a three-year investigation of contract negotiations via a survey and in-depth interviews.

My study begins from this point of knowledge but not from this point in time. My interest in publishing contract negotiations began over a decade ago when I became an accidental author in a particular editorial project. From that time, many more observations from a number of different perspectives – through freelance editing with both small and large publishers to my role as a mentor for aspirational writers – have prompted further investigation. I have realised that contracts tell stories about books, but these stories are not immediately apparent. As they say in editing, it's sometimes about what's *not* there. I've witnessed the conversations and struggles within the industry, which have illuminated how each clause and section echoes the author–publisher power dynamic.

What is revealed is steeped in historical practice and revolves around art, money and laws. The publishing contract has the capacity to fulfil or repress cultural and creative endeavours; however, in practice, it's hardly even looked at. It's a mystery – much like the operations of publishing houses are often a mystery for authors, particularly emerging or new authors. For many writers, publishing houses are fascinating, industrious spaces, where quick, pragmatic decisions are made alongside deliberate appraisal and development. Yet they are also insular; they are closed sites where the publisher, design team, production, sales and marketing and rights departments – all at the coalface of the creative synthesis – collaborate on a shared vision for each title. Somewhat surprisingly, the author is often absent from this process.

To the author these 'in-house' processes are intangible, but they have also contractually entrusted their work to the people within, and they hope it is respected, nurtured and distributed to its readers in the way they envisage. There is usually a vision for the book – a vision supposedly agreed upon via a list of promises and their acceptance; or, at the least, the parties will consent to the penalties for breaching those promises. Yet without the benefit of being 'inside', the author has no way of knowing if *their* plan for their book is the same as the publisher's. The trust the author places in their publisher is, for want of a better word, a 'gentleman's agreement': despite the minutiae of the contract, there is faith that the publisher will take the financial risk for the project and the author the creative risk. And though this agreement is also stipulated in the written terms of the contract, how it is understood explicitly can only be mapped out through the process of editing and producing the work. The more corporate the world of publishing becomes, the more concrete the barrier between the spaces inside and outside, and the gentleman's agreement more important than ever.

It would be remiss of me not to raise the gendered use of this term, which harkens back to a time when mainly men were publishers – gatekeepers to good literature and tastemakers for voracious readers. Nowadays the industry is predominantly female-oriented (Couper 2016, 27), and the relationships with authors still quite personal. Jason Epstein, famed American publisher and editor of authors such as Norman Mailer, Vladimir Nabokov, E.L. Doctorow, Philip Roth and Gore Vidal, describes Random House during the 60s as a more relaxed and personalised workplace where authors frequented the publishing office, sometimes slept in the office, and where editors had stronger relationships with their authors than they did their colleagues (Epstein 2001, 6). This is also not unlike the Lane Brothers of Penguin in the early part of the twentieth century, who used the bathroom at their Talbot Square flat as a meeting room and the centre of operations for their successful publishing house (Kells 2015, 112). Robin Freeman describes the 'courting rituals' between publishers and authors as deeply personal and that 'the exchanges . . . can sometimes lead to a lasting friendship between a writer and their editor' (Freeman 2001, 105). In the early days of commercial publishing, these relationships perhaps seemed more prominent, not just at Penguin Books or Random House. No doubt even in the contemporary industry, this is the way business is done in smaller houses.

The passion to nurture, produce and disseminate the written word has historically transcended the predictable confines of the corporate world, and the creative efforts of the writers *and* the publishing staff working together have, on occasion, tested those corporate barriers. Publishing staff are not just passionate about writing; they are highly trained and highly motivated (Thompson 2012, 6), often working for little pay. The work is vocational, creative and deeply rewarding, but it is not, and never has been, relative to some other businesses, lucrative (Epstein 2001, 6). Particularly in Australia, 'the industry still struggles to justify its importance to government, cultural and institutional bodies . . . to coordinate and finance a sustained strategy to address the major supply-chain issues that continue to undermine the profitability of the industry' (Richards 2016, 172).

Not quite shaking its cottage-industry roots, the people who publish books nevertheless find inventive opportunities beyond the margins. But perhaps the deeply human side of publishing and the connection of authors to the internal operations of the business have faded, at least for the most desirable publishers with the best resources and transnational reach. Many opine that this passion and dedication has dwindled with multinational conglomerates and companies with shareholders securing more of the market. Epstein describes when Random House became corporate in the 90s: 'In these new quarters with their carpeted offices we still operated independently of RCA, at least in theory, but a cottage industry within an industrial conglomerate makes no sense' (Epstein 2001, 8). More books are being published, there are fewer in-house editors as publishers merge and cut costs, and digital technology has transformed the sense of closeness – of family – that Epstein romanticises: the face-to-face contact. Word-processing tools and online software allow editors and authors to email back and forth their drafts and notes, for example (Freeman 2001, 115). Most books are almost entirely edited online – evidence of yet another barrier to the author connecting with their publisher. Attempts to regain what is lost, via nostalgia alone, seem disingenuous when the well-oiled publishing machine with its many cogs gains momentum. Even in a small, independent publishing house, you'll have to schedule a meeting, and there'll be a receptionist who asks you to sign in before someone comes to collect you. That's if you get a meeting in the first place. For an author this barrier is strongest at submission stage: just getting your life's work onto a publisher's desk is achievement itself. Who does it go to next? What will they do with it? As if that didn't make an author feel distant enough, once (and if) the work has been accepted, everyone has an opinion on what will happen to it – like a 'picked robin' Jo March exclaimed after having cut her masterpiece down by a third on the recommendation of the publisher, '[laying] her first-born on her table and [chopping] it up as ruthlessly as any ogre' (Alcott 1989, 270–71).

Susan Greenberg broaches the enigmatic practice of 'what happens next' by stating that '[t]he invisibility of production has an impact on our access to important detail, including that of specific, lived experience' (Greenberg 2018, 155), the lived experience being the shared and communicated act of negotiating the creation of a book. In the seemingly covert operations shrouded by industry jargon, specific workflow processes and a hierarchy not immediately evident, editors can still, of anyone in publishing, provide some communication between the author and other professionals in the in-house space. Not gatekeepers as such – their role is key-holder and ally. In a rather dubious comparison with base assumptions to the now more female-oriented profession, they have also been likened to midwives (Gross 1993) and workers in the 'cleaning and repairing business' (Commins 1978), responsible for 'mending' the manuscripts. They can also facilitate communication when authors' moral rights are challenged by commercial considerations. Author George R. R. Martin highlights the breadth of the editor's role and their importance to an author's career:

> A good editor offers you decent advances, and goes to bat with his publisher to make sure your book gets promoted, and returns your phone calls, and answers your letters. A good editor does work with his writers on their books. But only if the books need work. A good editor tries to figure out what the writer was trying to do, and helps him or her to do it better, rather than trying to change the book into something else entirely.
>
> (Martin 1979)

When I discuss the role of editors in this book, it is with the view that the sole editor is part of a larger editorial team. The editor might also be the publisher, and the publisher the commissioning editor. In some publishing houses, this distinction is even less apparent and could involve freelance editors, or perhaps the editing work has been completed by an assistant editor under supervision. So 'editor' in this study has quite a broad scope, and I utilise a range of terms to describe it: the editor, the publisher, the editor–publisher or publisher–editor, and the acquisitions editor. The editor can also be part of an editorial team that might include all the aforementioned roles. Freeman reiterates this interchangeability: [An editor]

> is someone who works for a publishing organisation, either as a commissioning editor . . . or . . . someone who takes a hands-on editorial role', and a publisher is 'the person . . . with responsibility for creating a particular list of titles, overseeing writing, design and production, and . . . marketing and sales of each title. Often this role is interchangeable with the role of commissioning editor.
>
> (Freeman 2001, 106)

On this point, it is necessary to also observe that the publisher can be viewed as an individual who works with creators to fine-tune their work and transform it into a book, but that the publisher is also a company or organisation that then takes that book and disseminates it to readers. Viewed distinctly as an individual, whichever term is being used, the operative word is 'hands-on' – the editor–publisher who works closely with the author on their vision for the book (as opposed to the more distant roles of the publicist and designer, for example).

The editor's influence and support will extend to promoting the work, too – to boosting the author's ego and to championing the work in-house. Additionally, and probably of most importance, editors offer writers their time. Time can be perceived differently: time can be a gift for authors when it allows them the freedom to finesse their text without rushing, and editors can negotiate more time for authors to do this; editors can spend time with authors to help them navigate the publishing process; editors can also manage time in-house, potentially facilitating opportunities for the author as a result. These time-related activities are not all connected to editing the written word. Most of an editor's activities reduce the time they are allocated to the text. Martin's quote cited earlier might even have us believe that writers do not want editors to touch their text at all. Susan Juby elaborates: 'Clearly, while the alteration of a word or two may not seem like a big issue to an editor who is short for time, such changes are seen by writers as a form of vandalism' (Juby 2005, 17). The perception of time, therefore, is fraught when seen through the individual lenses of the author and editor. Walter H Page also offered a more complex image of an editor's value: 'Almost every writer wishes to consult somebody. If they do not wish advice, they at least wish sympathy' (Greenberg 2018 quoting Walter, 97). Therefore, time to listen, understand and assist outside of the text is paramount to a more balanced author–publisher relationship, especially when the author is conflicted with their publishing house.

After a publishing contract is signed, the editor assists the author to maintain integrity in the work by way of balancing the publishing house's vision with the writer's sometimes contrasting vision, to manage expectations and to communicate in-house workflow processes, and to mediate disagreements. They are also integral to the success of the publishing list, assessing incoming manuscripts and proposals for their suitability to the house as well as their viability in the market (Thompson 2012, 144). The editors' and publishers' involvement in the whole process is the glue that binds the industrial to the aspirational. This is why the editorial team are in the best position to facilitate and negotiate the relationship an author has with their publishing house.

Though this relationship often begins with the signed contract, a change in circumstances can affect the terms originally set. The industry is iterative, evolving and idiosyncratic when confronted with a complex eco-system of digital advancement, new consumer pathways, economic and policy upheavals. Throughout my career, I have witnessed many disruptions and developments in publishing, one of the most devastating being the REDgroup collapse and an unforgiving exchange rate (for booksellers) during 2011 (Lim 2011), which fundamentally shifted the acquisitions choices made at the multinational for which I was then working. Discount department stores had become the biggest retail avenue for books, after growth from 24.8 per cent in 2007 to 35.8 in 2012 (Kong 2014, 40). My employer at the time utilised this market to the best of its ability, targeting the DDS and appeasing its buyers (Li 2010). As Foong Ling Kong wrote at the time: 'Publishers do what they can to ensure the package looks "DDS enough" for the stores' (Kong 2014, 41).

The editorial department in which I worked began to look at the list in a different light – cutting back on big-risk acquisitions and instead looking at the backlist to see what could be reissued and rebooted into a fresh market. Money for jam, so to speak. Non-fiction had already been on the rise, so anything from cookbooks to craft, wellness to sport and leisure, and memoir and biography suddenly became more viable. This non-fiction demand has been documented: an Australian study of non-fiction sales of books in the first decade of the noughties showed that 'biographies and autobiographies comprise roughly 18.8–21.5 per cent of the total top 5000' (Zwar 2013, 4). Digital developments have forced writers and publishers to rethink how to exploit the rights they have licensed and sub-licensed (Clark & Phillips 2014); sophisticated self-publishing platforms question the publisher as the key gatekeeper of literary decision-making (Levey 2016). Other entertainment streams have usurped reading as a prime leisure activity. Who would have foreseen the explosion of video streaming platforms traditional publishing now contends with, not to mention the array of content on a variety of different reading platforms, audio being one strong example? The gentleman's agreement from the nineteenth century that we still staunchly advocate stems from a cultural and social intersection starkly different to today.

The skillset needed to navigate the field now is informed and highly intuitive. A publisher's and editor's expertise nowadays does not stop at reading and assessing. They must also possess business acumen and an exceptional understanding of the market. Unlike other media that can rely on advertising to generate revenue, books rely solely on their financial return (Curtain 1993, 105). Publishers must make money as well as content – to be able to continue to create content. However, one doesn't always translate to the other – the eternal publishing dichotomy. As one publisher in this study relayed: '[W]e're burning our butts every day. And without going into it, the financial state of the industry at the moment is not good. It takes one bestseller to keep the whole frigging company afloat. . . . So if you don't find that bestseller . . . you are in all sorts of trouble.'

The 'bestseller', however, is a term riddled with uncertainty and differing interpretations, notoriously difficult to define. A bestseller could simply be higher-than-expected sales for a book that was considered 'quiet', in which case the sales might be far fewer than a Dan Brown and therefore comparatively very small. How do publishers view sales of 10,000 compared with 20,000? Perhaps bestseller is not an economic imperative but a question of transnational reach (Driscoll & Rehberg Sedo 2020, 245). As John Thompson says: 'What counts as a "big book" may differ from one agent to another and one house to another, but all agents and all houses want them' (Thompson 2012, 87). Regardless, publishers must make money to be able to afford to publish the small books as well as the big books; rather than print more books, it is more efficient to publish books that will sell.

Many authors, too, want to publish a 'big book' and believe that their book has the potential to be the one the publisher hangs their hopes on. The author might not be ready for the brutal economic reality of where their work is positioned in the market or for the inversion of their authorial significance when 'the value of the book corresponds to the economic investment in its promotion' (Glass 2004, 12). Such promotion could be in stark contrast to how the author views their work. From an editor in the study: 'Every author has Harry Potter on their hearts. That's what they imagine it could be'. Unfortunately, not every work *is* a Harry Potter. And, alternatively, a Harry Potter-type work might not be what the author had in mind anyway. There is good reason, therefore, for authors to feel anxious when the plan for their book isn't explicitly articulated to them – again that sense of being shut out of the decision-making process. Anne Richards describes this decision-making as having no definition or clear measure: 'There is no standard formula for these evaluation and endorsement processes; there is no valid measure of consistency – unless it is the final sales figures' (Richards 2016, 170).

I was fortunate to have an author experience, which is detailed in the next part of this introduction, and which also forms part of my direct involvement and observation of the post negotiation space from which this study of contracts was formed.

Reflections on a contract negotiation

In 2011, the year of the REDgroup collapse, I authored, and had published, a non-fiction title of my own. The experience changed my perspective of the author–editor relationship in a fundamental way and prompted me to think more critically about the author's and editor's roles in the publishing process.

I had pitched my idea at our monthly editorial meeting in late 2009, riding on the non-fiction wave with a project that initially proposed a collection of craft projects gathered from well-known 'crafty' people, with a one-off payment for each of the contributors. The one-off payments facilitated a series of simple contracts with no royalties and, hence, all money coming back to the publisher. A similar set of books of projects incorporating handcrafted soft toys had been commissioned from the Business Development (BD) department at the publishing house and was, at the time, a roaring success. Not to be outdone by the BD department or miss the crafty bandwagon, I set about costing the project.

It was while I was collecting potential crafts for the title that I realised I could write the book myself, and once that seed had been planted I kept feeding it until a week or so later when I struck up the courage to ask my publisher if I could write it. Reflecting on this moment I recall a startling shift in my own thinking, from confidant and resourceful editor to apologetic and insecure author. I had never had any desire to be an author. I admire writers for their tenacity and for their unflinching dedication to their craft – often without adequate payment.[1] To this day I still have no desire to be a writer, but this project had me in its grip and I felt responsible to it because I had conceived the idea and could therefore take more ownership of it. However, it was also a business proposition, and I would be able to separate my vision for it from what the publisher would decide to do with it. This presented a unique position for me: as an insider to the operations of the publishing house, I was acutely aware of workflow processes as well as the particular expertise of the publishing house – I knew the editors were excellent, and I knew that the design and production would be of a high quality; I also knew that sales and marketing could be fickle if the title was deemed 'unworthy' of an exhaustive sales and marketing plan. This is a view shared by Hugh Rawson, who states that '[t]he crucial, initial view that the company's sales reps receive of a book and of the size and composition of the audience for it comes from the sponsoring editor' (Rawson 1983, 275). My editor would be constrained by the 'size and composition' of the audience, as I had been for many of the titles I had edited. Still, I also knew that there was often a firm rationale for any sales and marketing plan based on this assessment of its audience, which was often undeniable. I was also working shoulder-to-shoulder with the people who would be producing the title if it was successful at 'acquisitions' (the meeting where decisions are made about what does and does not get published). I had a specific lived experience via my inside role in the company. While this should have made me feel powerful, instead I felt vulnerable. Luckily, the publisher thought it was a profitable idea.

Before a book goes to acquisitions, there are many steps taken to give it the best chance of being accepted at that meeting. This is a process undertaken by the editor if the author has not provided details about the format, cover design or any other distinguishing feature that tends to indicate the book's position in the market. It is a process Greenberg describes as 'discovery', with the editor acting as the intermediary:

> The intermediary might develop an idea from scratch and then give it to someone else for development or help a writer who brings in an idea to determine its overall direction. . . . Discovery can also occur in the list building of a publisher (through an acquisitions or commissioning editor), the creation of anthologies and series, the assembling of a recognisable group of contributors, the drafting of house style and the guidance for contributors and the definition of forms and sub-genres of content.
>
> (Greenberg 2018, 16)

Revisiting this process from an academic perspective, it is clear to me that what Greenberg refers to as 'discovery' forms part of what I now term 'pre negotiation' towards contract. In 'pre negotiation',[2] an author's ideas are developed, refined and rationalised within the business operations of the publishing house. The editor's and publisher's aims are to get the project accepted. To do that, they must justify the reasons they want to commission the work – its literary merit and its viability in the market. If it's not likely to be profitable, they must focus on its value to the cultural aims of the publishing house and sell its benefits to the list overall. Thompson affirms the level of knowledge that the contemporary editor now assumes: 'The importance of sales and the market is not something that is imposed on recalcitrant editors . . . it is something that editors themselves have internalised and incorporated into their practices' (Thompson 2012, 15). The decisions made in this 'pre negotiation' space have lasting effects: the pitch becomes a rhetoric that is perpetuated from the publishing director to the bookseller. Sometimes a publisher will walk into acquisitions with a specific idea and come out with an entirely different project. An author is never there to speak for themselves, and in their absence many decisions are made that inform the expectations of the book, which in turn inform the reasons behind it being contracted. While a contract doesn't even exist at this stage, the foundations are set for the level of investment from the company. Most of the time, the author isn't even aware that such a meeting exists.

Knowing how these meetings transpired, I set about being as specific as possible about the book idea even though I would not be physically present: it would be a Z-format and have a matte finish with simple illustrations and maybe even spiral binding. Also knowing the process involved in creating a book, I set to work putting together mock cover designs. I created separate files of the internal artwork and some photos of the projects in case they decided to use them instead of illustrations. I suggested the spiral binding, claiming that it would be 'easy to use' and 'lie flat when you are following the instructions', but I knew it was unlikely to be approved, given the cost of such a luxury feature. I also anticipated a handmade look and feel with a retro vibe (which turned out to be very on trend the following year after the success of Pip Lincolne's *Meet Me at Mike's*) (2012). In addition, I offered some comparisons – the closest was *The Crafty Minx* by Kelly Doust (2009).

The project was accepted at acquisitions. I assumed that the manuscript I had submitted was fully approved in the way it was presented, but I had no idea if this was the case. When I received my letter of offer, the description read, 'A non-fiction craft book (with photographs and illustrations) with step-by-step instructions on how to make simple projects without a sewing machine'. Delivery and approval proffered a little more information:

> The Proprietor undertakes to deliver to the Publisher . . . a clean typescript of the Work as described above . . . consisting of sufficient instructional text for approximately 16 craft projects together with sufficient step-by-step instructional illustrations and colour photographs in a form suitable for publication, for a book of 120 pages, as requested by and agreed with the Publisher.

Terms such as 'clean manuscript', 'sufficient' and 'suitable for publication' are subjective yet still dependent on key milestones, which can be flexible when you are aware of the production schedule and the team working on the project. But now, wearing an author's hat and without being able to snoop around inside another editor's files, these terms seemed vague. I wasn't sure what conversations had transpired at acquisitions and why the book suddenly incorporated both illustrations *and* photography.

Up until signing my own contract, my knowledge of contracts had focused around a few key areas: I knew delivery dates were important because without the finished manuscript you could not create the production schedule. The quality of the final draft was also important for the same reason. In addition to the delivery dates, the contract can sometimes offer the editor other valuable information such as price point, format and extent (though all of this information is not always available at the time). The other areas of copyright tended to interest me only if the title I was working on was being sold into other territories, or if there had been some negotiation around territories in subsequent books. Publishers always want to be able to exploit as many rights as possible, but savvy authors and authors with agents can sometimes wish to keep some territories to sell the work themselves. This has sometimes had the effect of straining the author–publisher relationship – on occasion to its eventual detriment. Limiting territories can be frustrating for a publishing team that has put many hours' work into the book. I therefore considered that offering world rights for my own title (or accepting the request for world rights) would be the right thing to do.

I was familiar with my publishing house's boilerplate contract and the expected terms of rights and the proportion of royalties. Based on my own costings of titles, I gauged an appropriate advance for my book – the minimum I was likely to receive. But armed with the ability to access a bounty of contracts, I spent an afternoon snooping around the old compactus where all the hardcopy files were kept. I imagine it's digital now, but back then you could get lost in the compactus (and sometimes even squashed if rights and permissions hurriedly rolled the wheel too quickly and sandwiched you in between L and M – or whichever aisle you happened to be in).

After reading a few more contracts, I had a clearer idea of many things in general – of who the publisher had invested in, who they hadn't invested in – and my suspicions of a fairly inflexible boilerplate were confirmed. There were a few random clauses pertaining to sales and marketing plans that diverged from the boilerplate. Each book is part of a larger list, and the sales, marketing and publicity teams have only so many resources they can allocate. With such experience and knowledge of the industry, publishers also know which books are selling and to whom. They will base their costings on these factors. Rawson says, 'After publication, the editor-marketer will keep at work, continually reminding people in the sales, rights, advertising and promotion departments of what can be done to support particular titles' (Rawson 1983, 276). But sometimes, despite all attempts to persuade, a publisher will have other ideas. Editors also know that you can't flog a dead horse, which is the difference between enthusiasm and delusion. Glancing over royalties and rights clauses, I could see that they stayed pretty firm. I knew even then that I could possibly negotiate a rising royalty, however. I also knew that an exact description of the book, and the look and feel, could likely be negotiated during the design process after the contract was signed. But this would hang on the vision. The look and feel of the book were important to me; I had a clear idea of my reader and what they would like to see.

It turns out that I didn't negotiate a thing. The book's specs were defined at a production meeting I never attended; the title was allocated to an editor and a designer, who attended meetings that, again, I did not attend. My job in this project was to write the book. I was now, clearly, on the outside. At the time of signing the contract, I was concerned that if I became too difficult about potential negotiations the publisher would lose interest. How often had I heard authors say the same thing? I had some hope that the book would sell, but I resigned myself to the fact that I knew publishing was a business of risk-taking and that there are no guarantees.

However, I felt I could have some control over the look of the book because I was working in close proximity to the people involved – the designer, editor and production team. Although I was an outsider, I was still within. I therefore went along with most of the decisions. An anxious author can impede progress and I didn't want to be *that author*. At the same time, I became acutely aware of how authors can be alienated from their own works. While I was grateful to the publishing team for their dedication, I also only *trusted* that they would understand my vision of the work and ensure it was reflected in the finished product. I experienced an unexpected sense of loss during this handover – a loss of intimacy with the work. It had now become a 'group' project. As an editor this feels okay: your titles are group projects from the outset because you don't create them; there is never a time when another individual is not involved. For the author who conceives the idea and has been working on it as a sole creator, this transferral – from author to the group – is unsettling.

One of the first things to happen that affirmed my outside position was that the company decided to change the title. Amusingly, my editor/colleague used editor-speak to tell me this: 'We want your wonderful title to have the best chance possible'. How could I argue with that? 'Of course!' I said. 'Whatever you think is best!' It all sounded so familiar, yet it was different being at the receiving end. The next thing to happen was a little more concerning. Everyone in publishing knows that costing a title successfully is finding the sweet spot – the balance of the number of copies and the price of the book. The bigger the print-run the cheaper you can price your book. The price per unit is also impacted by the cost of production, obviously. When the team returned from the program meeting, they were cautiously optimistic. The book had been priced at $24.95 and was going to be a perfect-bound paperback of 144 pages (24 more pages than I had stipulated in my brief) in 4-colour with a gloss lamination, as roughly prescribed in the contract.

I knew they had decided to make the book a lot more commercial than I had anticipated (based on the gloss lamination, 4-colour and perfect binding). For that reason, the price point was doomed. At $24.95 it would be too expensive for the Scholastic book club, which, if locked in as a firm sale at a discount, has the dual benefit of providing exposure to a large customer base and a higher volume of sales than would otherwise be anticipated. This was confirmed in the staff kitchenette (which was often the meeting room outside the meeting room) by the sales and marketing manager. My original vision of the handcrafted and retro look for this title was out the window. Some comparisons had been made, but they felt much more commercial. This was not surprising to me, and this decision did not concern me either. I knew that the publisher would likely see more opportunities for the title in this format, and after the global financial crisis of 2007–2008, it was not the time to be trying to promote something that hadn't been done before.

My position (as outsider within) allowed me some objectivity, which a true outsider would not benefit from. For a true outsider, there is no fully rounded perspective from which to adapt your creative view. Roberta Rosenthal Kwall describes this in terms of moral rights: 'When a work of authorship is understood as an embodiment of the author's personal meaning and message, the author's desire to maintain the original form and content of her work becomes manifest' (Rosenthal Kwall 2010, xiii). Kwall also highlights the effect on a writer when unilateral decisions are made about the work's appearance: 'It is human nature to care about how one's product is packaged for external consumption. And when the packaging violates the original author's vision of the work's meaning and message, there is an assault to the author's dignity' (Rosenthal Kwall 2010, 4). But while decisions were made about my title that I did not agree with, I was able to separate my personal meaning and message from the project as a business proposition, which is a perspective an author who does not work in-house is perhaps less likely to possess. This level of objectivity comes from an understanding of why decisions in publishing are made and that the outcome is reflective of the reasons why the publisher was first interested in the book. This is not always effectively communicated to authors, if at all. But it is fundamental to both parties' agreement to the plan for the book and their level of satisfaction with those decisions.

Next, I received some cover concepts. Cover concepts are decided upon very early because, again, the cover helps to position the book clearly in the market. My contract had stated the following: 'The views of the Proprietor concerning jacket design and copy will be welcomed and taken into consideration but the publisher reserves the right to make the final decision on all such matters'. I knew how hard the in-house designers worked to produce covers in line with the company's vision of each book. Cover meetings are notoriously tricky, but the experts present – directors of publishing and sales and marketing – have to be respected for their wealth of knowledge about what will and won't sell. Knowing this, I told my editor that I was pleased with all the cover concepts, and I then chose one. Again, I didn't want to 'rock the boat', but I also had a professional awareness and respect for the editor's and designer's positions. Once I had accepted the commercial vision, I switched back into business mode: it was not my life's work, after all. I had to remind myself that it had been a 'money-for-jam' title in its original incarnation when I had the idea of simply paying contributors a flat fee for their craft projects. There was definitely an opportunity to reject the concepts if I truly hated them. I had experienced these conversations many times during my career, and the publisher always capitulated. But the author's win was not often easy. There would be a number of conversations in which the editor and publisher would try to convince the author to accept a specific cover.

In revisiting this period from an academic perspective, I realise that many of the decisions about the book were made after signing the contract. Contrary to how it is perceived outside of the publishing house, I have observed that contract negotiations do not stop after the contract is signed. Rather, ongoing conversations that bend to a book's successes and failures, and determine a title's life in the publishing realm, continue. While this journey through my own author experience has focused on the appearance of the book, many other aspects of the contract can also be revisited. These include areas such as rights and royalties: the parties to the contract often cannot predict the industry or global changes that might affect the contract's terms, or account for all eventualities. The ongoing business relationship is more important than the fine print, and the parties find themselves adjusting terms to ensure they can continue to work together. Judge Michael McHugh JA said in *Integrated Computer Services Pty Ltd v Digital Equipment Corporation (Australia) Pty Ltd*:

> [I]n an ongoing relationship, it is not always easy to point to the precise moment when the legal criteria of the contract have been fulfilled. . . . In a dynamic commercial relationship new terms will be added or will supersede older terms. It is necessary therefore to look at the whole relationship not only what was said and done when the relationship was first formed.

There were many conversations between me, my editor and my publisher. One involved a US sale of the title with an underwhelming royalty cut – well below the norm but with a substantial print-run. Knowing how difficult it can be to get these deals over the line, I was quite content to sign the additional contract in order to simply pay out my advance. I knew my colleagues in the rights department had put time and effort into this negotiation, balancing its importance relative to the whole list. The rights assistant had pushed for a higher royalty, but the US publisher had resisted. It was a situation of take it or leave it.

The experience gave me insight into how little control an author has in the negotiations around their contract and what happens to their book after the contract is signed. Negotiations can and *do* happen, however, and the space where they take place is fluid but constrained by what the market for books dictates. I have defined these spaces in line with the dual narratives I presented at the beginning of this introduction:

Pre negotiation, where discussions around what might be included in the contract take place;

Post negotiation, where discussions about what has transpired and what is possible take place after the contract has been signed.

While 'pre negotiation' is important to set out the basic agreement and the terms upon which the book is produced, it is the 'post negotiation' space where my investigation is primarily focused. Of contracts, Albert Greco states that 'both sides have much to gain and lose whenever an agreement is executed; each party needs the other. So both of them surrender some control, some semblance of "sovereignty" to the other in order to have a business relationship that will profit both sides' (Greco 2005, 149). While this statement holds true for most contract negotiations, it is impossible in publishing to anticipate all the events that might influence a book's success (or not) or an author–publisher relationship into the future. It is also impossible to ascertain the level of knowledge an author brings to negotiations. In my own contract negotiations – both pre and post – I surrendered some control, knowing that in doing so I would make my publisher's life a little easier. But I am an exception, given my close contact with 'insiders' and with the process. In hindsight I can see that my own authors pushed back when they needed to, querying the process because they didn't understand the terms of the contract or the processes that they felt alienated by. What is agreed to at the time of signing is inevitably open to misinterpretation or misunderstanding. Greco summarises:

> Do contractual words and phrases stand 'as is'? Is there a possibility that a section could be 'interpreted' in a slightly different way? Are there 'industry practices' that are not incorporated into the agreement that both parties need to know? If a manuscript is to be delivered on June 1. . . and the author tenders it on July 30. . . was there a breach of contract because the agreement indicated clearly a June 1st submission date? What happens if an author signs an agreement to work with editor 'Z', who then leaves the house? Can the author ask to be released from this contract in order to follow the editor? Can editor 'Z' ask the house for permission to 'take' this author to the new publishing firm? The list of possible issues is literally endless.
>
> (Greco 2005, 150)

But *informed* surrendering is something quite different. With my own project, I knew the potential for misunderstanding from the outset. Therein lies another problem: if you don't ask, if you don't say anything, anything can happen – often things you don't expect or like. What this experience gave me was a clearer picture of how the power imbalance between authors and publishers is created and maintained, and why it happens. But I wanted to also explore the dynamics of this imbalance in some concrete form.

The contract reflects the power dynamic because it is the point at which the relationship begins and the ongoing discussion between author and publisher about what happens to their titles, and why. It is the point at which decisions are made about the vision for the title, the audience reach, and how the author and the book are positioned within the publisher's list. How the contract is used pre negotiation and post negotiation, I believe, is the key to understanding many other things about author–editor relationships. The contract is symbolic of something quite meaningful for the author – an endorsement of their work – as well as being a tool that reflects the business transaction and the title's economic potential. The contract is not just a legally binding agreement; it is an artefact that reflects the positions of the parties and industry norms and developments because it has the potential, being a secondary legal framework, to adapt to the evolving publishing landscape. It encompasses stages within the author–publisher relationship and can be used in-house (though not always) by commissioning editors and publishers to help foster long-term relationships with authors within this dynamic industry. Suchman summarises: 'Like most artifacts, contracts have material uses, and contract provisions often act as practical technologies; but again like most artifacts, contracts also have cultural meanings, and contract provisions sometimes act not as technologies but as symbols' (Suchman 2003, 92). The contract as artefact also presents the contract as a story. Other artefacts – an implement, adornment or natural object – will show markings over time that allude to their stories about who used them and why; a paper document such as a contract can have equally interesting properties that tell its story via the choices of words, the additions and the deletions.

Current contract analyses and copyright law is objective and quantitative, exposing the legal framework and the 'nuts and bolts' of negotiations but not interrogating these choices in the words, additions and deletions specific to publishing. Studies that focus on boilerplate contracts with no further investigation via qualitative research into the negotiations themselves cannot expose the true state of play; rather, they simply point out what is written in the contract according to copyright and contract law and the adjustments made to the boilerplate at the time of signing. Relying only on objective analysis to inform how we improve author–publisher relationships in publishing, and how we can sustain a thriving book industry, is short-sighted. Objective analysis does not factor in shades of grey, incremental change, possibilities; objective analysis, only, is too quantifiable in an area of business that relies on long-term relationships to create cultural products, which are arguably *un*quantifiable. In publishing the aim is, like other businesses, to minimise risk; but publishing success is unpredictable. David Throsby explains:

> books are not articles of commercial merchandise in the same way as footwear, beer or automobiles. Economists interested in the economics of art and culture classify books as cultural goods [but] . . . an objectively measurable cultural value of books, whether expressed in qualitative or quantitative terms, is a task that has challenged literary theorists and cultural economists for many years.
>
> (Throsby 2017, 2; see also Stuart Glover 2016)

The contract that binds the parties to an agreement about the production and dissemination of cultural goods requires a much deeper investigation than has been undertaken to date. I define this activity as taking place not within a 'contract' – as in 'post-contract'; in my view, this activity is a 'space' that is vulnerable to cultural, economic and policy factors and therefore necessarily fluid and flexible. Observing the contract from both a socio-legal and cultural perspective, therefore, helps us to understand how this agreement reflects industry practice and what it means to the parties who contribute to it.

A space of discovery: exploring publishing's black box

The retrospective above provides a personal motivation and narrative segue to researching the contract in more detail. It sets a scene – a premise – from which more questions are formed, and a framework for further investigation, which for me resulted in a three-year study. My findings combine the disciplines of cultural studies, law, publishing studies and cultural sociology in order to capture the differing author and publisher perspectives within contract negotiations, and I discovered that these findings add an important dimension to our understanding of the author–publisher relationship.

Most Australian publishing contracts appear quite rigid, unable to bridge the legal, economic and cultural divide described earlier. Practices and external pressures within the industry simply compound this difficulty. The contract's legal underpinnings contribute to its inflexibility, but this cannot be the sole reason for potentially stymied negotiations. The contract is not concrete until it is agreed upon, and in the interstices between the positions of the author and the publisher within this transformative landscape, renewed distinctions, positions and investments are possible. Ongoing dialogue between the negotiating parties in this landscape also produces ramifications for existing industry perspectives and practices.

While the standard publishing contract prescribes rigid parameters, its framework of parts, conversely, is unarticulated and unbound – evidenced by its gaps, which are open to misinterpretation but also further negotiation. Many publishers' contracts reflect previous scenarios in their drafting but often from a publisher's perspective. The drafting is also a narrative of cut-and-paste amendments that detail the many changes and developments in the original agreement. For the author, this narrative is complex and sometimes simply unnavigable. Such drafting also delineates 'group boundaries, facilitating the recognition of members and the stereotyping of non-members' (Calhoun 1989 in Suchman 2003, 113), the latter being where authors feel they are positioned. Authors also don't often care for such complex expressions of what they fundamentally feel the contract instils: an endorsement of their work – a stamp of approval that their writing has been accepted by the literary gatekeepers, the weight of which is manifested in the signed commitment (Hans & Mott 2000). With this in mind, the contract can represent many things – symbolically and actually. For this investigation, a few pertinent questions arose:

1 *What does the book-publishing contract represent for the contemporary author, and for the publisher? Does it have symbolic, legal and/or economic significance?*

In investigating this question from a scholarly and practical perspective, a number of theories can be tested:

1 the expression of copyright law within publishing contracts is beholden to significant historical influences, mostly dominated by publishers' needs but also reflective of a romantic view of the author;
2 these influences create conflicting perceptions of contract negotiations for authors and publishers;

3 globalisation and digitalisation have given authors greater flexibility and power to publish their works on their own terms;
4 despite this new power, authors still see the publishing contract as the ultimate endorsement of their work;
5 authors are not fully satisfied with the terms of their contracts.

This book reveals how our inherited institutions, and form and use of the contract as an instrument for the ultimate agreement between these parties, are applied in a contemporary publishing landscape. It delves into the distinctions between how publishers and authors perceive the terms of publishing contracts and asks what these distinctions tell us about industry developments: which particular areas of the contract have been shown to most convey commercial publishing's shifting landscape, and how?

While the author–publisher relationship is regarded within copyright and contract law specifically, I want to elaborate upon this frame of reference by interrogating the negotiations at the points where law and economics intersect with the symbolic representations embedded within the contract negotiation. The analysis is confined mostly to the 'post negotiation' space – after the contract is signed – as described earlier. To illustrate how the post negotiation space works in relation to publishing agreements' historical development, I borrow from existing 'black box' theory.[3]

My study posits the contract as comparable to the conceptual model of the black box system. Black box theory has been used predominantly in engineering and computing, to describe the phenomenon of what is not observable between the input and the output. The theory has also been adopted in psychology (Gigerenzer 2020), and even marketing, which provides the simplest example whereby the input of product, price and promotion results in a purchase (Lumen Learning 2020). What happens between the marketing and purchase, however, remains a mystery unless investigated.

In black box theory as it is applied in engineering, internal workings are not observable. Applying the theory to publishing presents an area ripe for critical examination because exploring what happens within the black box essentially reveals an area not seen before. This investigation lifts the lid on contract negotiations, rummages through the box and lifts out the contents to witness them, observe them from every angle, and assess their value. In my version of this model, the input represents the positions of the publisher and the author as prescribed in the initial negotiated terms of the contract; the output represents the terms of the contract as executed in the publishing process, and how this process might influence industry developments; the internal workings represents the under-researched post negotiation space – what happens between signing the contract and the published book.

These phases of contract negotiation mirror the pre and post negotiation spaces. For example, the input explores the legacy of the traditional publishing contract and considers the juxtaposition of authors' and publishers' understandings of contract negotiations and how their respective positions are consecrated in law, in the present. This is part of the 'pre negotiation space' because it informs the areas of struggle and the preconceived expectations and ideals that each party brings to contract negotiations at the time of signing. These expectations and ideals are considered from two perspectives: the contract as a symbolic artefact and as an instrument that sanctions the negotiating parties' economic and

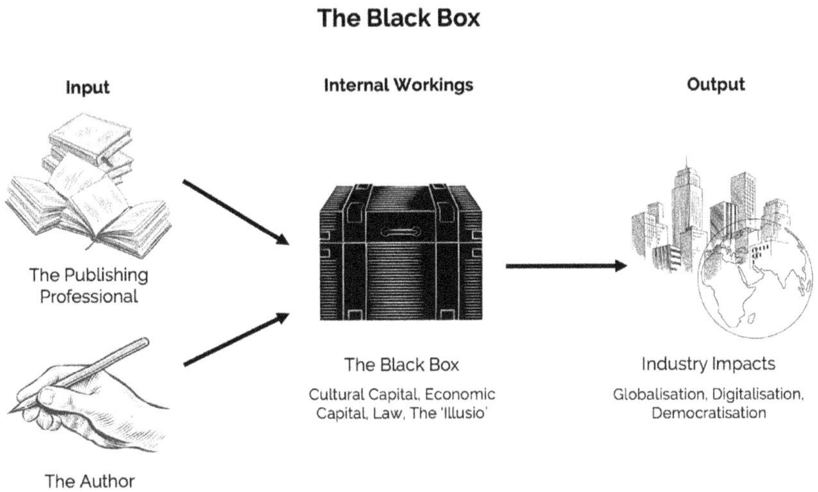

FIGURE 1.1 The black box

legal directives. Question 1 (aforementioned) guides the exploration of the 'pre negotiation space' – the input.

The internal workings represent the 'post negotiation space'. It is in this secondary space that expectations and ideals can be refined, reworked or even abandoned, and it is therefore the most dynamic. In assessing the internal workings – the post negotiation space – the following questions can be asked:

2 *How are the utilitarian and ideological spaces in book-publishing contracts negotiated?*
3 *What can the negotiation process tell us about relationships of power in book publishing?*

Finally, the internal workings can be assessed alongside the input and the output by analysing the gathered data and answering two final questions:

4 *How are contracts used within the publishing house after signing?*
5 *Is the contract still an effective tool for negotiations in the contemporary book-publishing landscape?*

The structure of this study integrates this conceptual model at its centre. First, a premise is established (power relations within publishing contract negotiations); second, the contract as a cultural artefact is studied; third, the authors' and publishers' perceptions of it are captured via a survey and in-depth interviews; finally, the analysis offers insight and recommendations. My close and directed examination of current publishing contracts, and observation of the power balance between authors and publishers in a contemporary publishing field, reveals the contracts' adaptability pursuant to the participating parties' desires and needs, and identifies areas of change and development within the industry.

The first step, then (discovering how contracts are used in-house, and how they function as tools for negotiation), is to examine our laws – where they have been perpetuated, and where they have been reshaped to influence current practices.

Notes

1 Throsby et al. (2015) describe the Australian book publishing market and comment that '*In this environment, writers struggle to make a living. A survey of Australian artists' incomes in 2009 found that "professional writers remain the least well rewarded artistic occupation for their creative work*'.

2 'Pre negotiation' and 'post negotiation' are not hyphenated because to hyphenate them would suggest that negotiation is complete. For example, a 'post-negotiation space' insinuates the time after negotiation has taken place, whereas 'post negotiation space' states that the negotiation is taking place after a prior negotiation.

3 In 'The Application of Black Box Theory to System Development', Green et al. describe the concept of a black box as 'a simple concept [with] a straightforward definition: we know the inputs and subsequent outputs to a system but the internal workings of the system are not visible to us' (2017).

2

A CONTEXTUAL DISCOVERY OF PUBLISHING AGREEMENTS

Copyright law underpins publishing activities and can be viewed, if somewhat rudimentarily, as possessing two fundamental pillars: pecuniary rights and, contrastingly, the moral rights of the author. Throughout the English-speaking territories, these pillars have been debated, modified and developed from as early as the late 1400s when the invention of the printing press transformed publishing into a thriving business (Zapata López 2002, 3). At the time, the advantages of mass production revealed commercial opportunities that publishers and writers would have been foolish not to exploit. However, these opportunities also became a tug-of-war between publishers, authors and booksellers: who owned the intellectual property and who had the right to benefit from its commercial prospects? For a time, the London Stationers' Company held the monopoly on the book trade in English-speaking territories, but the explosion of all forms and editions of existing works at the time proved stiff competition, and the Stationers were forced to concoct inventive ways to retain economic power even after copyright law became codified via the Statute of Anne in 1710.

From these rivalries, a very convincing argument emerged that pitched a romantic ideology of the author as a genius, who possessed distinct perpetual rights over their intellectual property. At a glance this might seem advantageous to authors, but the justification for asserting authors' rights was not just for their benefit. Isabella Alexander explains that 'those with a stake in the copyright industries [invoked] the rhetoric of romantic authorship, emphasising the natural rights of authors' (Alexander 2010, 292) with a view to substantiate their license of those rights. Furthermore, by arguing that protection of the rights advanced learning and general societal interests (Alexander 2010, 23), a cultural view of the author as a 'meaning-maker' (Craig 2011, 16) and 'originator' (Foucault 1997, 124) led to the ideology's eventual entrenchment in law and consecration via the landmark case *Donaldson v Becket*.

Donaldson v Becket

The case of *Donaldson v Becket* (1774) defined the author's focus. Thomas Becket argued that Alexander Donaldson's publication of James Thomson's collection of poetry – *The Seasons* – infringed Becket's (and some other London booksellers' and printers') copyright of the work.

DOI:10.4324/9781003336570-2

Although the wording in the Statute of Anne allowed for up to a 28-year maximum term for exclusive rights (14 years in the first instance and then an extended 14 years if desired by the author and publisher), Becket claimed that copyright was a common law right through which the author should enjoy the fruits of their labour – their intellectual property – in perpetuity (Rose 1994, 24). Again, although this appears to be a stance that invests in authors' interests, the argument was primarily based on the loss sustained by the Stationers if their copyrighted works could be reproduced by another party. Donaldson argued that the works were a mere assembly of ideas that should be readily available to all, and which did not warrant perpetual rights. This position was worth considering because it presented a public-interest element, which echoed the aims of the Statute more generally. The counter-argument from Becket's counsel was that the

> ideas could be common and shared widely, [but] the same was not true of the form in which the irreducible singularity of style and sentiment was expressed. The legitimation of literary property was thus based on a new aesthetic perception designating the work as an original creation recognizable by the specificity of its expression.
>
> (Chartier 1994, 15)

Their position was clear in asserting inalienable rights to the author, which they determined as very separate to the alienable rights (which were manifested in the physical books). In other words, the formation of ideas was undeniably unique and therefore inextricably linked to the author (Chartier 1994, 15). In considering what would happen if perpetuity were permitted, the judges presiding over *Becket* concluded that the Statute of Anne had replaced the common law right with a limited copyright. Not only was this a landmark decision legally, but it has also had a lasting cultural impact: first, it is difficult, even now, to separate an author from their work; second, and as an extension of the first point, it is difficult to pinpoint the demarcation of that work's legitimacy in the literary landscape as perceived by the author and the publisher, the latter with their own particular interests.

The author as 'original genius' continues to inform how we think about writers and even how the categorisation of the author is expressed in contracts. For example, contract terms still assert the author as having created an 'original' work by way of the 'Warranties and Indemnities' sections. While the author must warrant that the work is original, they must also indemnify the publisher should the work infringe copyright. Both would seem to question the genius of the author as original creator; however, once the contract is signed, the clauses effectively assert the author as having created something special. The 'Copyright Infringement' sections then permit the publisher to defend the copyright in the work should it be infringed by a third party. This would be an economic concern – one that asserts the publisher's monopoly and yet reflects the persistent author's ideology for the benefit of the publisher. If you consider this type of agreement in the present day, monopolies are questionable. The book-publishing industry is now saturated, and scope to be influenced by other works is more possible when those works can be more easily accessed.

New practices in old frameworks

The author as the sole creator has provided a perplexing dichotomy when considering their pecuniary rights and how the two pillars of copyright law are reflected in author contracts in contemporary publishing. Contemporary book publishing is now far more democratised, with authors often choosing to self-publish and create their own social-media platforms to reach their readers (Thompson 2012, 64). Authors might even have a clearer idea of their audience and potential reach than a publisher would. An author's perceived value of their work and entitlement to economic reward from it (Cantatore 2011, 4) does not necessarily sit well with the author as sole creator, however: democratisation provides choice, variety and an abundance of accessible material that can be adapted, integrated, modified and transformed into new works. The ability to mix and mash has permanently altered the ideal of the 'original' (Craig 2011, 23). Almost every new work can be attributed to something like it, and the trail of ideas more transparent. Indeed, 'appropriation, adaptation and reinterpretation of existing texts is an established mode of cultural meaning-making' (Craig 2011, 174), which has created a more 'communitarian' (Craig 2011, 25) landscape in which borrowing from others' creativity is encouraged – an echo of the challenges that the Stationers observed back in the eighteenth century but on a global scale.

For publishers, now, the variety of sources is still potentially challenging because authors don't view publishing houses as the only path to publication; the breadth of information, however, provides unprecedented resources for publishers that are also educational for their insight into markets and trends. These resources are auspicious in helping publishers position a work in the market. Nielsen Book data, for example, is a repository of sales that, when paid for and accessed, can help publishers to assess the viability of titles sometimes even before they are contracted (Magner 2012, 243). Publishers are tempted to pivot towards heteronomous content (Bode & Dixon 2009; Squires 2007, 47) by dismissing certain works that would be assessed as having a smaller readership; it can also result in a scattergun approach to publishing whereby publishers produce a variety of texts, based on Nielsen data, to 'see what sticks'. Authors who pursue traditional pathways experience the brunt of this saturated market in the way their work is received by a publisher and how the contract expresses the publisher's dedication to the work as a speculative transaction – mostly through a reduced print-run and format that mirrors the modest expectations. The author's belief in the degree of originality in their work may translate to a disproportionate commercial value (Torremans 2004, 99); what they perceive as a literary masterpiece may be a commercial burden in the eyes of a publisher, for example. And yet, the author as literary genius is maintained and the old Stationers' position preserved. This push and pull of traditional publishing practice and industry developments can be explained using Bourdieu's literary field, in which each player positions themselves relative to others in the field and their own work.

The field in depth

Bourdieu described the interplay between the publisher and the writer as a field of 'power' in which there is a 'space of relations of force between agents or between institutions having in common the possession of the capital necessary to occupy the dominant positions in different fields (notable economic or cultural)' (Bourdieu 1996, 210). He suggested that the field is 'characterized . . . by the extreme permeability of [its] boundaries and the extreme diversity of the diffusion of *posts* [it] offer[s] and the principle of legitimacy which confront each other there' (Bourdieu 1996, 220) This, he explained, results in a dynamic 'illusio' (Bourdieu 1996, 221), which is invested in, but also challenged, by the players in the field. Each player either accepts or provokes the illusio, in their attempts to define the 'distinctions' (Bourdieu 1996, 221) in their art and in their 'position-taking' (Bourdieu 1996, 226), challenging the 'problematic' to become a 'space of possibles': 'the struggle itself' (Bourdieu 1996, 226–228). It is, therefore, impossible to extract a fixed and dependable set of rules from the field, which the law invariably sets out to do. Bourdieu revealed: 'Each position is objectively defined by its objective relationship with other positions' (Bourdieu 1996, 224), and in defining the value of the work, '[t]he producer of the *value of the work of art* is not the artist but the field of production as a universe of belief which produces the value of the work of art as a *fetish* by producing the belief in the creative power of the artist' (Bourdieu 1996, 222). This statement would affirm the publisher's investment in the work and their influence in how the work is received by its audience. Bourdieu maintains that the work must be recognised by the dominant players in the field, who have the credibility to invest 'not only [in] the material production of the work but also the production of the value of the work or what amounts to the same thing, of the belief in the value of the work' (Bourdieu 1996, 223). But, as discussed, publishers, as agents in the game, are decidedly impacted by economics, too. Bourdieu refers to this as an economic illusio, which impacts on the artistic illusio and which publishers must renegotiate and challenge in order to inform their own habitus and position in the field. In 'impos[ing] the boundaries of the field most favourable to their own interests' (Bourdieu 1996, 217) (whether economic or cultural), Bourdieu suggests that publishers have contributed to the creation of two poles of literature – 'autonomous' (or prestigious) publishing, and 'heteronomous' (or middlebrow) publishing (Bourdieu 1996, 228) – and the 'monopoly of the power to say with authority who is authorised to call himself a writer . . . or, if you prefer, the monopoly of *power of consecration* of producers and products' (Bourdieu 1996, 218).

The 'capital' that individual publishers still possess continues to entice authors. This capital can be identified as economic or symbolic (Bourdieu 1996, 210) and determines how the author might be supported in their endeavour. Furthermore, the traditional publisher is still seen as a 'gatekeeper' of quality; the commercial publishers' expertise in the areas of editing and production, and rights exploitation and distribution, continue to attract authors (Seeber & Balkwill 2007). This is certainly so for commercial publishers, who have the ability to achieve the complex network of licensing arrangements that fundamentally characterise the universal success of prominent titles. In defining the value of the work, '[t]he producer of the *value of the work of art* is not the artist but the field of production as a universe of belief which produces the value of the work of art as a *fetish* by producing the belief in the creative power of the artist' (Bourdieu 1996, 222).

Bourdieu posits that this publisher monopoly is bound to be challenged – the 'ensemble of probable constraints' giving way to a set of 'possible uses' (Bourdieu 1996, 229). In other words, proof of what has gone before allows for the possibility of change – and existing structures must be acknowledged before a 'space of possibles' can be realised. Bourdieu uses the example of younger generations 'asserting their identity . . . by imposing new modes of thought and hence . . . destined to disconcert by their "obscurity" and their "gratuitousness"' (Bourdieu 1996, 233). Questions arise about what is considered literary in the changing field; perceptions of what constitutes 'highbrow' works are being challenged; and the 'illusio' of the literary field breached. This new landscape has shown that the democratisation of the industry has placed the author, potentially, in an unprecedented, powerful position. Yet, it could be that the romanticised notion of the author as literary genius still permeates the field in quite subtle ways. These permeations could be the very fact that the publishing contract signifies a certain value in the work – whatever that might be – and the book's eventual paratextual elements (the signifiers of genre, in particular) communicate that level of literariness. With publishers' economic capital influencing the production values inherent in literary works (be that a well-designed cover or expert editorial attention, for example), the breach could in fact be superficial.

All of these positions would, however, still indicate a completely reimagined illusio. The changes are perhaps not so revolutionary or sudden as we might believe. Indeed, Bourdieu suggests that '[t]he "profession" of the writer . . . is, in effect, one of the least codified there is; one of the least capable, too, of completely defining (and nourishing) those who claim it' (Bourdieu 1996, 221). This statement avows the identified conflict between the writer and the publisher, which is 'constantly being negotiated, rather than consecrated in law' (Bourdieu 1996, 220), and encapsulates the illusio in a way that allows a platform upon which to interrogate its incremental re-creation in publishing agreements. In essence, this new terrain embodies Bourdieu's literary field theory, where the 'space of possibles' has allowed the authors' and publishers' positions to evolve over time. In many ways this could be seen to expose their vulnerabilities further, or the renewed space of possibles, by virtue of its challenging the status quo, allowing both authors and publishers to take advantage of the new ways in which works are created, adapted and distributed in publishing today. The author, then, might not have the desire to extricate themselves entirely from established publishers if they can work together in new and more collaborative ways. For the author this collaboration is most fruitful when respect for the work is evident, which is where an author's moral rights would intersect with their pecuniary rights. It should be in the contract *negotiations* where moral rights can be parlayed.

Moral rights in practice

When weighing up moral rights versus pecuniary interests, Jane Ginsburg suggests that moral rights are more important for the author because the material gain is contingent on the explicit or implicit recognition of the author's moral rights (Ginsburg 1990, 3). This position, based on her analysis of the French translation of *dommage moral*, from which moral rights emerged, and which translates as 'non-material damage', includes 'encroachments upon the personality, such as emotional distress, loss of amenities, injury to honor or diminution of a person's reputation' (Ginsburg 1990, 3) The most interesting aspect of this definition, in Ginsburg's view, focuses again on the author-subject, whereby the work:

> incorporates the personality of the author because the authorial persona permeates and invades the work. Therefore, when something happens to the work – such as deformation or mutilation – that constitutes an attack on the person or personality of the author herself.
>
> (Ginsburg 1990, 3)

In Australia (unlike the UK), moral rights are assumed and are viewed as independent of economic rights (Arts Law 2018). However, they were not codified in Australia until 2010. Although there is often no specific clause in publishing contracts that affirms moral rights, they are part of the overarching rights that authors possess. They can, however, be waived in some circumstances (e.g. where an author waives their rights to the work to allow for a screenplay, serialisation or abridged version). In other jurisdictions such as in France, moral rights are treated very differently, and 'although intellectual works are capable of commodification, the author retains general rights of personality that survive market exploitation of the external work' (Rosenthal Kwall 2010, 39). In France, Germany and Italy, authors also have the right of withdrawal as part of their suite moral rights – meaning that the author can ask for the work to be withdrawn from the public 'if it no longer reflects the author's convictions of spirit' (Rosenthal Kwall 2010, 44). However,

> [i]n adjudicating the validity of waivers as a defense in actions for alleged right of integrity violations, the French judiciary tends to enforce contracts allowing reasonable alterations that do not distort the spirit of the author's work, particularly with respect to adaptations and contributions to collective works.
>
> (Rosenthal Kwall 2010, 45)

Thinking again about the breadth of information and material available to reading audiences, who also have other entertainment options to explore, the pressure to diversify a single source of creativity is inevitable. The diversification, too, allows authors to exploit their works extensively. Commercial appeal, therefore, can sometimes supersede an author's wish to uphold their moral rights. Much of the time they are not aware of the repercussions.

Ginsburg discusses the problematic structure of these types of waivers in publishing contracts and admits that 'defacto waivers are likely to occur' through authors' willingness to allow publishers control over works to better exploit them (Ginsburg 1990, 11). She suggests, however, that '[t]he artist is protected under a regime requiring specificity of waivers better than under one where an ideologically pure no-waiver law is in fact rarely observed' (Ginsburg 1990, 11). Louise Buckingham supports this view:

> Although there is a defence of reasonableness from a publisher's perspective if any alterations of any kind . . . are likely to be necessary in the publication of the work, it's best to build this into an agreement. If there is a later alteration that needs to be made and it goes beyond what has already been agreed, it's important to get consent in writing to that specific change from the creator. As well as being best practice and the most appropriate way to ensure a good long-term relationship between you and your authors and illustrators, in legal terms this is the creator's consent to waive their moral rights and it is important that you abide by it.
>
> (Buckingham 2013, 36)

This statement still inadvertently affirms the existence of the authorial persona by way of the publisher's responsibility to essentially 'check in' with the author if further changes need to be made to the work. Derivative, borrowed and adapted works are therefore not possible without the permission of the creator. This can only be possible because the contract, as a secondary legal framework, is created by the parties who wish to form business relations. In theory all of the aforementioned can be written into the contract before signing; in reality neither the publisher nor the author can usually predict the circumstances they would encounter that require specific clauses. How the author and publisher broach these circumstances will be discussed, but first an outline of the contract as a secondary legal framework provides some context.

The contract as a legacy

The law of contract is a secondary legal structure that acts as a mediating set of rules between what the law of copyright (as codified law) may have intended (author's rights) and what transpires. The contract, therefore, has the potential to empower individuals to create a more sophisticated, nuanced arrangement within a larger, primary legal framework (codified, positive law) (Hart 1994, 92).

The contract's focus on pecuniary interests signifies a preference even now towards the publisher's rights, yet the author, as has been established, still appears to seek the contract as a means of legitimising their work. Thompson maintains that a publisher's investment in the editing, production, rights exploitation and distribution of a manuscript is assurance of their enthusiasm and endorsement (Thompson 2012, 43), which plays to the author's own sense of value in their work. As this investment unfolds, however, the author and publisher's perception of the value of the work may differ, resulting in potentially conflicting ideas about the positioning of the work and its respective markets (Bourdieu 1996, 5), to which the author still appears at the mercy of the publisher.

The romantic ideology of the author still influences the publishing contract as a tool for negotiation within copyright legislation, and its mediating qualities as a secondary legal structure, by allowing the publisher to impose degrees of literary genius and genre, as well as an active distinction between literary hierarchies. Is the contract simply an amalgam of the same complex struggle that our inherited copyright law framework has seemingly failed to reconcile, despite the contract's promise as a flexible platform made to 'ascertain, introduce and eliminate' the primary structure (Hart 1994, 92)?

Author–publisher relations in context

In his influential book *Contract and Promise*, Fried describes the contract as a private agreement between two parties, which elaborates upon a criterion of consent, with enforceable conditions (Fried 2007, 2), and requires a 'meeting of minds' (Fried 1981, 16) on the 'reasonable' interpretation of its terms (Fried 2007, 16). Fried's highly regarded theory of 'contract as promise' (Fried 2007, 4) discusses and reflects upon the various aims of the parties – in particular on the 'will' of each, entering the contract. Fried reimagines 'will' as 'promise', whereby 'persons may impose on themselves obligations where none existed before' (Fried 2007, 16). He describes this concept of 'will' as '[a]n individual [being] morally bound to keep his promise because he has intentionally invoked a convention whose function it is to give grounds – moral grounds – for another to expect the promised performance' (Fried 2007, 16). This theory bridges the particularities of book-publishing contracts with a more fundamental philosophy underpinning legal agreements, which allows us to observe the possible inherent tensions between them.

The negotiable aspects of publishing contracts converge around the specific areas of assignment of copyright, and licences. But, in signing the contract, the parties also show a general intention 'to create legal relations' (Butler et al. 2017, 182), which commits them to their individual understandings of the agreement. Of contracts in cultural production, Fried says they are 'an interdependent, distinct part of the structure of value' but, also, 'if the legal foundation is to support the whole, then the ideals and values must constrain, limit, inform and inspire the foundation – but no more' (Fried 2007, 17), essentially affirming the conflict between negotiating cultural products and enforcing legal obligations.

In 'Contract Is Not Promise; Contract Is Consent', Barnett argues that Fried's 'moral' principle is problematic. This is because it must support the terms of the contract, and the desire of the promisor to perform these terms is 'freely assumed' (Barnett 2011, 5). Barnett says that the promisor understands these terms subjectively, which means, in essence, that the sanction is imposed, not chosen. Barnett suggests that the 'promise' cannot be sustained, as a result; rather, the contract is one of 'consent'. However, Barnett also affirms that the contract signifies a 'manifested intention to create a legal relation' (Barnett 2011, 10).

This traditional framework of will and morality, of promise or consent, translates awkwardly to publishing, where the value of cultural production is fluid and not as clearly articulated as the value of products in other businesses. No publisher can definitively pick a bestseller, though many try by assessing Bookscan data or consulting booksellers about reading trends. Many publishers also look to other media and general news for information on what consumers want. Books have become a luxury for many – costly compared to the content/value ratio in competing entertainment streams (Throsby et al. 2017, 10 and Peschel 2019). The value of stories/content is continually a subjective field, which constantly changes and requires research as well as an ability to ride the trends when they hit their peak. There are, as a result, dualities embedded in publishing contracts (indeed in contract law in general): 'market versus community, individualism versus altruism, self versus other, form versus substance' (Paterson et al. 2009, 18). Classical contract theory perhaps inadequately reflects actual agreements in publishing practice, because publishing practice is a business conducive to long-term relationships, and arguably a business in which the sanctioning properties of contracts can be revisited and used 'as a starting point for renegotiation and adjustment when circumstances change or difficulties arise' (Kimel 2007 in Mouzas & Furmston 2008, 37). Relational contract theory presents a framework where 'the parties are relying heavily on social conventions or because the parties are involved in a long-term relationship' (Paterson et al. 2009, 25) and presents publishing contracts as an '"incremental process" in which the parties "gather increasing information and gradually agree to more and more as they proceed"' (Paterson et al. 2009, 28).

Relational contract theory

When discussing contracts in this book, it is important to know that contract law, as a secondary legal framework, is also supported by rigorous scholarly theory on how the secondary legal framework operates. We tend to think of contracts as being rigid – much like a mortgage contract, for example. Rather, contracts fall on a spectrum from highly discreet, whereby the terms of the contract are very strictly applied and adhered to, to quite relational (Macaulay 2003; Macneil 1985). It is at this end of the spectrum that the contract's terms require negotiation and where the terms outline the way in which the relationship between the contracted parties will engage in these negotiations. It is at the relational end of the spectrum where, I argue, publishing contracts are situated.

Developing Macaulay's 1960s paper that introduced this theory, Macneil proposed that contracts 'will almost always be "incomplete" because they contain some "third-party unenforceable" elements' (Mouzas & Blois 2008 quoting Macneil, 2). These elements incorporate a number of aspects of any business venture that might not be concrete at the time of signing, so

> instead of planning for various contingencies at the outset, the parties deal with problems as they arise by adjusting their obligations and granting concessions in relation to time of performance or price. It may even be expected that one party will release the other from his or her contractual obligations altogether in order to preserve the broader relationship between the parties or one party's reputation within the industry.
>
> (Paterson et al. 2009, 26)

In publishing, each book is treated as an individual project with its own particularities, and because it is difficult to predict the success of an individual title – an endeavour that claims anomalies both successful and unsuccessful. It would appear, then, that relational contract theory could facilitate the many commercial and cultural transactions that take place between the author and the publisher throughout the book production process. This is not to say that the whole contract is relational: publishing contract clauses might vary – some being 'discrete' and some being 'highly relational' (Macneil 1985, 490); the discrete clauses can also be regulated to varying degrees by the parties, as Macneil observed:

> the sole function of discrete exchange is the transfer of control of capital and labor, of goods and services. This is a limited economic function, albeit one essential to the physical production itself of goods and services and necessary for enhancing the value of those goods and services. Because of the limited nature of this function and because it can be and is also carried on by relational exchange, it is inevitably a very small part of the overall economic activities of any given society.
>
> (Macneil 1985, 490)

Any stage in the production of each title could trigger the need to negotiate existing agreements – the incidence of which Macneil described as 'internal patterns of relational exchange' (Macneil 1985, 490). These types of internal patterns of exchange also require trust, which is integral to the author–publisher relationship. Business relationships of trust are therefore a key factor in relational contract theory and indicate 'contractual rights and obligations are not always the most important factors influencing businesspeople planning transactions, adjusting agreements and resolving disputes' (Paterson et al. 2009, 24). This is where relational contract theory also explains the existence of boilerplate contracts, which provide an existing template as a point of reference that can remain untouched or be moulded when necessary (Mouzas & Furmston 2008, 38–39). If an author feels that their relationship with their publisher is one that is built on trust, they might potentially feel less inclined to '[insist] on their contractual rights and not [take] too seriously the option of litigation' (Kimel 2007, 250). The kind of trust that parties to the contract might experience in publishing is derived from a culture of collaboration that runs through the business as a cultural expectation; while the contract framework is necessary as a formality to stipulate the initial terms, it clinical foil hides an approach to practice that allows each party 'norms from their relationship to guide their behaviour' as well as the continuing agreement (Leib 2013, 264).

The agreement to continue to negotiate is, however, part of the problem. Mouzas and Blois broach this stumbling block by stating that

> contracting parties may have a) divergent expectations, b) they may hold asymmetric information, c) they may be uncertain about the structure of their interaction with others or whether the deal is possible and d) they might have locked themselves in other irreversible commitments.
>
> (Mouzas & Blois 2008, 13)

A relationship of trust and a 'meeting of minds' could be considered altruistic when one party holds more knowledge of the processes of the business than the other. This is so for publishers versus authors (Maskin & Tirole 1999 in Mouzas & Blois 2008, 4; Akerlof 1970, 488). Asymmetry of information problematises fairness because 'a transaction is [only] fair if it is one which the parties would have reached had they had sufficient knowledge to understand all the relevant aspects' (Levin & McDowell 1983, 31). Robin Freeman highlights the complexity of expectations upon which the agreement is initiated, suggesting that the asymmetry of information weighs most heavily on the emerging author:

> In the traditional trade model the control of these negotiations has depended on the commercial weight attributed to the individual or to the publishing company and the perception of who will be of most benefit to whom. A first-time author, inexperienced in matters of contracts and eager to get that first book published, is not in the same position when negotiating a contract with a large multinational publisher, as is an established writer with over half a dozen best-selling titles to their credit.
>
> (Freeman 2001, 107)

Emerging writers will always be presented with the boilerplate contract, which presents as a fait accompli in most cases. Through another lens, the boilerplate is simply a reflection of past agreements and scenarios through which the publisher and previously contracted author emerge as more knowledgeable. These umbrella agreements 'transform explicit norms, which are embedded in customs and business practices into explicit, basic rules and principles for business interaction' (Mouzas & Furmston 2008, 38–39). The umbrella agreement might appear impermeable, but it is not. Rather, these basic rules and principles form a fascinating tapestry of publishing's history and culture with regard to author–publisher relationships and negotiations, which presents the contract as impressionable. In this sense, the contract is more symbolic than sanctioning. Observing the contract's symbolic qualities, therefore, prompts a different kind of analysis of contracts as 'social artifacts' (Suchman 2003, 92).

The contract as symbolic artefact

Mark Suchman claims the contract is a cultural artefact that deserves 'serious scholarly consideration' because it has the capacity to convey the specific principles held most important within a particular social community as well as express the experiences of those within that community (Suchman 2003, 100). Cultural artefacts are not a new phenomenon in sociological studies: Klaus Bruhn Jensen describes how '[c]ultural artefacts and other vehicles of meaning provide people with a sense of identity, a position from which to exercise agency, and a means of orienting oneself in social interaction' (Jensen et al. 1997, 236). Suchman elaborates on this theory with the contract as being representative of 'reference points for stage managing complex, multilayer productions' (Suchman 2003, 99–100), in this instance the author–publisher relationship and the production of a book. In the event of the author not having any intrinsic knowledge of this process, or the doctrines and principles that the publishing industry tends to follow, the mere act of signing a contract, as an 'artefact', has symbolic meaning. Suchman describes this process as a kind of ceremony whereby 'drafting and signing a contract may reenact and reinforce elements of faith, both about the transaction itself and about the larger social order' (Suchman 2003, 111–112). The ceremony or ritual of contract signing then becomes somewhat reassuring to the parties and symbolises some sense of control within a mutual relationship (Suchman 2003, 111–112). And '[a]lthough these reassurances may often prove more mystical than factual, they can nonetheless shape legal consciousness and hence legal behaviour' (Suchman 2003, 111–112).

However, similar to Bourdieu's theory of the 'space of possibles' whereby the players can rupture existing norms and processes, so too can the umbrella agreement be transformative. This movement can be witnessed in the additional phrases, addendums and other paratextual evidence in the contract, further exemplifying its function as an artefact. The waves of movement across the agreements eventually become embedded as 'behavioural scripts' and 'increasingly routinized . . . taken for granted, and . . . coordinated with other elements of accepted practice until, eventually, the rationality of the new regime becomes a self-fulfilling prophecy' (Suchman 2003, 129). And it is precisely the new challenges of 'economic, religious, and political tides' (Kahan & Klausner 1997, 743–744) that create this contractual landscape – in this instance those challenges being globalisation, reading trends, conglomeration, democratisation, digitalisation and any other force that has directly affected book publishing in the contemporary landscape. The contract as a physical document, therefore, is worthy of close analysis to highlight the aforementioned incidences and ask how they happen to become a part of various contract templates and why they might also be omitted, over time, as part of the contract's relational orientation. Contracts have the capacity to tell the story of the book's journey in publishing, as well as the story of the relationship between the publisher and the author.

***

The democratised literary landscape has facilitated new platforms to self-publish as well as provided access to works and information globally. This new context inadvertently undermines the ideal of author as creator and genius, the upshot of which also alters how we connect moral rights to authors. The contract, as a secondary legal framework, has the capacity to incorporate the expectations of the contributing parties in this changing landscape. However, the embedded cultural perceptions of who an author is and what a publisher represents continue to reflect what they were back in the eighteenth century. The contract could be seen to have more symbolic meaning for an author – an endorsement of their work – as well as sanctioning properties, via its legal parameters as a reflection of copyright law. These contrasting arms are enmeshed with the 'industrial' (Carter 2016, 10) considerations of the publisher and the 'aspirational' (Barnett 2011 citing Fried, 20) ideals of the author, exacerbating contract negotiations and defining two camps of thought: the publishing contract as a ***symbol***[1] and the publishing contract as a ***sanction***.[2] For the author, the contract represents validation in the cultural 'space' (Bourdieu 1984, 95); for the publisher (and the author), it presents a level of protection from 'misunderstandings, broken promises, or the ability of a party to extricate itself from a project in which it is no longer interested' (Simensky et al. 2003, 152). These understandings are of course problematic in the contemporary sphere.

The contract's symbolism juxtaposed against its sanctioning properties have not yet been fully identified by scholarly research, nor have they been interrogated adequately in the industry. Contract theory focuses mostly on the legal repercussions of failed contracts, and relational contract theory has been applied mostly to contracts in businesses other than publishing. For industry, contracts are a part of a much larger operation in which individuals have other focuses around trends and tastes, deadlines and production. The contract is not always at the forefront of the publishing process. While current literature reiterates the strain between authors and publishers in terms of the work, and via an objective assessment of publishing contract agreements from a legal perspective, the agreements have not been explored in depth, in a subjective and qualitative way, to ascertain why the tension between the parties persists, in which specific areas, and what it reveals about the industry in a global and digital realm.

I have witnessed a power imbalance between authors and publishing houses, whereby the author, on the outside of publishing workflow, is unable to understand the decisions that are made around the publication of their title, while the publisher takes for granted the knowledge they possess of this process. Yet a relationship persists, facilitated most by the editor–publisher – the author and the editor–publisher relying on each other to realise the success of the work. Looking at the contract from this perspective, we see that it reflects the historic role of patronage – of a 'gentleman's agreement' in its most nostalgic ideal.

For Australian authors and publishers, the Australian Society of Authors' (ASA) provides an analysis of the terms of publishing contracts, which identifies specific areas where development in negotiations may have occurred. Other organisations such as the Authors Guild in the US also continue to educate authors about contracts and author rights. But this information and the scholarly literature fail to offer a nuanced voice to the current players in the field from all perspectives – the ways in which they negotiate at the point of signing and beyond, and the particular expressions of these negotiations. The research and findings in this book explore these nuanced relationships qualitatively. The contract might simply be an industry framework that reflects existing power relations and provides a tool in the post negotiation space, precisely because of its clear limitations and vague clauses. A more extensive analysis of standard contracts and new contracts could highlight manipulation in these areas and reveal that the status quo is satisfactory. Objective and detailed clauses would tend to hold parties to the contract to the exact wording. Vague clauses, on the other hand, are open to interpretation. What the contract says and how it is used are quite different, and authors', agents' and publishing professionals' responses to potentially negotiable areas need to be examined qualitatively than simply analysing the document as a disconnected and an isolated artefact. The following research, therefore, has been formulated to delve into the post negotiation space and connect with the players in the field directly.

Notes

1 'Something used or regarded as standing for or representing something else; a material object representing something immaterial; an emblem, token, or sign.' Macquarie Dictionary, 6th edition.

2 'Binding force given, or something which gives binding force, as to an oath, rule of conduct, etc.' Macquarie Dictionary, 6th edition.

3

VIEWING THE ARTEFACT

An overview of publishing boilerplates

The contract (being 'the vehicle of meaning') can be viewed as an 'artefact' and critically evaluated with respect to its standard 'parts'. Doing so helps to contextualise the perspectives from the research participants in the survey and interviews in the following chapters. Conducting a contract overview also prompts hypotheses about why contracts are constructed in particular ways and the underlying meaning behind those particular constructions. For example, ' "best efforts" clauses become statements of suspicion; negotiated revisions become shows of mutuality, and reprinted forms become indicators of oppression; warranties become emblems of quality, and disclaimers become marks of deficiency' (Suchman 2003, 100). The following overview of typical boilerplate-type contracts also assists the reader to understand the various clauses in the contract in order to successfully interpret the survey data and interview findings in the following chapters.

As already defined, the contract is an agreement with an intention on both sides to create legal relations between two parties (Mitchell 2009, 683). Publishing boilerplate contracts are wide-ranging, and the myriad ways in which these contracts can be negotiated to satisfy the signing parties are not all reflected in this chapter. However, most trade publishers' contracts will reflect industry norms, and studying the various parts of a standard publishing contract offers insight into how these areas have helped ascertain how copyright law and the contract as a secondary legal framework have been combined to create these industry standards.

In this contract overview, a summary of the various 'parts' helps to contextualise the scope and purpose of publishing contracts overall, and clauses that might signify symbolic and/or sanctioning power. The parts include 'Copyright and Rights/Licences', 'Subsidiary Rights', 'Delivery and Publication', 'Moral Rights and Editorial Input', 'Warrants and Indemnities', 'Royalties' and 'Termination and Reversion'.

This contract overview was also positioned and viewed in a particular context in the pre negotiation and post negotiation spaces to illustrate potential areas for adaptation – before and after signing. This context presumed a literal interpretation of the contract's terms (the pre negotiation space) as well as a subjective application of these terms in a real-life scenario (the post negotiation space). These perspectives are substantiated with further literature.

DOI:10.4324/9781003336570-3

Copyright and rights/licences granted

Boilerplate publishing contracts begin with an introduction or 'part' designed to clearly state the parties to the agreement and the date the contract is signed. This part will usually contain four key elements of the contract: that there is an agreement; that there is an intention to create legal relations; that there is consideration; and, finally, that the parties have a legal capacity to make the agreement (though the latter might also fall under the warrants and indemnities section of the contract) (Butler et al. 2017, 183). Despite some variation, most boilerplates also cover the intellectual property of the author, the rights that will be granted to the publisher, and delivery of the work.

An author owns their work (except in circumstances where it is jointly owned or has been created in the course of their employment, in Australian law for example) but may transfer rights to a third party (often exclusively). Literary agent Alex Adsett describes this process:

> If someone rents a house from you, they have the exclusive right to live in the house, and even though you are the owner/landlord, you cannot do certain things with your property while it is leased to someone else. If you grant the publisher an exclusive licence for the copyright then you cannot take advantage of whatever specific rights you have granted to the publisher for as long as the publisher has those rights.
>
> (Adsett 2018)

This means that the author cannot simultaneously publish the work while it has been licensed to the publisher. This prohibition would include excerpts or parts of the text (as per the subsidiary rights section). Publishers granted the licence, on the other hand, can reproduce, communicate and distribute the work (Butler et al. 2017, 114). In addition, they can license the work to others to do the same. Publishers, therefore, will want to claim as many rights as possible to exploit the work successfully with the aim of getting a return on their investment. Rarely would an author *assign* full copyright to a publisher, and this is an industry norm. This is not to say that there would not be other publishers who would, and could, ask the author to assign copyright. There is nothing in Australian law to prevent an author from assigning rights in a secondary framework such as a contract, though doing so completely disempowers the author from having any control over the production and distribution of their work. Many boilerplate contracts, however, state that the author will provide an 'exclusive' license, which means that no other party can publish the work except the signed publisher. More recently, the Australian Society of Authors standard template has included a specific Indigenous Cultural and Intellectual Property (ICIP) section and states that 'ownership of ICIP will at all times remain with the traditional owners or custodians of the ICIP', distinguishing this cultural content.

In terms of what rights are licensed and for how long, boilerplate clauses might state 'for the Term' and 'in the Languages and in the Territory' leaving open the negotiation of what the Languages, the Territory, and the Term, will be. Other contracts might prescribe the full term of copyright: 'for the legal period/term of copyright' and 'for the full term of the copyright of the Work' and 'during the legal term of copyright (including any renewals or extensions)', which would indicate a potential monopoly on any extension of copyright beyond the 70+ years after the death of the author (Jones & Benson 2011, 37).

In addition to the open language with regard to territories and the term of copyright, specifics about the Work can be itemised: as a 'Print Book', 'Ebook' and 'Audiobook', for example, sometimes with instructions to delete 'Audiobook' if the publisher intends to sub-license the audio production. Other contracts might state 'in all forms and editions' and 'in any form and by any means' – leaving open not only the decision to publish the work in any form if so desired but also the scope for future technological developments that might result in a variety of 'forms' not yet existing. These forms are also often offered 'throughout the world' but sometimes leaving this rights area open, with a range of options for the publisher and the author to negotiate. Gaining 'world rights' allows the publisher to sell the book in other territories and therefore exploit it maximally.

In Australia, the UK and the US, territorial copyright still exists (Cantatore 2014, 11). Depending on the publisher's power in the market, a company's strong international business relationships might mean that they are in the best position to be able to sell the book overseas. If so, the author should consider offering these rights to the publisher. Lynette Owen explains: 'It should . . . be remembered that the total package of rights offered to the hardback publishing house will certainly affect its decision on whether to take the work on at all' (Owen 2010, 61).

If the author's agent thinks they are in a better position to exploit the work, however, the author may choose to keep rights in some territories. The presence of an agent can certainly affect negotiations in this area, but if the wording of the contract prohibits negotiations in the first instance, then these negotiations could be strained. Some publishers eliminate the option to negotiate this right, even when they might be the least likely to have the transnational reach (such as a small independent publisher). On the other hand, an independent publisher might also be more willing to work harder to obtain international deals; a multinational would consider a midlist title not worth the effort (when compared with the potential revenue of a highly commercial book from a well-known author).

The next 'Subsidiary rights' area of the contract highlights the various rights on offer for exploitation.

Subsidiary rights

In addition to assigning exclusive economic rights to a publisher, an author may allow the publisher to exploit a number of other rights bundled into a category called subsidiary rights. These rights include such things as television and merchandising rights, English language rights, translation rights, serial rights, book club rights, dramatic rights and audio rights (to name a few). Digital rights can also fall under this category (Jones & Benson 2011, 92–94).

In contrast to the rights and licences explained earlier, which the publisher pays for with an advance and royalty, subsidiary rights income is shared between the author and publisher when the publisher has sublicensed these rights to a third party (providing the author has granted the rights to the primary publisher in the first place) (Jones & Benson 2011, 91).

For film and television rights, producers option the rights to a manuscript after the publisher has pitched it to them (option fees vary). Once the rights are assigned to the producer, the film and television rights belong to the producer, with ongoing income to the publisher and author. In many cases, the screenplay requires extensive reworking of the manuscript, and the publisher, in wanting the deal to be finalised, might encourage the author to forfeit their moral rights in the adapted work to facilitate this rework.

Most boilerplates detail the various subsidiary rights that will be granted to the publisher, albeit with much variation. These include first serial rights and second and subsequent serial rights; digest rights (some contracts prescribe, specifically, that these rights be extended to any mechanical, electronic or digital means); translation rights; electronic and digital reproduction rights (though these rights tend to be prescribed in either the 'Rights Granted' sections or the 'Subsidiary Rights' sections. A contract might also state these rights as 'mechanical or electronic . . . whether now known or which are yet to be invented', 'other delivery technology now known or later invented' or 'any electronic or digital means'); dramatic and film rights; television rights; merchandising rights; other mechanical rights; reprint rights; rights for formats for print disabled readers; and audio rights. To cover the whole suite of rights, which might not yet be identified, a contract might also state '*Any other right* which is vested in the Publishers during the term of the licence granted in [clause] – a percentage to be agreed' or, more vaguely, 'Any other sublicence contemplated by this agreement'.

The development of new technologies offers even more opportunities to exploit the work. Owen says:

> Few people could have imagined forty years ago that today it would be possible to license rights for the adaptation of a science fiction novel into a computer game, for a famous author to be heard reading his own book on an audiobook downloaded to an iPod.
>
> (Owen 2010, 38)

It is interesting to observe that publishers have attempted to predict that new formats will emerge, and they have asked for these rights to be assigned to them even though they don't yet exist.

Publishers effectively manage third-party licenses that could threaten other editions of the work if not handled in a timely fashion. For example,

> [t]he release of a Dutch translation very soon after publication of the original English-language hardback edition . . . could have a detrimental effect of sales on an early export edition of the UK paperback edition in the open market.
>
> (Owen 2010, 62)

Cannibalisation is an area that the author might not handle well without the assistance of an experienced publisher. For example, if an author keeps their rights to produce an ebook, their production of the ebook could cannibalise the print edition. It might be better, then, to leave the strategic release of editions to one party who manages them all (the publisher). But not all authors feel comfortable with the publisher acting as the middleperson in these negotiations if their work changes drastically (as noted previously, in television and movie rights). Also, due to the slight differences in what might be contained in the subsidiary 'bundle' of rights, authors aren't always aware of what they are licensing to publishers. Perhaps the agent plays a more significant role in the negotiations for these rights. Audiobook rights is certainly one aspect of the subsidiary rights area that has been highlighted as showing a shift in negotiations.

Audiobooks have seen significant growth in the market, boosted by the emergence of Audible. As a result, publishers are considering requesting this specific right as a primary right and producing their own audiobooks cheaply and efficiently. The recent production of Michelle's and Barak Obama's respective memoirs, for example, were recorded in-house at Penguin Random House, with the Obamas narrating their own works. Currently, authors receive around 10–15 per cent of net receipts, or a percentage, as noted earlier, of a third-party license. But it has been suggested that the recent growth in audiobooks is '[leading] to a shift in attitude amongst authors' agents, who are no longer so inclined to include audiobook rights automatically in the publisher's package of rights' (Owen 2010, 269). The broad and non-exhaustive list of subsidiary rights the publisher wishes to secure has, perhaps, in the past, not always been utilised effectively (if at all). Evidence of contestation in the areas of 'Rights and Territories' might also indicate how subsidiary rights are utilised in relation to digital reproductions of content in a global publishing market.

English language is also a subsidiary right many authors choose to allow their agents (as opposed to publishers) to exploit. From a publisher's perspective, this can be frustrating. For example, for titles that have not had strong sales domestically, territorial rights can often help the publisher recoup income internationally, and publishers can be very effective in finding possibilities for titles outside of their territory. An author's moral rights could be adversely affected via the third-party licensing of subsidiary rights, however. For example, does the author have a say in which translator will be used for translation rights? Can they choose who to hire to write the stage adaption of their book? It should be imperative for rights agents in publishing houses to work closely with the editorial department to ensure they have the perspective of the author when negotiating deals to third parties. But it is not always practical to keep the author in mind when trying to secure the best deal possible. The author is also not always present to inform the rights agent about their preferences. It is easier for rights agents to think of the publisher when the author is absent from negotiations, particularly because it is their job to sell rights. This perhaps highlights the role of editors as one of the most important mediators in the 'post negotiation space'. In response to my analysis of this particular area of the contract, 'Rights and Territories' and 'Subsidiary Rights' would likely present in the surveys as contested areas of the contract *before* the contract is signed – pre negotiation, as well as an area of contestation and perhaps regret/disappointment post negotiation.

Delivery and publication

There are usually fairly detailed requirements for the delivery of the work to the publisher. These details include a firm date for the delivery and the format in which the work shall be delivered (usually electronic), as well as some very general terms used to explain what is meant by 'satisfactory' work: 'suitable for publication', 'of publishable quality', 'satisfactory to the Publisher' and 'sufficient'. Even when the description of the work is fairly comprehensive, it is usually the case that 'the Publisher has final say with respect to the matters outlined' but that 'the Publisher must take into account the Author's reasonable views on the matters and act reasonably in making its decision about such matters'. Some contracts expressly prohibit the Author from decisions regarding production and sales.

The express prohibition of final decisions in price point, layout, print paper and bind (PPB), and sales and marketing, in some publishing contracts, could also affect the authors' moral rights because the publisher has the final say over the paratextual elements that signify genre and the published book's position in the market. There is, of course, the possibility that the author and the publisher will agree on these details prior to the contract being signed. If not, they are not accounted for in writing. It is rare that a publisher would give the author full 'approval' as opposed to 'consent'. It could be surmised that publishers consider it unnecessary to prescribe such strict parameters about the book's production and that the details of the paratextual elements of the book are always open to interpretation, in which editorial input could be advantageous in determining how communication of expectations will transpire. But willingness to negotiate does not mitigate the publisher having the final say. What is clear is that there is minimal detail in this area about what the publisher plans for each title. What is not clear is if the lack of detail is intentional, and, if it is, why. Charles Fried states: 'Most contract disputes have to do with disagreements about interpretation, and the topics of good faith and the effect of writing can be gathered under the rubric' (Fried 1981, 134). In a show of good faith to correct miscommunication, it is possible that the parties to the publishing contract can *re*communicate post negotiation.

In addition to the specifications for the production of the book, many contracts also prescribe a strict blanket rule with regard to editorial intervention, often in the author's favour. Clauses such as 'No alterations will be made to the title of the Work without the Author's consent' and 'The Publisher must consult the Author on editorial decisions and the Publisher must take into account the Author's reasonable views in making a decision about such matters. The Publisher will not publish the Work until any reasonable differences in editing have been resolved' are not uncommon. While this appears very prescriptive, what is deemed 'reasonable' might be very different from the publisher's and the author's perspectives. In other words, its assertion could be misleading in that it suggests that the author has more power to veto changes. If we look at what would be reasonable by industry standards, it has been suggested that, in the event of conflict, the law may find in favour of the publisher. Maree Sainsbury describes this dilemma:

> The implication of a term limiting the alterations which can be made to a work depends on two main considerations. *First*, the express terms of the contract must be considered – a contract granting a right to alter the work will be enforced according to its terms, regardless of what the alterations are. . . . *Secondly*, the extent of such a term will depend on the subject matter of the contract. . . . It may also be possible to argue that such a term ought to be implied as a matter of custom in the industry, such that everyone in that situation can be reasonably presumed to have imported that term into the contract.
>
> (Sainsbury 2003, 75)

Being an outsider to the in-house workflow processes of a publishing company, an author, especially a first-time author, might be at a disadvantage when it comes to defining what is customary.

Moral rights and editorial input

Australia has only recently recognised moral rights in its Copyright Act, but other countries have had a moral rights framework that has been finessed over time. UK publishing contracts, for example, allow for more freedom to waive rights. Overall, moral rights are assumed without authors having to assert these rights. Moral rights include:

> The right to be identified as the author of the work.
> The right not to have authorship of the work falsely attributed.
> The right not to have the work altered in a prejudicial way (Copyright Act (Australia)).

Notwithstanding the UK's flexibility with waiving rights, moral rights in general cannot be assigned or licensed to another person, which means that they cannot be passed to the publisher. While in book publishing the right to attribution is generally uncontested (due to the author's name being clearly placed on the covers of their titles), the right of integrity is less clear but possibly the most important, in terms of its application in the normal processes of book production and editing. Sainsbury claims that '[t]he right to integrity limits the circumstances in which alterations can be made to the work' (Sainsbury 2003, 23), yet s 195AS of the Australian Copyright Act states that the right to integrity has not been infringed if it was reasonable to do so.[1] An example of this might be casting the text into another format, such as an ebook. Sainsbury says: 'The moral rights of an author may be infringed, not by any alteration of the actual text or images, but by the way in which they are presented. When a work is converted into digital form, it is difficult to guarantee that the layout will stay the same' (Sainsbury 2003, 143). Also, in typical workflow practice, categorisation of genre and subsequent editing are decided on within the in-house discussions and assessment of the manuscript. These determinations may not necessarily be in line with the author's perception of their writing, and there could be grounds for termination of the contract if there is evidence of inadvertent misunderstandings about the editing of the work based on its initial evaluation. Without the express disclosure of things like layout and publishing decisions, an author has, perhaps, minimal control over the presentation of the work and their particular personality inherent within it. This is where the author can broach such things with their editor and publisher, post negotiation.

For there to be a moral infringement, it must be proven that the 'treatment of the work prejudices the creator's honour or reputation' (Butler et al. 2017, 136) and that 'the derogatory treatment of the Work must have occurred to a substantial part' (Section 195A1 (2) of the Australian Copyright Act 1968). This is undoubtedly difficult to prove, and the Berne Convention provides requirements for determination. As such, and with Article 6*bis* of the Berne Convention adopting a minimalist approach to determining honour and reputation, it is more likely that 'the test will incorporate some objective judgement of prejudice, as in a defamation action' (Sainsbury 2003, 57). This statement suggests that more detail within publishing contracts could uphold the author's moral rights in a secondary legal framework and be further supported via effective communication between the author and the publisher in contract negotiations.

In analysing how moral rights have been communicated in publishing boilerplate contracts, some express them explicitly, while others do not state the rights but, rather, assume them. The most recent ASA contract also asserts the right of traditional owners or custodians of ICIP to 'be recognised and attributed in the Work as owners'. Some boilerplates include an 'Acknowledgement' part, whereby the author will have the work attributed to them, and the contract will follow the provisions of the Universal Copyright Convention or refer the signatories to the overarching laws pertaining to copyright in general. While these oblique references to moral rights are perhaps sufficient on the surface, there is an assumption of a consensus on what amounts to infringement. These references also assume that the author has asserted their moral rights in other territories, where moral rights might need to be actively defended.

While some contracts prescribe a rather strict blanket rule around editorial intervention at the developmental editing stage *before* the text is typeset into page proofs, other contracts may choose to keep the degree of editorial intervention (as a written prescription) vague.

This stage of the editing process is fundamental in that it confirms the position of the book in the market, in terms of its genre and market expectations. At the structural editing stage, substantial redrafting can sometimes amount to complete recasting of POV (point-of-view) characters as well as cuts and vastly reworked plotlines, to bring the writing up to the expectations of its projected audience. Many contracts, however, regard this work as a process outside of the contractual terms. The expectations of what editorial work constitutes can therefore be misunderstood between the parties. It might be better, then, not to have such a clause in the contract, thereby leaving such alterations open for discussion throughout the editorial process.

Despite the vague outline of the editorial process at the infant stages of book production, there are generally some clauses to guide perusal of page proofs. Within these clauses, there is little variation, and the degree of corrections allowed generally falls within 15 per cent for author corrections (for the overall work). The publisher's contribution to the mark-up of page proofs is almost always, notably, absent.

It is necessary to explore how editorial processes balance the rights of the publisher and the author, as well as their specific interests, both within the contract negotiation and beyond it. Does effective communication about expectations around editorial intervention, post negotiation, help to uphold the author's rights *and* provide the most flexibility possible for the publisher? Or would detailing the editorial process in the contract (e.g. insisting on hardcopy edits so the work can't be easily distributed, and corrections can be identified more easily – made without Track Changes) be more effective? As Sainsbury suggests, perhaps such a term should, or is, rather, implied (Sainsbury 2003, 75). Yet, again, that does not necessarily assist someone outside of the specific customs and ways of working within the publishing house.

Moral rights can of course be waived, and there is, in some instances, economic justification for this to occur (such as the sale of film rights) (Jones & Benson 2011, 48). To maximise revenue for a title, publishers might encourage authors to abandon moral rights, which could involve conciliating the author's assertions. Publishers are arguably in the best position to ascertain how an author's moral rights could affect the economic potential of their titles. Publishers and rights agents are, after all, the ones on the ground selling the work into other territories and in a variety of different formats. There is usually no evidence, however, of the possibility of such discussions or of rights being waived for the purpose of exploiting the work. This could be because the possibilities for a work, at the time of contracting, have not yet been imagined, or perhaps they are not apparent. But if a movie option is raised, it will be up to the publisher to convince the author that screenwriting, as an entirely different genre, might require extensive intervention. In this situation, the publisher will have to 'persuade the author to forego some or all of his protection. This persuasion could take the form of an economic incentive' (Sainsbury 2003, 21).

Warrants and indemnities

The warrants and indemnities sections of the contract assist the publisher in protecting themselves from potentially litigious content. Almost all boilerplate contracts now, therefore, contain a warrants clause. In this clause, the author warrants to the publisher that the work is original, that the author is the sole proprietor of the work, that the work does not infringe on existing copyright, that the work is true (if applicable) and does not contain any defamatory content, and that the author has power to enter into the agreement. The latter concerns the author's 'capacity' to enter into the contract, which means, legally, that they are not minors and are not mentally impaired (Butler et al. 2017, 187). What this clause does *not* address is authors who might, post contract, feel that they were not informed of the contract's terms at the time of signing it. However, under Australian consumer law (s 18), as an example, an author can rescind a contract if he/she can show that they were in a position of 'special disadvantage' and that the other party knew of that disadvantage. Des Butler explains:

> A position of 'special disadvantage' has been interpreted as meaning a position which seriously affects the ability of an innocent party to make a judgment about his or her interests, with relevant circumstances including the innocent party's age, drunkenness, infirmity of mind or body, illiteracy or lack of education and lack of assistance or explanation where assistance or explanation is necessary.
>
> (Butler et al. 2017, 196)

This clause puts the onus entirely in the publisher's hands. The 'lack of education and lack of assistance or explanation where assistance or explanation is necessary' might therefore cover an author not practised in contract negotiations. Authors could be especially disadvantaged if they lack knowledge, or interest in, this area of the contract. But disinterest, in particular, would not necessarily be considered a special disadvantage. Publishers have the option of refusing to enter into the agreement if the author will not warrant that the work does not contain any content that might prompt litigation. Publishers aren't always immediately aware of such content, and there is also the possibility of the author adding more content to the already submitted manuscript. It might be possible, then, for both parties to find a way to revisit this clause post negotiation. It is not feasible to expect all authors to have agents or to employ a lawyer to look over their contracts. In this respect, they could be considered 'rationally ignorant' (Barnett 2011, 16) and agree to specific terms, if breaking a vague or subjective term is deemed to be not as significant as the cost of clarifying it.

Most contracts will also require the author to warrant that the work is not in breach of any other laws, such as privacy or official secrets laws, as well as having no content that would cause injury to the user, usually 'to the best of his/her/their knowledge', which provides room for error of judgement. Publishing contract clauses will also require the author to indemnify the publisher against any loss, injury or damage with respect to the warrants. If the contract contains a 'Legal Review' clause, however, negotiation between the author and the publisher about vetting content that might pose a legal threat to both parties will be encouraged. With non-fiction proving to be an established popular genre, there is more reason to ensure that non-fiction titles are factual and non-defamatory. The warrants and indemnities section of the contract, therefore, is very important to many publishers, who are in more danger of being sued because of their relative financial strength and their position as secondary infringers. Its importance is reflected in the precise wording of this section in boilerplate contracts, and at the least a willingness to discuss potential problems, via the 'Legal Review' section, before publication.

Royalties

Royalties are presented in both the subsidiary rights and royalties sections of most publishing contracts, and they relate to the publisher's specific territory – usually for the first printing of the book. The royalty rate for reprints is also stated in the contract, and will either be a little higher, as a gesture to reward the author for the success of their title, or, in some cases, lower – particularly if the reprint is small. This should not be assumed, however. Some contracts also provide a separate royalty for small reprints, which are to be negotiated at the time when a decision to reprint is made.

Although the royalty percentages are, in theory, negotiable, the publisher usually sets the percentage at 10 per cent of the recommended retail price of the title at both the first printing and the reprint, which doesn't reward the author if sales grow. It is not uncommon for the royalty to rise to 12.5 per cent on sales for 5001–15,000 copies and 15 per cent thereafter on copies sold (other than high discount). For well-known and successful authors (in terms of sales), the royalty might be slightly higher as the print-runs increase on subsequent titles. These risers would suggest that the author is being rewarded for the sales success of their titles *if* the sales are significant in the eyes of the publisher.

Ebook royalties are always higher at around 20–25 per cent, which is consistent across most standard contracts. Bulk discounted stock is also generally a percentage of net receipts. The benefits of bulk stock could be that the book has a wider distribution and therefore a potentially bigger market. This can sometimes be seen in dump bins at large orders in discount department stores (DDS) or for book clubs such as Scholastic. Such large orders are often offset by a discounted price.

For subsidiary rights, the percentage that will be shared with the author, of net amounts of money earned from these rights, is documented. The proportion to the author generally ranges between 50 and 80 per cent, and the individual publishers' strengths in different markets and their relationships with international agencies, as explained under the 'Subsidiary Rights' subheading, could inform the different percentages.

The wording of clauses for small print-runs is of particular interest. To keep the book in print, the author may have to forego the standard royalty expected. This positions the publisher as something of a saviour in their efforts to ensure the longevity of the title when it would otherwise have become out of print (OP). An author, then, has the option, in negotiations, of prohibiting the publisher from reprinting if a royalty cannot be negotiated, or acquiescing. If the publisher feels that the potential of the title has been exhausted, they will usually pulp the remaining stock, or sell the stock to the author at a discounted price, while still maintaining copyright of the Work. Another solution is for the publisher to revert the rights back to the author if the author feels that the publisher is not fulfilling their duties in marketing and selling the work effectively. Reversion, as a solution to unsuccessful contracts or relationships, or in the event of a book not reaching its potential (however that is perceived), is discussed next.

Termination and reversion

Publishing is a business that attempts to minimise risk (Thompson 2005, 15). Most publishers and acquisitions editors will keep abreast of trends and try to predict the market, but nobody ever really knows if a book will be a bestseller, a solid midlist title or sell only a few copies. For this reason, a publisher will attempt to secure rights for the work usually for the full term of copyright. But in the case of works that don't sell, this could mean the book is left languishing with a publisher who no longer has a commercial interest in it. In this situation, the contract might offer a reversion clause that allows the author to regain the rights they have licensed to the publisher and potentially relicense those rights to another party who might be more successful in exploiting them. This could also result in self-publishing opportunities, too, for the author, who, having developed a stronger platform after the primary negotiations took place, might be in a good position to exploit the Work. Conversely, if the book is a huge success, the author may feel that they should have the opportunity to renegotiate the terms of the contract and recoup more from the success of their work. Rebecca Giblin notes:

> there is no reason why the author and publisher should not be able to mutually agree to terminate the previous grant and enter into a fresh one for a new period of up to another twenty-five years – this time each with much better knowledge of what the work is worth.
>
> (Giblin 2018, 398)

The obvious benefit for the author is that they are remunerated for the unprecedented success of the work or perhaps they initially underestimated the commercial strength of the work and now want to capitalise on its success (after the fact). The downside for the publisher is that they might have to pay a higher royalty or provide other benefits to the author that they were not required to do in the primary contract. Not all publishing contracts prescribe a specific reversion clause as a separate right; however, most contracts will usually contain a clause that outlines when a title will be considered out of print (OP). When a book becomes OP, it is an unspoken agreement that the author can ask for their rights to be reverted and that the reversion is often obliged. Outlines of what is considered OP range from fewer than 20 copies for hardback editions, fewer than 50 copies for paperback, or fewer than 100 copies of any edition that has been sold in the previous two accounting periods. A reversion clause such as this appears to provide a fair deal to the author, but close inspection of the wording of the clauses reveals that, in all likelihood, the work may never go OP. Giblin shares this perspective and quotes the Authors Guild:

> [P]ublishers have cleverly managed to craft 'out of print' clauses that make it almost impossible for authors to recapture their rights. Classic contract language states that a book is not out of print as long as it is 'available for sale in any edition.' So publishers 'release' the book in a print-on-demand or electronic edition that's always available, even if few copies are actually sold. By relying on language originally intended to provide a real reversionary right, a publisher can now hold onto a book forever even if it's not actually doing anything with it. That is not how 'out of print' was supposed to work.[2]

Not all contracts are so specific, and they may instead offer clauses such as 'the Work is out of print when the royalty paid for gross combined sales of print and ebook editions in the previous twelve-month royalty period is less than $100' and 'a Work shall be deemed out of print where combined gross sales of the hardback, paperback and the ebook editions across any two successive accounting periods total less than 50 (fifty) copies'. Given the possibility of small print-runs, and the multiple editions of the work, in a number of different territories, the publisher, if diligent, can ensure that the work never goes out of print. But if the work is not selling well, it begs the question: Why would publishers want to hang onto it anyway? Giblin offers some context:

> imagine a book author who enters a contract with a publisher to publish the book, granting exclusive rights to reproduce the text for twenty-five years and reserving the film rights. In the twenty-fourth year of the publication contract, a film adaptation is released. This would be a great opportunity to re-market the book, but the publisher may be reluctant to make those investments knowing that their exclusivity period was about to lapse.
>
> (Giblin 2018, 398)

Authors, however, seldom broach this aspect of contract negotiations and don't always consider reversion as something that allows them to maintain some control over the exploitation of their work – effectively prompting the publisher to do the best they can for the work, or lose it – at least not in initial contract negotiations. Some contracts certainly cover such an agreement by suggesting that authors negotiate a right of termination if sales drop below expectations. Authors might still tacitly accept terms so they don't jeopardise the negotiation altogether. Or authors are so confident in their publisher's ability to exploit the work that they would grant them the full term of copyright, with no reversion clause if circumstances change. Or it might be that authors are not even aware of the benefits of reversion. So what scope is there for outright termination, not just for books OP, but for other reasons such as the author being unsatisfied with how the work was edited, or the current royalty breakdown?

With regard to termination, most contract clauses focus on the publisher's *non-compliance* with the agreement: for example, if the publisher goes into liquidation or claims by the publisher that the author has not complied with the agreement. While most contracts will indicate what will happen in the event of the terms of the contract not being met, there might still be room for negotiations, even in the post negotiation space. Oliver Black states: '[A] contract may exist even though an agreement only appears to – in which case there can be a contract without an agreement' (Black 2012, 238). This would suggest that it is expected that contracts are simply unable to be interpreted by both parties in exactly the same way. Charles Fried also supports this theory in saying that (in the area of tort and restitution) '[t]he language of mistake suggests that certainty is the paradigm, but in fact contracts are largely a deliberate attempt to deal with uncertainty' (Fried 1981, 59). This assumes, however, that there is a general consensus on the terms of the contract and that the individual *interpretation* by the vested parties is subjective. But what if the terms are understood and the author is effectively assenting to terms they don't like? Black raises this possibility in saying that 'it seems that a person may make an agreement, contractual or not, against his will and yet without being subject to any coercion as would exclude his being obligated to perform' (Black 2012, 221). For example, it would appear that the author should initially be in a more powerful position during negotiations of the terms of the contract. This is because it is the publisher who recognises the work as valuable and believes that they can exploit it (Fried 1981, 13). They are 'promising' the author to do so and will have the author's best 'economic' interests when trying to sell the work to other territories and in other formats. In the pre negotiation space, it is the author who usually seeks to submit their work in the hope that it will be accepted. This immediately reverses the power dynamic in that the author is now promising the publisher exclusive economic rights by way of being grateful for the chance to be published. In this scenario, challenging the contract could prove risky for the author. If any terms in the contract are not accepted and a renegotiation is instigated, this could jeopardise the agreement and place the author back at square one. In this instance, the author's acceptance of the terms is, essentially, tacit. Fried likens this scenario to an electrical current with two switches – one switch for the promisor (the author in this case) and one switch for the promisee (the publisher). I have constructed two diagrams to help illustrate this scenario: in a 'pre negotiation space', if the promisor closes their switch, they are vulnerable because the circuit can be fully closed by the promisee accepting the promise. For example, if the author promises to indemnify the publisher for any legal costs in relation to potentially defamatory material in the manuscript, they are effectively closing their switch. If the publisher accepts their promise and also closes their switch, then the deal is done. But if the author does not agree to indemnify the publisher, their switch is open for renegotiation. And if it is open (before acceptance), the acceptance by itself is insufficient to complete the circuit.

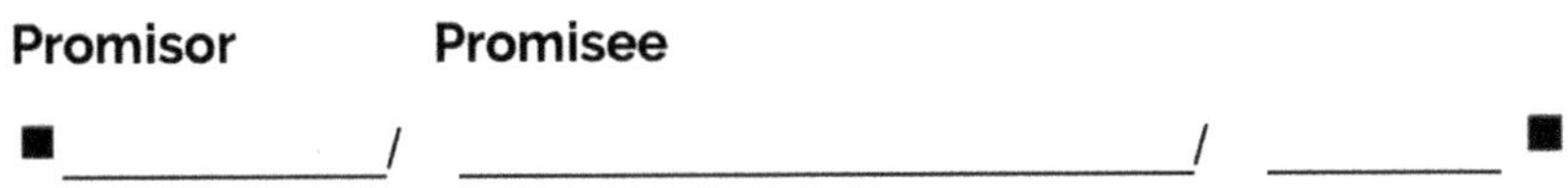

FIGURE 3.1 Contract agreement diagram A

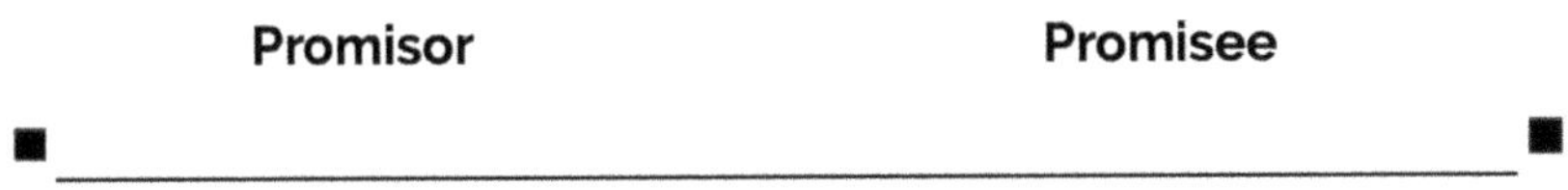

FIGURE 3.2 Contract agreement diagram B

This is all dependent on agreement about the explicit and implicit terms of the contract. And in the pre negotiation space, consensus on these meanings may never be reached. It could be in this scenario that we are more likely to witness the author's tacit position again. Black describes that '[v]arious writers note that the etymology of "obligation" (*ob-ligare*) includes the idea of a bond, and some have drawn attention to the distinction between being bound (a normative matter) and feeling bound (a matter of psychology)' (Black 2012, 95). There might come a point at which the author will take their chances and rely on the circumstances of the event in which a promise might be seen to have been broken, and assume fairness from the publisher. Fried says: '[W]hether each can be sure that the other meant what he seemed to mean, or heard what he seemed to hear, is a problem that no amount of confirmation or reconfirmation can solve completely' (Fried 1981, 50). In post negotiation, there are two possibilities towards resolution: a) that the promisee is willing to negotiate in light of a broken promise due to misunderstanding or b) that the promisor accepts the punishment if they do not deliver on their promise.

***

Publishers will request as many rights as possible in most contract negotiations. This is obviously in an attempt to gain more opportunities for them to recoup on their investment. In many cases, publishers will have a clear idea of the potential for the book before a letter of offer is made and will be confident of their relationships with agents in other territories, as well as their ability to market the book successfully. But authors can actively challenge their publisher's ability to exhaust all of these rights, and authors can also make distinctions between publishers and know which are in a better position to sell their work. For publishers, a clear awareness of their position in the field allows them to make realistic decisions around the print-run, format and price of certain titles. Independents may also be in a strong position to exhaust all possibilities for a midlist title that would otherwise be lost among the commercial titles in a larger publisher's list.

Undoubtedly, a publisher might also have a better overall strategy to handle third-party licenses. Even with an agent, an author must ensure that different editions in different territories do not cannibalise each other, which is easier to manage when all of the rights are in the same place and not divided and sold to various licensees. The danger, of course, is relinquishing control and leaving the publisher to make the deals – some that might result in extensive rewriting of the story to fit the particular structure and style of a film script, for example. There is little evidence to suggest that authors are, in fact, happy to waive their moral rights in order to gain more economic benefits – precisely because this negotiating detail is often not present in standard publishing contracts, and it appears that authors would be willing to offer all rights to a publisher they think can exhaust them effectively. If an author is completely unaware of the power their particular publisher has in the field – and of how the publisher goes about their business – then we might see authors accepting the terms simply because they do not understand the potential for the work, they do not have an agent to advise on the potential, or they trust that the publisher is in the best position to exploit the work. For the latter, authors might be more mindful of their pecuniary interests than the literature would suggest. If so, then a shift in position-taking of the author, by way of them demanding performance from the publisher, or seeking alternatives to that of granting the publisher full rights, is observed.

The reversion clause of the contract might, as an extension of the author's negotiating power, also be an area of contestation. If a book does well after publication, the author might want to reassess the original contract after the book's unprecedented success. Reversion would allow for this level of reassessment, and its implementation in a contract offers a much more equal playing field for the author and the publisher. Unlike unilateral termination, with reversion negotiation is likely – particularly if the publisher wants to keep the author on their list.

Also evident in many boilerplates is the very precise wording in the delivery and publication section deeming the publisher to be in full control over the final decision about the print, paper and bind (PPB). In determining some of the important paratextual aspects of the book, the publisher controls the position of the book in the market. If the author disagrees, they often have little room to assert their own vision, potentially highlighting a chasm in the way a book is envisioned by the author and the publisher. The publisher might project a commercial title and package the work as such; the author might see a literary title and resist the publisher's vision. Looking back on my own experience, I know that the publishing house's vision for my book was different to my own, but I made the decision to adopt the publisher's vision. Another author's inability to understand or negotiate the vision, however, would place them in a position of tacit obligation or complete faith in their publisher's assessment of the work. Many contracts display only the basic terms around moral rights, as outlined in copyright law, without considering other territories and the integrity aspect of moral rights, in particular. But perhaps publishers and authors have other ways of negotiating moral rights without the need for this detail, and the editor's role in supporting and managing the author's expectations is a key factor in the satisfaction of the parties in this area. Yet it certainly is not prescriptive within many contracts.

In the warrants and indemnities section of contracts, authors often carry the burden of responsibility of defamatory content in the manuscript. Some contracts promote negotiation between the author and the publisher over the manuscript's 'legalling' and encourage the author to consider the publisher's position in this respect.

Finally, the particular wording of the royalty sections in many boilerplates indicates more power for the publisher to maintain exclusive rights to the author's work. The small print-runs clauses, in particular, prevent authors from exerting control after the contract is signed. One would imagine that this would have a knock-on effect if reversion has not been considered, in which case it would be a contested area.

The standardisation of most commercial trade publishing boilerplates indicates that authors rarely challenge contracts and that the same clauses are repeated over time. Perhaps authors don't challenge the contract's terms because they don't want to jeopardise the negotiation. Or perhaps they are happy with the agreements. The division of rights speaks to the pecuniary interests of the author, as do the 'Royalties' and 'Rights Reversion' sections. But if these areas of the contract are uncontested, authors might find other ways to exert some degree of power in the post negotiation space. The editor would play a significant role in this respect, and would be the key to successful relationships within publishing houses, revealing the contract as a 'guide' and not necessarily a sanction. But while the editor's management of the editorial and book production process might uphold the moral rights of the author, the author's pecuniary interests are still locked into the specific wording of the contract. The authors' tacit positions on negotiations in this area points to it being less important than their moral rights inherent in the work, in which case there could be seen to be a general consensus that any contract with a publisher would always only focus on pecuniary interests and the author then concedes of their position in this scenario. This new position-taking might not be so much a question of challenging the status quo as much as a shift in values, by way of the author having to adapt to a changing landscape. The question, then, would be of whom to publish with – preferably a publisher with more power in the market. Alternatively, the author may seek a publisher that upholds values that align with their own.

It is enlightening that authors might be far more concerned with their pecuniary interests in the contract than would be anticipated (whether by concession or re-evaluation) and that this concern has potentially reframed the historical construction of the romanticised author as genius and creator. Rather than using this construction to substantiate value in the work, is it possible that authors are acquiescing to the publishers' requests, which are notably pecuniary but also employing these pecuniary parameters? Authors are now better positioned to understand publishing as a business (a direct result of globalisation and global communication). Knowing that the publisher will approach the contract from this position, the author can negotiate areas important to them. For example, the author can expect, and will possibly ask for, performance from their publishers for marketing their work and finding opportunities in various territories. Bourdieu expresses this position by suggesting that it is naïve to think one can enter into 'a *specific code* of conduct and expression' and experience '*freedom under constraints* and *objective potentialities*' (Bourdieu 1996, 229). Rather, the author is aware of the constraints, which

> define and delimit the universe of the thinkable and the unthinkable, that is to say, both the finite universe of potentialities capable of being thought and realized at any given moment – freedom – and the system of constraints inside which is determined what is to be done and to be thought – necessity.
>
> (Bourdieu 1996, 229)

In other words, proof of what has gone before – in this example, the construction of the terms of the standard contract, as well as its utilitarian foundations based on our understanding of the dynamics of the publishing field – influences a new perception of author as creator *and* entrepreneur. In this instance, the author circumscribes the highly constrained paradigm (the contract) – a structure that could borrow from Bourdieu's term 'historical transcendental'. This highlights a gradual perceptive shift in the author's position-taking. The author is no longer *actively* and abruptly oppositional to the historical construction of 'writer'; rather, development of the author's renewed position is incremental. In re-negotiating Bourdieu's field (and recasting themselves as artists concerned with the cultural value of their work but *not* at the expense of the economic value of the work), the author, by extension, subconsciously re-negotiates the contract. In effect, the author creates a stronger link between the sanctioning aspects of the contract and their expectations of what it means to be a writer.

The next stage of this study analysed the results of the surveys, which were designed to add further context to the overview provided earlier and answer some of the questions posed, test the theories and identify areas in need of further investigation via in-depth interviews.

Notes

1 The Australian Copyright Act (1968) describes what is reasonable treatment of the work: editing or reworking a draft document, translation, using work as for parody or burlesque.

2 See 'A Publishing Contract Should Not Be Forever', Authors Guild (July 28, 2015), https://perma.cc/67DE-JQBN. in Giblin, R 2018, 'Reclaiming Lost Culture and Getting Authors Paid', 41 COLUM. J.L. & ARTS, vol. 369, pp. 403.

4

ASSESSING THE FIELD

What the survey says

The next step in the research design was to survey 100 participants representative of the literary field, which encompassed authors (unpublished and published), and publishing professionals (literary agents, publishers and rights agents). This sample also mirrors Bourdieu's players in the literary field, which enables the theoretical framework to be directly investigated in context: the 'populations' within the field (writers, publishers and agents) (Jensen 2002, 238), and like Bourdieu's literary field, the 'strategic junctures may be hierarchical or spatial (in terms of the structure of the organisation) or they may be temporal'. (Jensen 2002, 239)

The survey sample was based on a cross-sectional design within the following genres: children's, young adult, adult fiction and non-fiction, and comprised two main groups: 'Authors' (which includes subgroups 'Established Authors', 'New Authors', 'Self-Published and Hybrid Authors', and 'Emerging/Unpublished Authors') and 'Publishing Professionals' (which included subgroups 'Agents, Legal Representatives and Rights and Permissions Agents', and 'Publishers'). The subgroups were defined by the following characteristics: 'Established Authors' will have published 4+ titles, in which they may have had an opportunity to witness change in contract negotiations, including changing publishing houses, securing an agent or negotiating specific areas of the contract based on previous experiences. 'New Authors' will have published 1–3 titles. It was anticipated that this group was perhaps on the verge of considering the negotiations stated for 'Established Writers', thus in the process of exploring their options. 'Self-Published and Hybrid Authors' created the variable, representing the democratised field, and in this capacity, it was hoped, would shed some light on developments in the industry, indicating abandonment of traditional models. The final group, the 'Unpublished Authors', like the 'New Authors', potentially offered an example of a facet of the field on the cusp of potential contract negotiations or on the outer circle – watching the field as it transpires and hopefully cultivating some opinions regarding what they are witnessing. Excluded from the sample were editors, booksellers and sales and marketing professionals, the latter not directly involved in contract negotiations.

In collating the sample, I had anticipated that the groups within it would be refined as the research progressed (e.g. further subsets of publishers i.e. the commercial publisher, the

DOI:10.4324/9781003336570-4

self-publisher and the independent publisher, and further subsets of authors – the commercial author, the literary author). It was my intention to allow the research to determine the subsets as they emerged, rather than impose the subsets before the commencement of interviews. Brannen cautions of this risk in saying that 'the current turn to reflexivity in qualitative research in respect of the focus upon the researcher risks neglecting research participants' (Brannen 2004, 283).

With a list prepared of a cross section of the literary field, the next step was to devise a survey that would be open enough to pinpoint areas for further investigation via the interviews. I used two self-administered questionnaires as my survey instrument: the Author Survey (AS) and the Publishing Professionals Survey (PPS), and adopted a descriptive design that reflected existing phenomena in publishing (such as work hierarchies, genre identifications, as a few examples) (Fink 1995, 25). I also defined the distinct characteristics of the sample, to make valuable comparisons between them (Fink 2003). These characteristics (variables) assisted me in developing an 'understanding of what may cause a phenomenon . . . by looking at variation in that variable across cases, and looking for other characteristics which are systematically linked with it' (De Vaus 2002, 5). The purposive sample attempted to provide the variables to direct the content of the questionnaires, which were designed to be specific to the subgroups within the 'Author' and 'Publishing Professional' groups.

To identify the variables more clearly and determine what they might signify, I devised four objectives for the survey and then developed the list of questions for the survey instrument (Fink 1995, 17). To do this, I asked the following: what do these theories tell me that I can integrate into the survey instrument? In what direction does the literature steer me? What can I define for the survey questions? What do I want to discover?

Based on the existing literature, I was able to make some assumptions before devising the questions, and these assumptions defined the subgroups of the sample. For example, I was able to distinguish a commercial publisher from an independent publisher, and an emerging writer from an established writer, by way of discreet characteristics. An example might be that an independent publisher works for a publishing house that is perhaps partly government subsidised and is not a listed company. I was also able to assume that the historical development of copyright law is expressed in contracts. I did not seek to define these concepts/terms in the survey. Knowing that the purpose of the survey was to test initial theories and further define the eligibility of the units of analysis, my questionnaire, rather, attempted the following:

1 to determine within the sample the level of involvement with book contracts;
2 to determine the degree to which authors still seek a publishing contract, and with whom;
3 to determine if contract negotiations had occurred, and in which areas of the contract;
4 to ascertain the level of satisfaction in contract negotiations;
5 to ascertain if alternatives to publishing contracts have been sought, and which alternatives.

In compiling the survey questions, I attempted to eliminate ambiguous terms and concepts (Fink 1995, 8). Although I had a clear understanding of the variables in my cross section of the literary field, I was mindful that not all subgroups would have the same understanding of conceptual terms. For example, can I define a book contract? Who is a writer? Who is a publishing professional? What constitutes negotiation? These concepts were refined and given context at the time the questions were devised. They were then added to the survey to assist the respondents with their answers. The definitions were a combination of my own understanding of these terms from my experience as a publishing professional and from the ways in which they have been defined in scholarly studies.

The survey also aimed to identify central themes that might emerge from the participants' responses (Patton 2002, 234–235), from which further discovery could be sought via in-depth interviews. To help me extract these themes, I embedded the survey with subsections which were not made explicit to the participants. This was arranged discreetly so as not to influence the participants' responses. The subsections in the 'Author Survey' (AS) corresponded with the 'Publishing Professional Survey' (PPS) but with some variation due to the unique roles of each participant group. I wanted to create a basis for cross-checking answers. For the 'Unpublished Authors', I focused on the following:

Questions 12, 14, 15 – These questions established responses to the main questions of perceptions of publishers, contracts and agents, generally.

Questions 8, 16, 19 – These questions indicated the level of understanding of the parts of the contract and copyright in general. Even 'no' or 'don't know' answers, then, in these questions, might indicate areas for further research. These particular questions also closely corresponded with the PPS in the hope that they might show similarities or differences, and, in doing so, a perceived difference in values and expectations.

Question 18 – This question was designed to ascertain the unpublished author's understanding/perception of an agent's role/influence in contract negotiations. This question aimed to have a dual purpose in that it supports questions 8, 16 and 19 – either the author will say they 'don't know' in the box below, or they will have an opinion. If they ticked the box that stated that they think having an agent is beneficial, in 15, then I would expect that they would number the boxes in 16. The answers would then point to some regard for the agent's role in contract negotiations. Again, these corresponded to similar questions in the PPS, to highlight similarities/differences.

Questions 20, 21 – These questions looked at the alternatives for authors. Have they abandoned/or are thinking about abandoning traditional publishing avenues altogether? And why would they do so? The aim, here, was to gauge whether unpublished authors would consider self-publishing. There were also corresponding questions in the PPS.

Question 24 – This question was quite an important question for the unpublished author to answer because I hoped to compare the answers, here, with the publisher's answers for the same question (in the corresponding survey), and distinguish any similarities and differences.

Questions 5, 6, 7, 9, 10, 11, 13 – I expected the unpublished authors to leave these blank.

There were also some overall sections, which helped when compiling the data. These sections were:

SECTION A – Overview (AS Qs 1–5, PPS Qs 1–6)
SECTION B – Contract status and copyright (AS Qs 8–11, 16, 19, PPS Qs 8–16, 19)
SECTION C – Literary agents (AS Qs 6–7, 15, 17–18, PPS Qs 17–18)
SECTION D – Perceptions of industry values (AS Qs 12–14, 24, PPS Qs 7, 20, 21)
SECTION E – Self-publishing (AS Qs 20–23, PPS Qs 22, 23)

Survey data analysis

Section A – overview

(AS Qs 1–5, PPS Qs 1–6)

I gathered 100 responses to the survey (from global English-speaking territories): 71 responses to the AS and 29 responses to the PPS. In the AS, 70 per cent of the respondents were female and 28 per cent male, with 1 respondent identifying as non-binary. In the PPS, there was a high proportion of female participants (83 per cent of respondents were female). This data reflects the current employee gender balance in trade book publishing, and in writing generally. A recent Australian study, for example, concluded that an overwhelming 87 per cent of employees in publishing were female (*Books+Publishing* 2018). Likewise, a Macquarie University 2015 study of working authors showed that over 73 per cent of respondents identified as female (Throsby et al. 2015, 8).

A large proportion of participants in both surveys were in the 41–50 years age bracket (38 per cent in the AS and 46 per cent in the PPS), with only 8 per cent between the ages of 18–30 in the AS and none between these ages in the PPS. Ages 31–40 showed 23 per cent in the PPS and 51–60 at 31 per cent. In the AS, 23 per cent of respondents were aged 31–40 and 30 per cent 51–60. This data is unsurprising, given the vocational nature of publishing and the likelihood of publishing professionals and writers having post-graduate education. The aforementioned *Books+Publishing* survey concluded that over 93 per cent of respondents who work in the publishing industry have a tertiary qualification (*Books+Publishing* 2018). The 2015 Macquarie University study showed that over half of the writers surveyed for that study had a post-graduate degree, and more than 80 per cent had attended university (Throsby et al. 2015, 12)).

Of the AS, 69 per cent were published writers, and some of these published writers had also self-published (13 respondents checked both published and self-published) (Q.3). Six respondents had *only* self-published. Eight per cent of writers surveyed said they were unpublished. In the PPS, publishers made up 69 per cent of the respondents, Rights and Permissions Employees 13 per cent, and Agents 16 per cent. The remaining respondents in the PPS classified themselves as 'Publishing Consultants' (Q.3).

In the AS, there was an even spread of writing genres overall: between 17 per cent and 19 per cent in each of the categories of Adult Literary Fiction, Adult Commercial Fiction and Adult Non-fiction, and 22 per cent for Young Adult Fiction and 22 per cent Children's. Three per cent of respondents added screenwriting, poetry and corporate writing (Q.4). An even spread was also reflected in the body of genres across the PPS, with the bulk of participants working in Literary Fiction and Adult Non-Fiction (22 per cent and 25 per cent, respectively), with Adult Commercial Fiction at 15 per cent and Children's and Young Adult Fiction both at 18 per cent. One respondent also published religious texts (Q.5). There was obviously some crossover with many publishers representing lists of all genres – likewise with authors writing in more than one genre.

Seventy-one per cent of respondents in the PPS represented an 'Independent Publisher', 14 per cent 'University Presses' and 10 per cent 'Multinationals' (reflective of current market spread). Sixty-three per cent of the publishing professionals surveyed said that they thought authors were reasonably well aware of the types of books on their lists (Q.6).

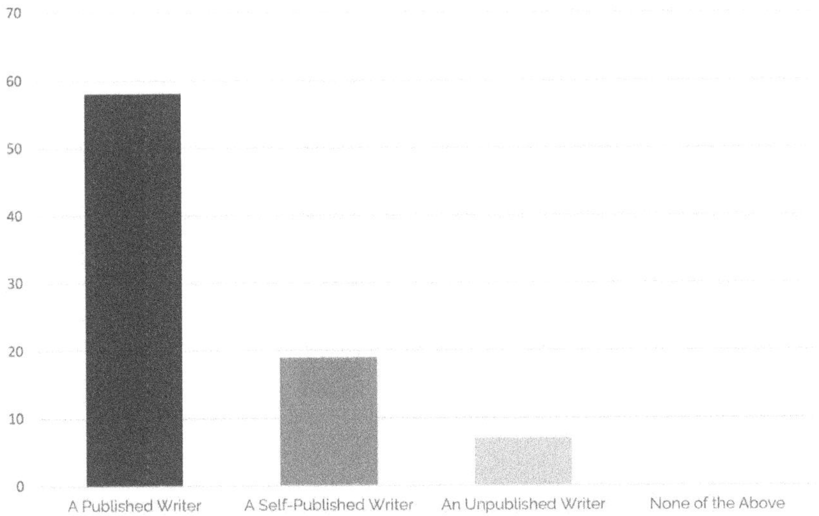

FIGURE 4.1 AS Q3 – Are you (tick all applicable boxes)

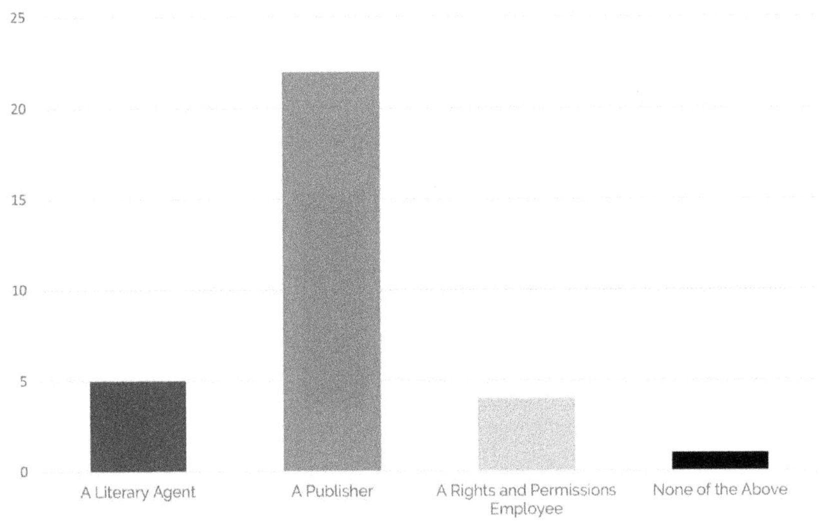

FIGURE 4.2 PPS Q3 – Are you (tick all applicable boxes)

There were few comments about the categories of genres within the survey. Although the participants in the AS indicated that they were writing in a number of genres, the only genres outside of those specified were corporate writing, scriptwriting and poetry. From this, I deduce that the categories were uncontested on the whole, which might indicate that the authors were easily able to position their works in the market within these genre categories. This was the same for the publishers, who didn't offer alternative categories except religious texts.

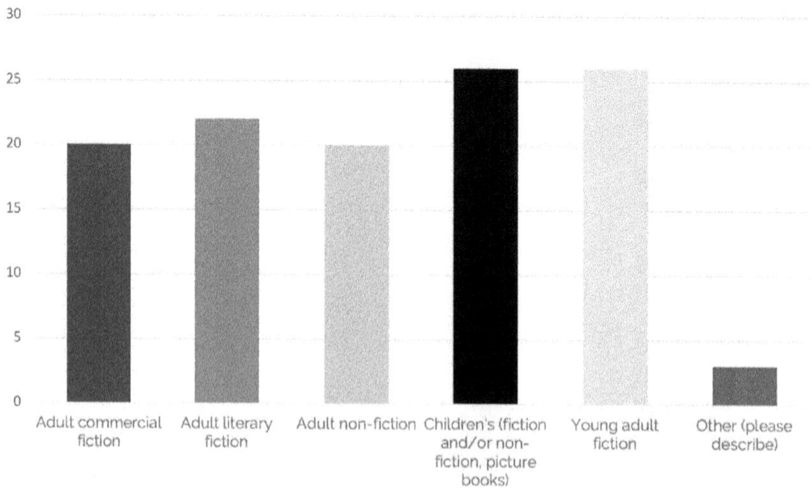

FIGURE 4.3 AS Q4 – Which of the following genres best describes your writing? (tick all applicable boxes)

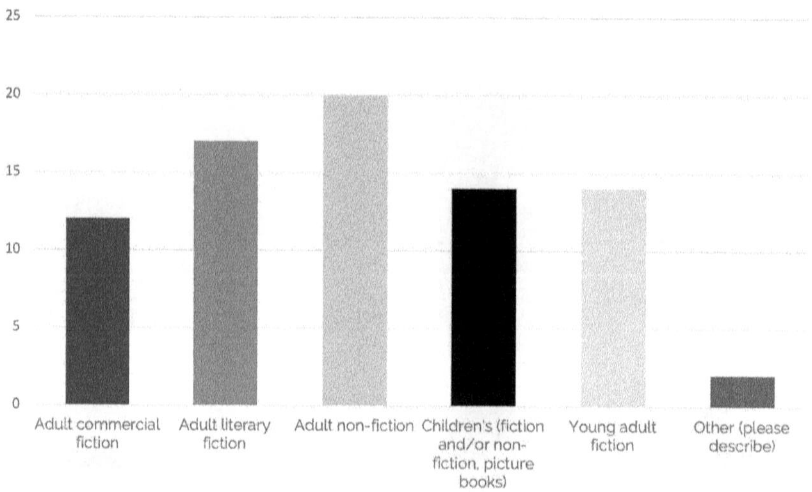

FIGURE 4.4 PPS Q5 – How would you categorise your list or the titles you represent? (tick all applicable boxes)

Section B – contract status and copyright

(AS Qs 8–11, 16, 19, PPS Qs 8–16, 19)

Most published authors had published 4+ titles (56 per cent) and the rest between 1 and 3 titles (44 per cent) (Q.5). Eighty-two per cent of writers had been involved in a publishing contract negotiation (which reflects the proportion of published to unpublished authors in the survey) (Q.7a).

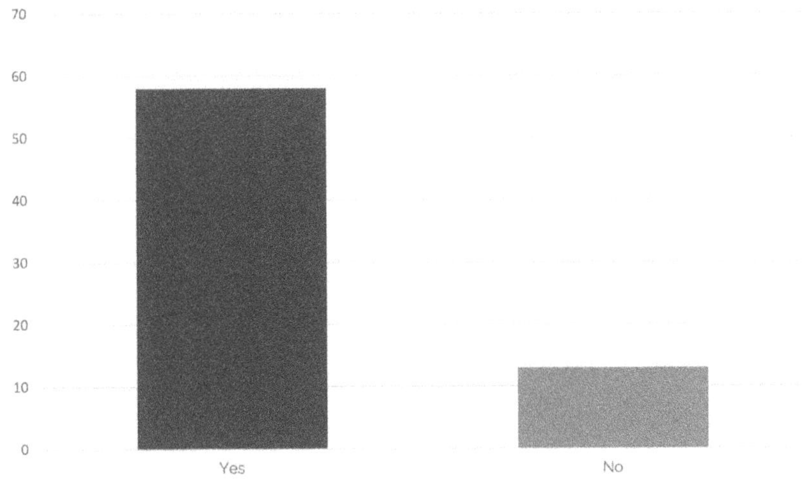

FIGURE 4.5 AS Q7a – Have you ever been involved in a publishing contract negotiation – either directly or via a literary agent?

Contrastingly, all respondents in the PPS had been involved in a contract negotiation (Q.8a), with 100 per cent also having been involved in more than 11 negotiations.

These results show a significant level of experience in contract negotiations from the authors and publishing professionals surveyed, which could be considered important in ascertaining how informed the respondents are in providing their responses. There was, however, a mixed response regarding knowledge of advocate standard publishing contract templates (the ASA in Australia, or equivalent in your respective country) (Q.8 AS and Q.9 PPS): 38 per cent of respondents in the PPS and 54 per cent in the AS were not familiar with advocates' standard contract (or equivalent) templates.

FIGURE 4.6 AS Q8 – Are you familiar with the Australian Society of Authors trade publishing agreement template (or equivalent in your respective country)?

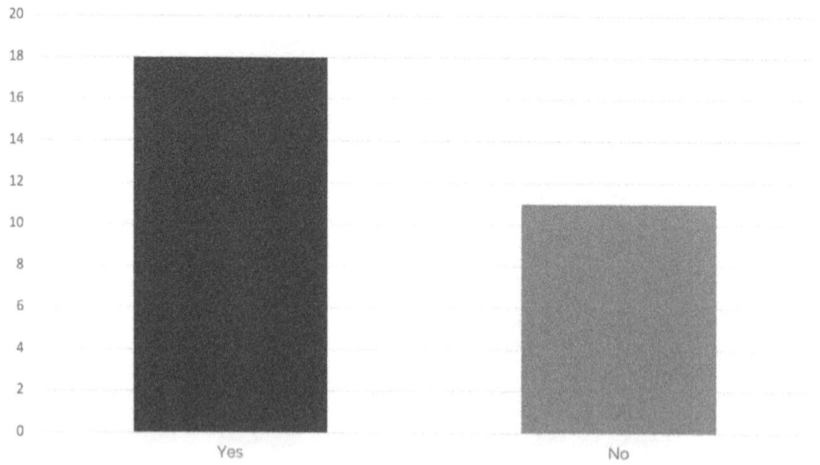

FIGURE 4.7 PPS Q9 – Are you familiar with the new Australian Society of Authors standard contract template (or equivalent in your respective country)?

Breaking this down further, unsurprisingly none of the self-published authors were aware of standard contract templates, which contrasted with a little less than 50 per cent of unpublished authors being familiar with these types of advocate contracts. Also unsurprisingly, all literary agents were familiar with standard advocate contract templates, bar one respondent. Interestingly, not one of the multinational publishers was familiar with a standard contract template (such as the ASA), and almost half of the independent publishers were also unfamiliar with this type of contract. Most publishers have their own boilerplates and are therefore are less likely to consult with alternatives outside of terms their particular publishing house has experience with. It does show a preference for those terms without considering the alternatives from an author's perspective, however.

Sixty-one per cent of publishing professionals indicated that they felt authors were only a little familiar with the terms of a standard book-publishing contract, and 32 per cent said they thought authors were reasonably well aware of the terms of a standard advocate contract such as the ASA (or equivalent). (Q.10) Despite the mixed response, there was a strong response to knowledge of the specific areas of the contract and to the experience of contract negotiations overall, in subsequent questions. This could be due to authors only experiencing interest in publishing contracts at the point of negotiation and publishers only experiencing interest in the contracts available at the publishing houses in which they work, as mentioned earlier.

With regard to satisfaction in contract negotiations, respondents in the PPS were either very satisfied or moderately satisfied (Q.11a) (52 per cent and 48 per cent, respectively). Comparing this to the AS, only 25 per cent of authors said they were very satisfied with their contract negotiations (Q.9a).

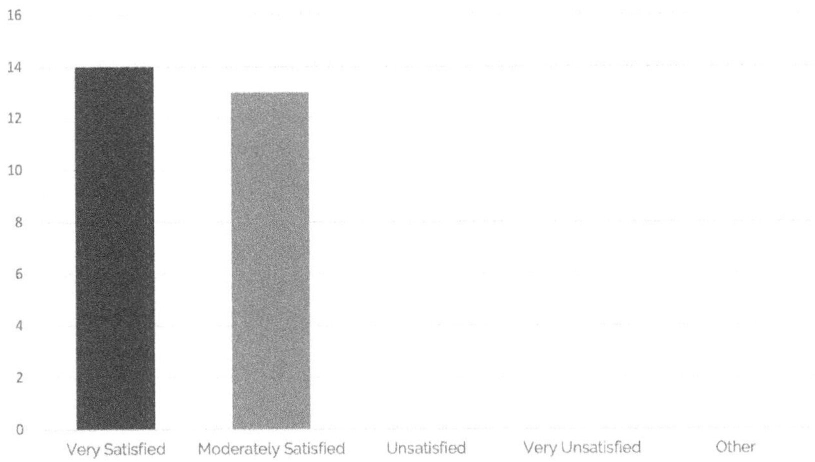

FIGURE 4.8 PPS Q11a – If you have been directly involved in a book-publishing contract negotiation/s, how would you rate your level of satisfaction with the negotiation/s overall?

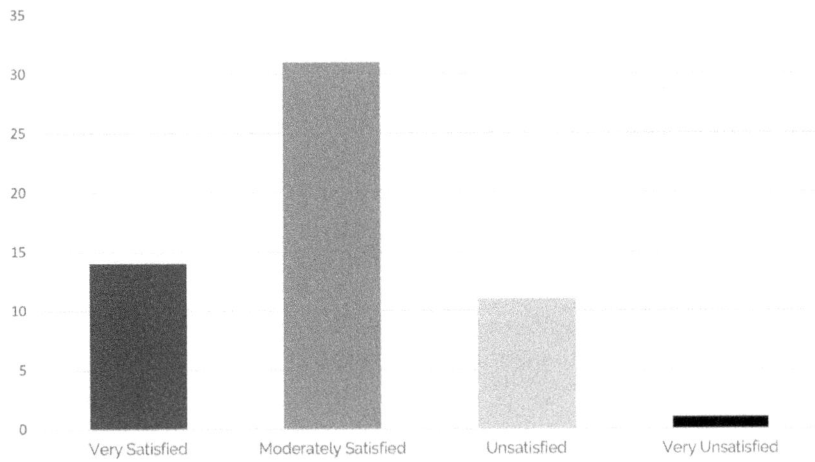

FIGURE 4.9 AS Q9a – If you are a writer who has been involved in a publishing contract negotiation/s, how would you rate your level of satisfaction with the negotiation/s overall?

This shows a 27 per cent difference in the level of satisfaction between authors and publishing professionals. Nineteen per cent of respondents in the AS said they were unsatisfied with their contract negotiation and 2 per cent were very unsatisfied. This is compared with a 0 per cent unsatisfactory experience with the publishing professionals. Authors' reasons for unsatisfactory negotiations almost always indicated a power imbalance between author and publisher. A sample of responses is as follows:

> It feels as if contract negotiations only really tweak minor things around the edges of a deal rather than making a substantial difference to an author's position. The publisher ultimately almost always holds the power and is mostly unwilling to budge.
>
> I felt that often certain publishers tried to bulldoze me into accepting terms that favoured them rather than me, that they didn't want to answer questions, and that they only changed things begrudgingly, or simply refused with a take it or leave it attitude.
>
> My contract was the only one I was ever going to receive, at that moment in my career, and I felt as though I was unable to ask for more. . . . I felt as though asking for more money would seem ungrateful somehow, and jeopardise my contract.
>
> A writer has little power in a publishing contract.
>
> My publisher was unhappy that I got guidance on the contract from a friend who is also a literary agent. In general, my publisher did not see this as a negotiation but an accept it or don't scenario.
>
> I do not feel as if I had any power to enforce the contract, so the negotiation didn't have any real effect.
>
> The terms that protect the publisher are always in the contract (e.g. joint accounting). However, terms that benefit the author (e.g. promises of more marketing support) are usually not. Therefore, publishers are free to change their minds.
>
> Publishers are often inflexible and offer pretty terrible contracts. I've lost contracts because I wasn't willing to meet unreasonable demands.

These responses speak of authors' feelings of powerlessness, which indicates that publishers tend to stick very closely to their boilerplates. Words and phrases used such as 'inflexible' and 'unwilling to budge' suggest that publishers are relying on the umbrella terms of the contract perhaps too stubbornly. It appears that the authors have tried negotiations because they feel the terms are unequal and more favourable to publishers, but they have failed due to publishers' inflexibility. I also observed that the reference to 'publisher' was unclear and in most cases directed more to the publishing house as an organisation, rather than an individual. I feel that this distinction indicates that authors feel very acutely that contracts come from the 'company' perspective, which of course they do. But the fact that they are being delivered by an individual who will most likely be working with them on their next book – even 'on the page' – does not register at this contractual stage. The individual publisher, therefore, is very separate to the organisational publisher, and perhaps this separation posits the individual publisher as someone who also lacks agency and is therefore more sympathetic to the author's position.

A cross reference of the 'moderately satisfied' to 'very satisfied' answers to the genres represented shows that children's and literary fiction authors were most satisfied (10 responses for children's and 11 responses for literary fiction), while commercial fiction authors were the least satisfied (4 responses of 'unsatisfied'). There doesn't appear to be any reason for this disparity but it could be put down to the fact that the expectations of market value are different for different genres.

Thirteen per cent of respondents indicated that 'Subsidiary Rights' was a problem area. The other areas of investigation – 'Copyright Provisions', 'Moral Rights', 'Rights Reversion', 'Warranties and Indemnities', and 'Editorial and Production Input' rated between 3 per cent and 9 per cent, while 'Manuscript Delivery and Publication Dates' scored 0 per cent. For this question, participants were able to nominate more than one problem area.

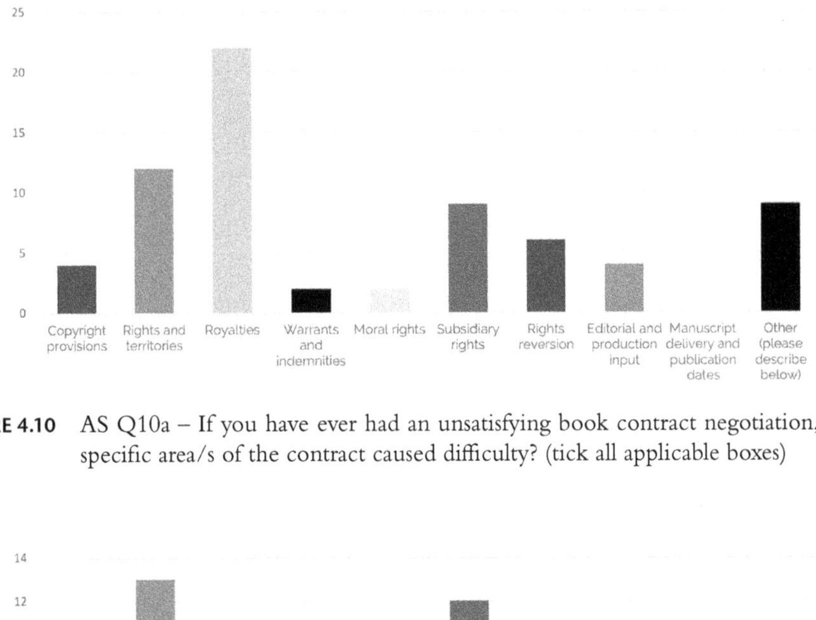

FIGURE 4.10 AS Q10a – If you have ever had an unsatisfying book contract negotiation, which specific area/s of the contract caused difficulty? (tick all applicable boxes)

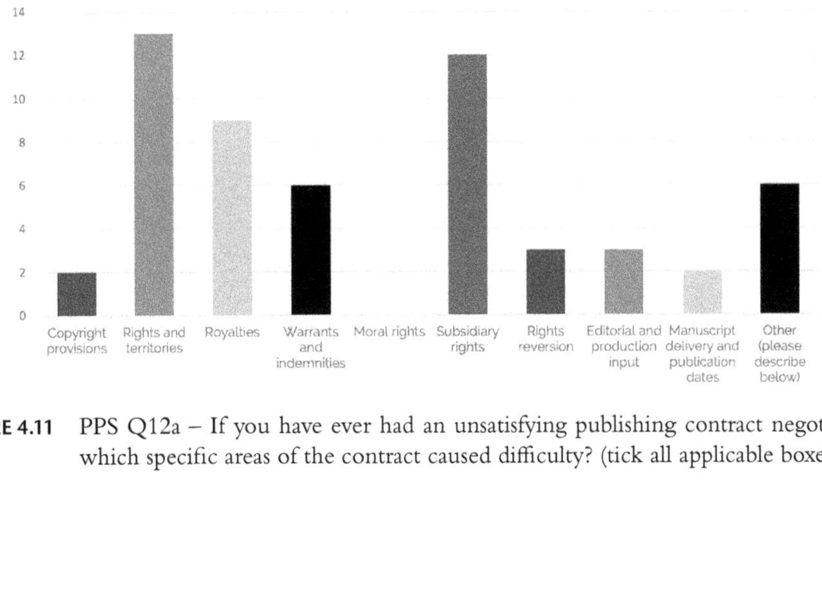

FIGURE 4.11 PPS Q12a – If you have ever had an unsatisfying publishing contract negotiation, which specific areas of the contract caused difficulty? (tick all applicable boxes)

Although no respondent in the PPS claimed to be unhappy with their contract negotiations, they did highlight some areas where there had been difficulties in negotiations (Q.12a): 'Rights and Territories' and 'Subsidiary Rights' were seen as the most problematic (at 23 per cent and 22 per cent, respectively). These results are comparable with the AS results. 'Royalties' also ranked quite highly at 16 per cent.

'Other' included the following:

> Contract negotiations are made trickier when authors don't understand what is standard in the publishing industry. It's difficult when they hire lawyers who have no experience in publishing, to advise on their contracts. Lots of time and money is wasted.

> Contract termination clauses: I've had an issue around whether a signature advance is recoupable by the publisher.

> Agents are often wanting to retain all rights ex-ANZ, which often makes the project unworkable for us.

> Where the high discount clause engages, lower royalty on sales to NZ, Lower royalty on subsequent editions. Including an Inspection of Account clauses, Competing Works and Option clauses.

There are a couple of areas worth highlighting here: most notably, the explanation for queries about royalties being linked to discount clauses, as suspected; there is also suggestion that authors are not familiar with standard publishing practice, and this could explain why they also feel that the boilerplate contracts, which cover standard publishing scenarios, mostly, are also unfair. In addition, in the AS, when asked which areas of the contract had caused the most difficulties in negotiations (Q.10a), for authors who had experienced an unsatisfying negotiation 'Royalties' rated highly at 32 per cent and 'Rights and Territories' also rated highly at 17 per cent and, most interestingly, children's authors displayed the highest count for these areas (11 respondents for 'Royalties' and 7 respondents for 'Rights and Territories'). This is compared with only 1–3 responses for the areas of commercial fiction, adult literary fiction and adult non-fiction, and 0 responses for YA. Discount clauses are prevalent in children's publishing due to opportunities for bulk purchases such as for Australia Post or Scholastic book club, which might account for the dissatisfaction with royalties – where authors might receive less money for bulk stock that is sold at a reduced RRP. All but one of the literary agents also placed 'Royalties' as the No. 1 query from authors. The literary agent who didn't place it at No. 1 nominated 'Reversion' as the No. 1 query. However, 'Reversion' rated very low overall. The most queries overall from authors (Q.13) shows 'Royalties' as 38 per cent out of 9 ranked areas. 'Moral Rights' was the least ranked (47 per cent at No. 9). While 'Editorial and Production Input' had a strong ranking at No. 1, it was ranked low at No. 2. 'Rights and Territories', however, was ranked high at both No. 1 and No. 2 (14 per cent and 31 per cent, respectively). These figures indicate consistency in both surveys across two clear areas of contention: 'Royalties' and 'Rights and Territories'. 'Other' is shown at No. 1 and included written responses in support of individuals' rankings.

These findings are compatible with the assessment of the contract types in the contract analysis. While most boilerplate contracts would suggest that the royalty rate is an area that the publisher will be unlikely to negotiate and quite standard across most publishing houses as 10 per cent of the RRP, it being raised as an area of contention might suggest the following: that the royalty is based on net receipts as opposed to RRP, that the royalty is set at a lower percentage for smaller reprints that the author has locked themselves into (as mentioned earlier in the contract overview), that the royalty is being awarded on discounted stock, that there is no rising royalty (as a reward for a sudden success) or that the percentages for the subsidiary rights are unsatisfactory to the author. Lynette Own explains: '[L]icensing [in paperback editions only] has largely been abandoned in favour of "vertical publishing", where the same publisher first publishes a hardback edition and then, after an interval of about a year, the cheaper paperback version' (Owen 2010, 37). The ability to negotiate the royalties, if the publisher sells the rights in other territories, is unlikely to be specified in the first contract with the primary publisher. What will be specified, however, is the division of payments between the author and the primary publisher, for these sales. This means that if the author offers full global rights to the primary publisher, they will take a cut of the sale (as well as the publisher in another territory). Sometimes the agent will also take a cut. With this in mind, the significant percentage for 'Rights and Territories' as a contested area (14 per cent at No. 1 and 31 per cent at No. 2) would seem warranted.

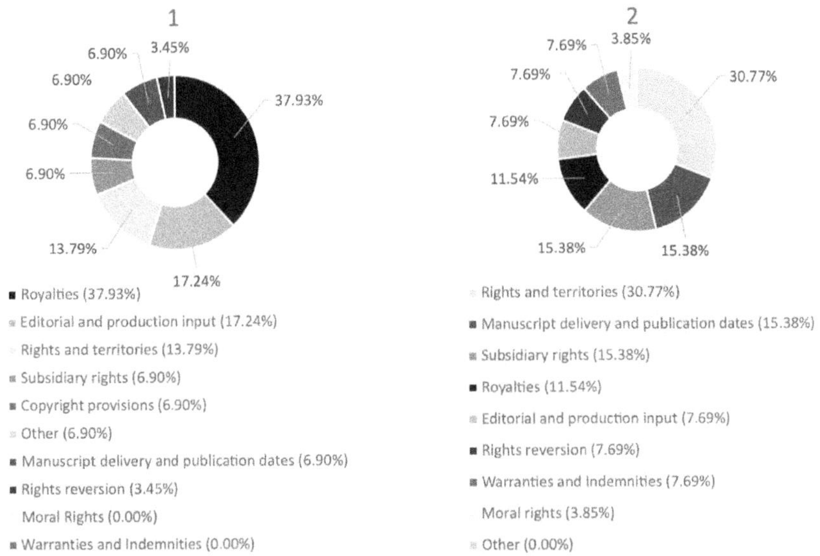

FIGURE 4.12 PPS Q13a – If you have ever been involved directly in a publishing contract negotiation/s, which areas elicited the most queries from authors? (number boxes from 1 to 9, with 1 being the highest)

Despite this, the AS survey showed that 80 per cent of negotiations had resulted in a signed contract 'All of the time' (Q.11) and in the PPS, respondents claimed that 57 per cent of negotiations had resulted in signed contracts all of the time and 39 per cent most of the time. Four per cent in the PPS claimed that the negotiation resulted in a signed contract some of the time (Q.14.).

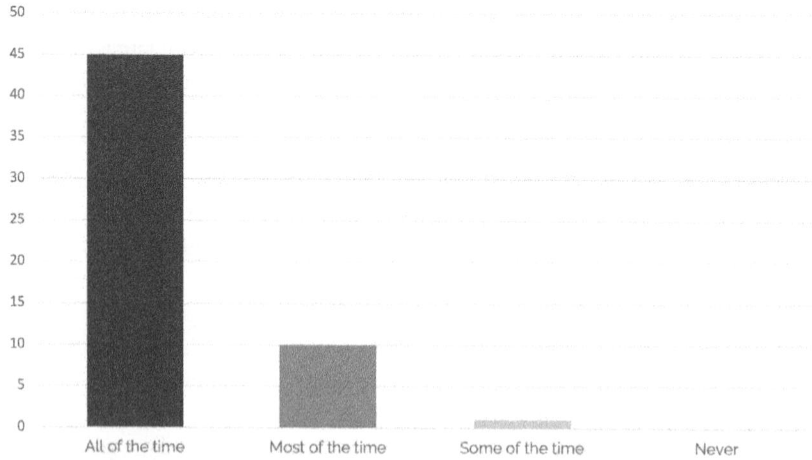

FIGURE 4.13 AS Q11 – If you are a writer who has been involved in a publishing contract negotiation/s, did the negotiation/s result in a signed contract?

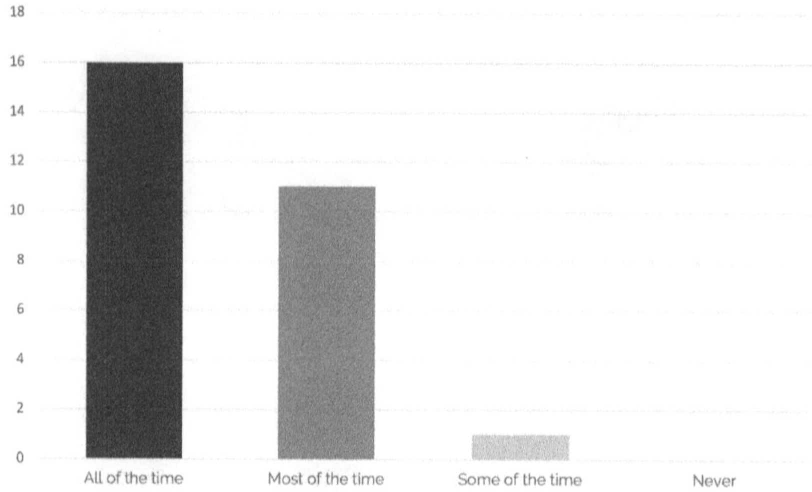

FIGURE 4.14 PPS Q14 – Did the negotiations you have been involved in result in signed contracts?

These findings show that authors are *not* walking away from contracts that don't suit them. The authors' dissatisfaction also indicates that they might acquiesce in areas of the negotiation that are important to them (as clearly expressed in the written feedback). The contested areas are clearly pecuniary – 'Royalties' and 'Rights and Territories'. To the AS Q.16a – 'Which areas of author/publisher contracts are/would be most important to you?' – 44 per cent out of 37 responses ranked 'Royalties' as No. 1 (out of 9 ranked contract areas). A cross reference to writing categories showed that children's writers, mostly, ranked royalties as most important (9 respondents), with adult literary fiction and commercial fiction following (5 respondents each) The second-highest ranked areas were 'Editorial and Production Input' and 'Copyright Provisions' at 15 per cent each. 'Rights and Territories' was again ranked high for No. 1 and No. 2 combined (12 per cent at No. 1 and 24 per cent at No. 2). This response emphasises the contested areas listed in Q.10a of the AS and Qs.12a and 13a of the PPS.

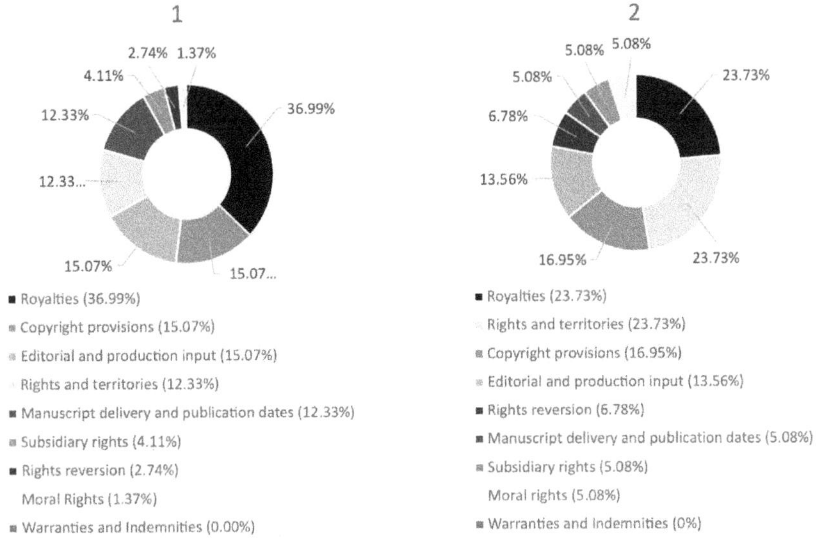

FIGURE 4.15 AS Q16a – Which areas of author/publisher contracts are/would be most important to you? (Number boxes from 1–9 with 1 being the highest)

'Warrants and Indemnities' ranked least important with 28 per cent placing it at No. 8 and 35 per cent placing it at No. 9.

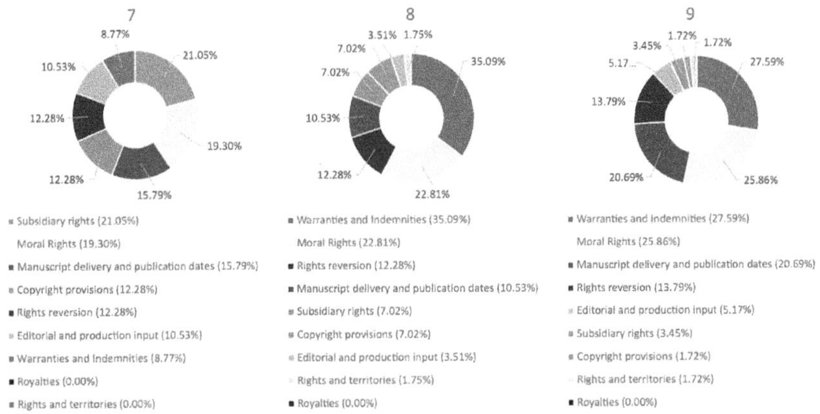

FIGURE 4.16 AS Q16a – Which areas of author/publisher contracts are/would be most important to you? (Number boxes from 1–9 with 1 being the highest)

This response might reflect the lack of knowledge about the legal repercussions of defamatory content and/or a 'rationally ignorant' perspective (as raised by Butler et al. and Barnett (previously)), or it might simply be that the proportion of fiction writers in the sample was larger than the non-fiction writers.

'Moral Rights' also ranked low at 26 per cent at 8 and 23 per cent at 9. It should again be noted that moral rights and copyright are formalised in copyright law and could be seen as granted rights in which they might not need to be explicitly asserted in the contract. They were included as areas in this survey, however, to ascertain authors' and publishers' understandings of their importance. Some responses were:

> I believe moral rights are very important but I have only worked with quality publishers who respect my moral rights.

> While I didn't answer 'none' or 'I don't know', I must point out I don't know what moral rights are.

> I have rated moral and copyright rights lower purely because I wouldn't work with a publisher who didn't accept these as a given.

From these results, a few possible conclusions can be drawn: either that authors assume that their moral rights are respected or that they are unaware of what their moral rights are (as indicated in the written feedback) or that they *don't* expect their moral rights to be respected. This might explain the clear focus on pecuniary rights, particularly in the 'Royalties' and 'Rights and Territories' sections. If moral rights are not paramount, focus will shift elsewhere. Alternatively, if authors are more concerned with their pecuniary rights, then moral rights will be a secondary focus.

Twelve respondents from the AS did not answer Q.16a and indicated that they did not know which areas of the contract are/would be most important to them. The written responses next were all generated from the AS Q.16a and indicate that some authors are not aware of the contract's terms (from a mix of published and unpublished writers) and, in some cases, place all their trust in the publisher or their agent:

> I really don't understand a great deal about this industry. I may be naive, but I just trust that I am getting a fair deal.

> As an emerging author. . . . I am still at a stage where any contract is a good thing. I am yet to be affected by, or experience, these particular areas.

> I haven't really thought about it yet, but suspect it is something that I need to think about.

> I've never dealt with or seen author/publisher contracts, so I'm not sure what is in them.

> Haven't researched the topic. I suspect all highly important.

There was a very clear response with regard to the term of copyright (AS Q.19a). Sixty-eight per cent of authors indicated that they thought the term of Copyright should not be changed (it is currently for the life of the author, plus 70 years).

When asked to provide a reason, the most common response was legacy:

> I expect to be able to earn money from my work for as long as possible and to pass on that earning to my family or a trust post-death.
>
> Authors' descendants should benefit as from other assets.
>
> I think copyright should remain with the author until death, and then pass to their next of kin as dictated by their will. If there is no provision in their will for their copyright, I think it should become public domain.
>
> I believe an author should be able to pass their works and the earnings of such works to their family, like other property.
>
> A writer's work is their intellectual property legacy similar to the way others would leave property to family. Copyright also protects the format and ways in which the work might be adapted.
>
> Legacy. Copyright should be owned by the author's estate and especially if original contract was negotiated under company law.
>
> An author's work may not earn any money until after his or her death, in which case the family's rights to those earnings are, at least in theory, protected by the current copyright provisions.

These responses again speak to the pecuniary rights of the author with many comparing the right to their intellectual property akin to the right of property ownership in other forms (such as land). Further analysis via the in-depth interviews will aim to contextualise this sense of ownership, within contract negotiations and also within the authors' own perceptions of themselves as writers, and how proprietary concerns can straddle both the financial and the creative. When offering publishers their works for the term of copyright, how willing are authors to work with their publisher's vision for the work, for financial reward?

Only one respondent expressed that the term of copyright 'also protects the format and ways in which the work might be adapted', which refers to the effect of adaptions on the integrity of the work. Authors might or might not be so concerned with what happens to the work after they die, as long as it is providing income for their heirs. Or perhaps, in the balance, the income derived from their works is slightly more important than the integrity inherent in the works. The latter would certainly explain the focus on pecuniary rights in the negotiation process. Again, the self-published authors surveyed were predictably less concerned with the term of copyright and were the ones to challenge the current term (13 per cent):

> I believe extending copyright beyond 70 years offers little or no benefit to the heirs of those who created the work. It does create the potential for large companies to exploit copyright.

> Publishers profit from authors' work and there should be a shorter cap on the ownership of the copyright.

> The current arrangement protects large corporate entities more than it protects individual, living copyright holders and enables the fair distribution of art and the continued production of ideas and artworks. Large corporate entities behave psychopathically in the free market and need obstacles and restrictions, not affordances and protections.

> As far as I can tell, this term only exists so that big corporations (i.e. Disney) can keep their cash cows. Lifetime + 20 years would be plenty.

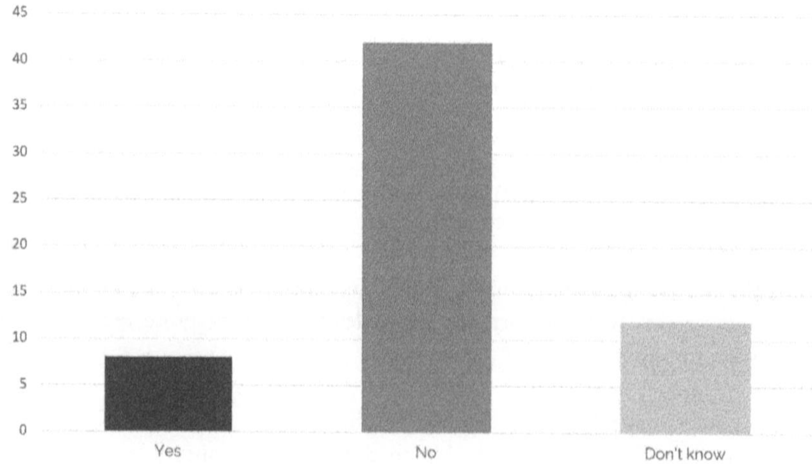

FIGURE 4.17 AS Q19a – Do you think the term of copyright should be changed to less than it is currently? (Please refer to your respective country). In Australia and the UK: for the life of the author, plus 70 years. In the US: 95 years from first publication or 120 years from creation, whichever is shortest

Also, on closer inspection, the survey showed that adult non-fiction writers were most likely to not know the copyright terms. Again, while there doesn't appear to be any identifiable reason, it was noted for future reference throughout the rest of the study. When asked in the PPS if the term of copyright should be changed (Q.19a), 63 per cent of respondents said that it shouldn't. The most frequently cited reason was the likelihood of a reduction in authors' incomes:

> I think it is entirely appropriate that an author's copyright/intellectual property is protected (and preserved for their estate) for 70 years after their death, given that their creation is often their life's work and a contribution to our culture.

Authors are often not well-off and royalties may be the only significant estate they can leave, it is only right that they have the right to bequeath their intellectual property, as well as have the benefit of it when they are alive.

Potential negative effects on authors' incomes.

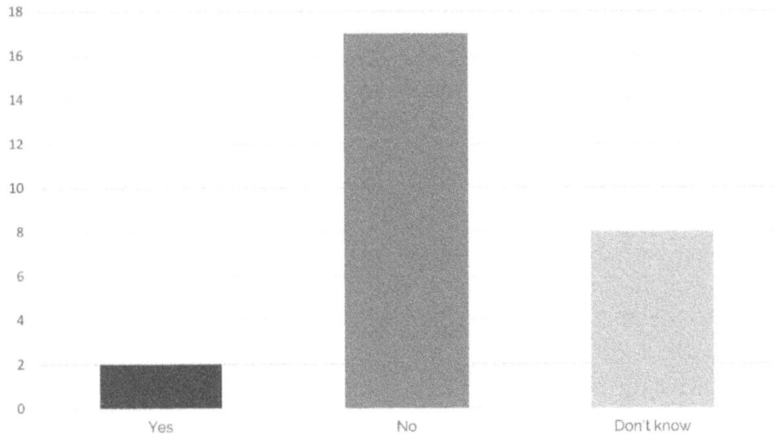

FIGURE 4.18 PPS Q19a – Do you think the term of copyright should be changed to less than it is currently? (Please refer to your respective country). In Australia and the UK: for the life of the author, plus 70 years. In the US: 95 years from first publication or 120 years from creation, whichever is shortest

Alternately, some respondents thought the term of copyright should be changed (7 per cent in the PPS). From the PPS perspective, the following feedback was gathered:

> It should be reduced because the only entity to gain from these long periods are multinational publishing houses.

> The long term of 70 years after an author's death significantly affects our authors' ability to include quotes from poems and songs and which are genres that have a lot to say about the spiritual state of humanity. As the majority of our authors do not make much money from writing, they cannot afford to pay what are often very high licence fees. It means that a lot of this valuable material cannot be used in our publication as the fees are prohibitive.

One respondent also mentioned the importance of the author's estate in maintaining integrity in the work after the term of copyright:

> In most cases I find an estate looks after the moral rights of the author, and it is important to have this control. There are exceptions of course, where the estate is not

> managed by someone with a good understanding of the business, and they can needlessly block opportunities or make bad decisions.

Most authors seem informed enough about the law to have an opinion about ownership of their intellectual property, but unpublished authors are obviously the most likely to not have an opinion. Publishers mostly support the longest term of the authors' ownership of their intellectual property. This is consistent with current literature surrounding intellectual property ownership in book publishing throughout history, but it also raises the question about the lack of a contested rights reversion clause in the contract. 'Rights Reversion' was quite low in the list of important areas of the contract (Qs.10a and 16a of the AS), and teamed with a preference for maintaining the status quo with regard to the term of copyright it could be assumed that authors either haven't considered having their rights reverted back to them or they are satisfied with the publishers keeping the work for the term of copyright. Given the authors' dissatisfaction with contract negotiations, the former would perhaps be more likely. Conversely, if the author feels that they would not be able to exploit the work as well as the publisher or that asking for a shorter term might put the negotiation in jeopardy, they might concede and offer the work for the full copyright term.

Notwithstanding the relatively concrete results indicated earlier, this study recognises the limited scope for more nuanced responses, and it is reiterated that this data is designed to indicate areas of interest warranting further research via more qualitative methods in the form of in-depth interviews. What the data does suggest is that many, if not most, authors (especially published authors) appear to have a sound understanding of some of the contract's terms, while some authors (particularly unpublished authors) possess very little knowledge. From the PPS perspective, the understanding of the contract's terms for publishers is based on the individual professionals' *experience* of negotiations (given the large number of negotiations occurring). This would also be the case for the AS responses, though the authors' experiences reflect an inability to assert their requests to the same degree as the publishers. Even with a sound knowledge of the contract's terms, the authors express impotence in negotiations. In contrast, the publishers claim that contract negotiations are mostly successful.

There are also some consistently problematic areas, namely 'Royalties' and 'Rights and Territories'. Another area of note is 'Moral Rights', which, given its consistently low ranking, is assumed or conceded and, therefore, perhaps inadequately exercised.

Literary agents could assist in negotiations. How do publishing professionals and authors perceive of literary agents and their role in contract negotiations?

Section C – literary agents

(AS Qs 6–7, 15, 17–18, PPS Qs 17–18)

Almost half (42 per cent) of respondents in the AS had a literary agent (Q.6), and an agent was present for approximately 143 negotiations (Q.7c). When asked how important it is to have a literary agent (Q.15a), there was a 100 per cent response with 21 per cent stating that it was Very Important and 48 per cent Moderately Important. Twelve per cent claimed it was Not Important.

Many of the written responses to this question indicated that an agent is helpful in presenting the author's work to publishers, particularly at the beginning of their career:

> I think it's more important at the beginning of a career.
>
> Industry contacts; help plan career.
>
> I don't think it's essential these days, but can be helpful, especially with contracts and having an extra foot in the door when pursuing a range a publishers.
>
> Some publishers are closed to un-agented authors. Getting chosen from a slush pile is difficult.
>
> I don't have an agent, but I imagine it would help to get a foot in the door.
>
> I think it could be helpful, especially when it comes to multiple submissions and receiving an offer of interest.
>
> The larger, more prominent publishers, especially in Australia, do not take unsolicited manuscripts so an agent is the only access to a lot of publishing houses.
>
> If a writer hasn't been published then an agent is a good way to get your work in front of a publisher. But sometimes you can be lucky and get picked off the slush pile. Agents are great for negotiating contracts.

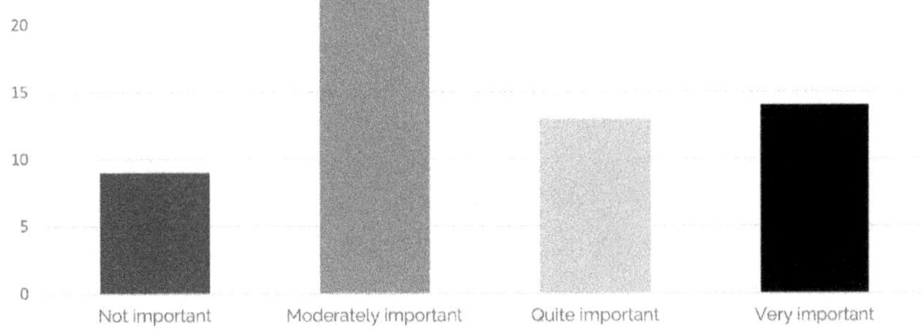

FIGURE 4.19 AS Q15a – How important is it for a writer to have a literary agent?

There was very little mention of actual contract negotiations; rather, the agent was seen as someone who had the necessary connections to help an author 'get a foot in the door' and garner interest for their manuscript. Many authors, in fact, felt that an agent was superfluous:

> It's not important for me because these days any writer can self-publish on a platform such as Amazon, either as an ebook on Kindle or as print on demand paper copies. There are companies providing publishing support to self-published writers if the writer needs help and wants to spend the money. Agents don't always reply or return a manuscript so treat writers with disdain.

> I was published initially because I had a prominent profile. I have never needed an agent, because of this profile and 20+ years in the publishing industry. Publishers talk directly to me.

> In this day and age, it's easy to submit a MS yourself. It's usually passed through some form of critique before it reaches the submission stage. Good publishers can see if a story has a strong possibility of sales (after a structural edit etc. first, of course!).

Many responses pertaining to an agent's importance came from unpublished and self-published authors, which reflects and perhaps supports the belief that agents help authors to get their manuscripts onto a publisher's desk. While many commercial publishing houses accept unsolicited submissions, due to the sheer quantity and quality of writing available, now, the work must be almost exactly what the publisher is looking for or be exceptional. Agents are often seen as playing an important role in the sifting process – identifying the types of writing certain publishers are looking for. This process reduces the time the publisher needs to assess the unsolicited pile and is a valued addition to the acquisitions process. When a manuscript is sent via an agent, therefore, it is immediately given priority.

Once published, however, authors see agents as having other benefits mostly to do with negotiating on their behalf so that they don't have to. In navigating contracts and deals, some authors expressed that they preferred their agent to do so:

> There's . . . the relief of not having to negotiate yourself (it's a very stressful position to be in and not all writers will be good at understanding contracts and being able to advocate for their position). I also think it's important to have a third party who is always on your side and while I love my editor and I trust her, ultimately when it comes to contract negotiation, the publisher will put their needs first and you need someone who can always put your needs first. I also feel I am in a better financial position when I can carve up the rights and have my agent responsible for selling into other territories as, from my experience, my agent has done a better job in this area than my publisher.

> I like having a buffer person for that stuff, and I value my agent's advice. Our relationship has grown and improved a lot, and I feel he is on my side.

> As I said above, contract negotiations are stressful for a writer who is afraid to scare off the contract. An agent does the hard yards, there.

> Having an agent means I don't have to discuss the business end directly with the publisher, who might well be the same person doing the structural edit on the ms. That way there's never any tension and we can focus on the actual work. I hate the business stuff!

Still, the emphasis, here, is not so much on the success of the negotiation itself; rather, it is on the reliance of the agent as a 'buffer' to the negotiations (apart from the first response, which delineated that agent's expertise with dividing rights) because the negotiation process is stressful for the author. An agent's advantage as mostly initiating contact with publishers could explain why the majority of respondents in the AS who have a literary agent said they are very satisfied with their agent (42 per cent), with only 6 per cent very unsatisfied (Q.17a).

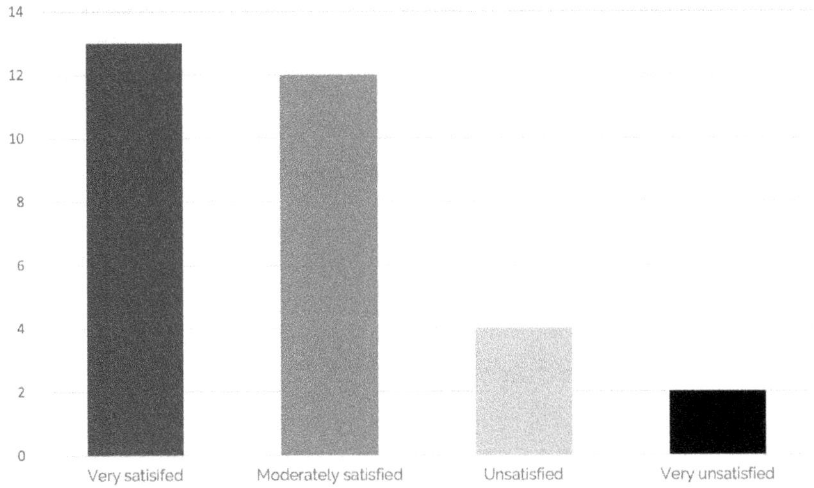

FIGURE 4.20 AS Q17a – If you have a literary agent, how would you rate your level of satisfaction with them?

These results suggest that authors clearly see the agent as integral to helping them get noticed by a publisher, which is perhaps more important to the author than the contract negotiation itself. It is clear that the authors feel uncomfortable with the negotiation process, too, in which case the agent can be a buffer for potential conflict. It does seem, however, at least from the surveyed authors' perspectives, that agents are perhaps not as effective in changing terms that do not suit the author. This is reflected in the fact that most authors are unhappy with the terms of their contracts despite a large portion of them having an agent. Evidence of this also points to a reluctance to challenge areas that they find unsatisfactory, as opposed to simply not knowing how the terms affect the outcome of publishing decisions.

Contrastingly, 50 per cent of publishing professionals think that it is 'Not Important' for an author to have an agent (Q.17a), and 25 per cent think it is only 'Moderately Important'. This response reflects the high ratio of publishers to literary agents in the survey but also a significant gap in the perceived importance of the literary agent when comparing the AS and the PPS. The responses show a 38 per cent difference in whether the literary agent is 'Not Important'.

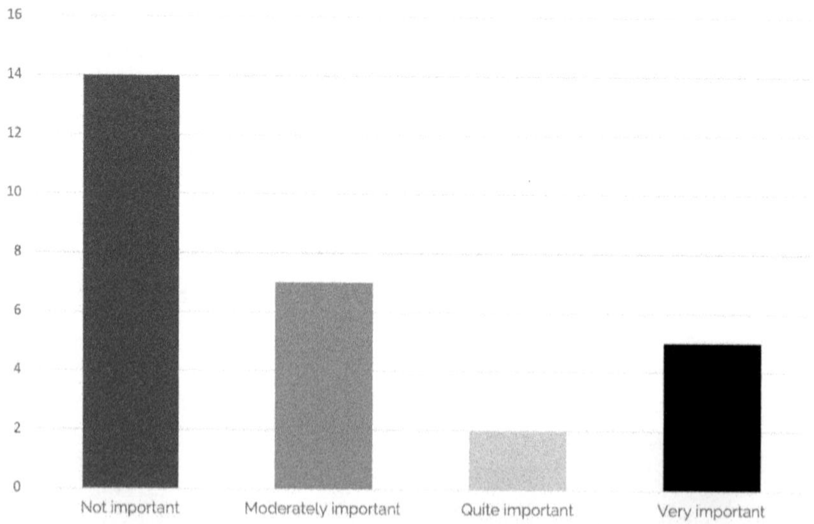

FIGURE 4.21 PPS Q17a – How important is it for writers to have a literary agent?

Reasons from the publishers' perspectives were as follows:

> As a publisher who is also a writer I am aware of what the contract means and have to be able to explain parts of it if an author has questions. That is part of my professional skill. A contract is not fair if one side feels cheated. So agreement must be reached.

> At [publisher] our authors don't need an agent, as we tend to represent them here and overseas. . . . Having said that, if an author becomes very well known, they are sometimes overwhelmed by attention and need a gatekeeper to filter for them. That's where an agent can be useful.

> I prefer to work with authors who haven't found representation, because I build really strong relationships with my authors. When an agent is involved, there's another layer . . . my goal is to give underrepresented voices a home, and many debut authors don't yet have agents . . . if an author wants a contract with a big house, or if they have a contract offer and want help, agents can be great.

> A true literary agent can be valuable for a writer. Many agents I deal with are not literary agents, however, and they can unwittingly be an obstacle in the way of negotiating a good deal for both parties. In addition there are many writers who do not need a literary agent in order to strike a good deal directly with a publisher.

> It's not important if you have a reputable publisher with an international rights department and most will do their absolute best on behalf of the author and only increase/improve in terms negotiated by an agent will usually be swallowed up by the commission. It may be important/helpful for an unpublished writer or one with a small publisher.

Publishers believe they can effectively negotiate agreements with authors. But this belief also assumes that authors share with publishers an awareness of the terms of their contract, on an equal playing field. It is not equal if authors conceal their dissatisfaction. Publishers can then only *assume* that the terms of the contract have been agreed upon. An author's frustration, therefore, might be due to them not having had the chance *at all* to query the contract. The opportunity to ask questions and challenge clauses, via an agent, might, for the author, be worth the 10–15 per cent commission – even if no changes ensue. Authors' expectations of publishers keeping their end of the bargain in doing all they can for the work – both editorially and in the market (or both) – are inevitably quite high. The in-depth interviews will explore where the pre negotiation space and the post negotiation space intersect, in this manner, and investigate the *position* of the author in both spaces, separately, as being fundamental to how they perceive the negotiation *overall*. The agent, therefore, might also have quite a different position to how their role is understood, in theory. The editorial relationship might help facilitate author satisfaction in this space in the event that pre negotiations are less than ideal. Agents had a different perspective in assessing agents' effectiveness:

> I believe literary agents act as an important buffer between author and publisher, as many authors feel daunted and mystified by the publishing process. I don't believe publishers are always very transparent or communicative about the publishing process and literary agents can act as an intermediary, and keep the relationship between author and publisher as harmonious as possible.

> Often find that authors are inexperienced in reading publishing contracts and understanding what is, and is not, standard. Often authors, particularly debut authors, are so grateful for a publishing contract offer that they are unwilling to ask for changes/improvements in contract terms.

These responses do not pinpoint specific areas of negotiation; rather, they discuss how agents can interpret the contract for the author and facilitate effective communication between the author and the publisher. Remarks such as 'I don't believe publishers are always transparent' implies that some authors believe that publishers are not forthcoming with all the information they have. But perhaps the publishers are simply assuming that the author understands the terms of the contract as it is explained to them. And if the author is 'unwilling to ask for changes/improvements in contract terms', then the publisher is unlikely to ever see that there is a problem. The agent, then, becomes a mediator as opposed to a negotiator, which is consistent with the authors' perception of their role, too. If the agent has explained the terms of the contract and the author understands them and consents to the terms, then this survey is again highlighting that the author is aware but tacit in negotiations. And publishers cannot, perhaps, be blamed for being oblivious to conflicts of interest. When asked where a literary agent is most likely to be helpful in a contract negotiation (Q.18a), 55 per cent of respondents in the PPS ranked 'Rights and Territories' at No. 1. This figure comprised half of the independent publishers and all but one of the multinational publishers. 'Royalties' came in a close second with 23 per cent ranking it at No. 1 and 44 per cent at No. 2, comprising only 4 independents and 1 each of multinational, university press and literary agent.

Subsidiary rights also ranked highly at No. 2 (28 per cent). In terms of agents having the least impact in specific areas, there were no significant results. 'Other' appears at No. 1 and responses included 'Don't know' and 'None'.

The only other significant anomaly in the responses to this question, which has not been seen in the responses to the other questions, at least to this degree, is the emergence of reversion as an area of value (and thus worthy of negotiating). 'Rights Reversion' was ranked 20 per cent at No. 3 and 44 per cent at No. 4.

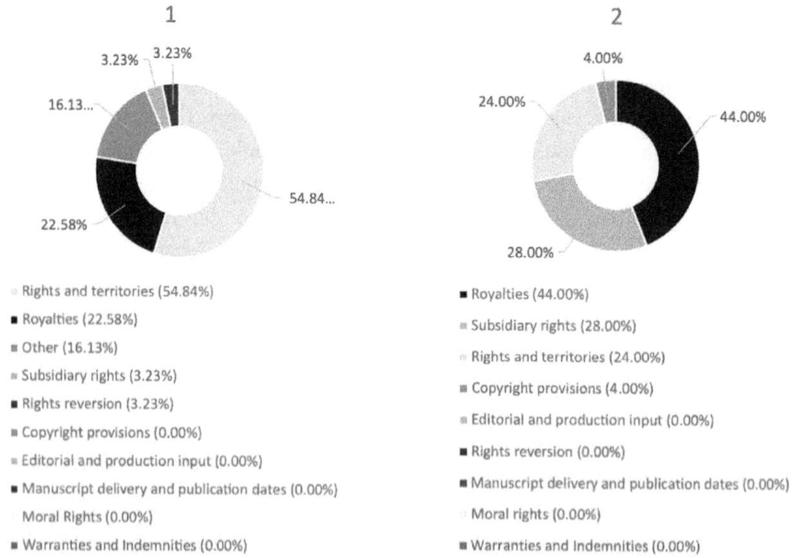

FIGURE 4.22 PPS Q18a – In which areas of publishing contract negotiations is a literary agent most likely to have an impact? (Number boxes from 1–9, with 1 being the highest)

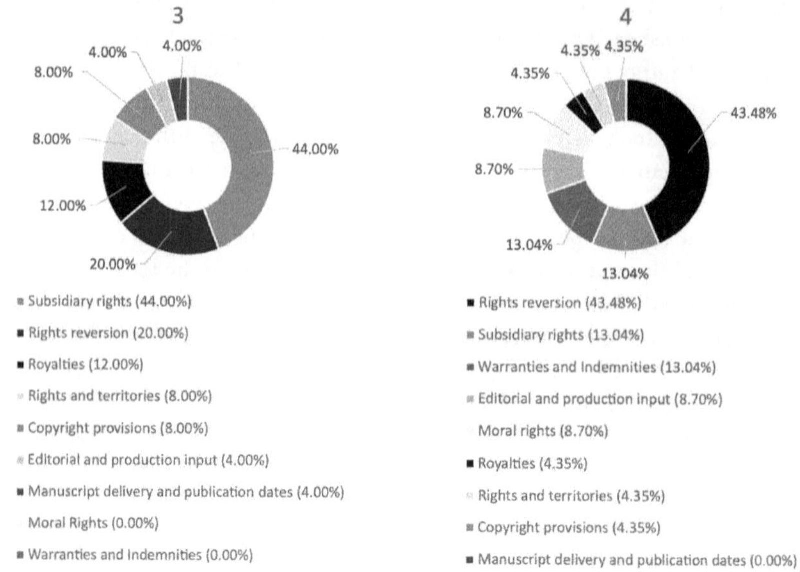

FIGURE 4.23 PPS Q18a – In which areas of publishing contract negotiations is a literary agent most likely to have an impact? (Number boxes from 1–9, with 1 being the highest)

This affirms that the agent has a deeper knowledge of the capacity of various parts of contracts and how they can be better framed to suit the author. But, along with the results of other questions, it also indicates that this knowledge is arguably ineffectual to the outcomes of signed contracts.

In the AS, when asked the same question (Q.18a), 49 per cent of 58 respondents placed 'Royalties' at No. 1. The next highest ranked area was 'Rights and Territories' (20 per cent at No. 1 and 42 per cent at No. 2). Once again, children's authors accounted for most of the No. 1 'Royalties' rankings (9 respondents); however, it is also interesting to note that half of the self-published authors also placed 'Royalties' as the No. 1 area where a literary agent could help with negotiations.

These responses are consistent with the answers at Q.10a in the AS (indicating areas of importance in the contract) and also consistent with the publishing professionals' responses in Q.18a, though with 'Rights and Territories' and 'Royalties' reversed. The surveys also indicate a disparity in the reception of literary agents (according to authors and publishers), which can be investigated further via the interview process. The question of why 'Royalties' and 'Rights and Territories' are so emphasised and contentious, but not resolved in negotiations even with a literary agent as a mediator, is also explored in the interviews. Given the high proportion of children's authors ranking 'Royalties' as high, it is my assessment that discount clauses have contributed to the dissatisfaction. Also, in the case of territories, the written responses indicate that agents are advising authors to withhold territories. Even with publishers being in a better position to exploit these rights, the negotiations result in a stalemate, to which the author often succumbs.

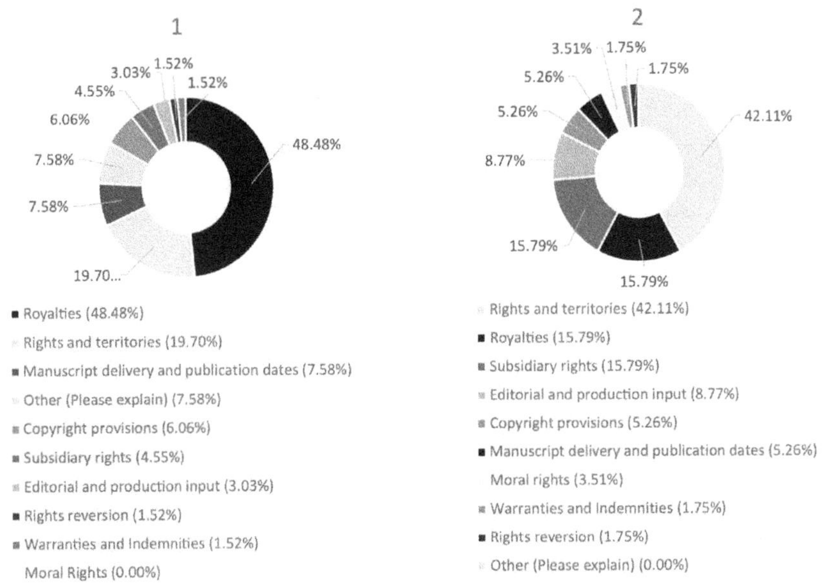

FIGURE 4.24 AS Q18a – In your opinion, where is a literary agent most likely to have an impact in contract negotiations? (number boxes from 1 to 9, with 1 being the highest)

Overall, authors continue to agree to/sign contracts that fail to satisfy them, but perhaps they also don't perceive of the work in the same way their publisher does. What are authors' expectations of the contract in the pre negotiating space that they seem so disillusioned in the post negotiating space? The presence of an agent seems to mitigate a less-than-satisfactory deal, but only by way of the author understanding their impotent position a little better, it would seem. Or perhaps it's the misaligned expectations of the position of the work in the market that the parties cannot reconcile. However, given the publisher is the party investing in the book, the author perhaps feels they have no choice but to agree to the publisher's terms. The next section of the survey seeks to illuminate this tension and discover some reasons for it.

Section D – perceptions of industry values

(AS Qs 12–14, 24, PPS Qs 7, 20, 21)

Sixty-three per cent of writers surveyed have a preferred publisher (Q.12a). When asked to name the preferred publisher, 28 publishers were named but 33 per cent placed Penguin Random House as one of their No. 1 preferences (7 respondents had more than one preferred publisher). Eleven per cent nominated Allen and Unwin as their preferred publisher and 7 per cent nominated Harper Collins. The rest were split at approximately 2 per cent each, excluding self-published authors of which the total said they had no preferred publisher. Given their decision to publish on their own, this is unsurprising.

In the written responses, there was a clear regard for editorial input and quality as being a prime reason for their choice, and words and phrases such as 'excellent editing' and 'editorial reputation' were common and consistent:

> Quality of books, great editing team, small publisher so more personal.
>
> I like my editor. She tells me what will and won't work . . . before I write the book. This sort of inside information helps the book go through fewer rewrites. I also think the publisher is able to weave her way through a very difficult market in America to get books on shelves. I have confidence in her and the publication house.
>
> Long-term relationship with editor.
>
> Editorial team.
>
> I like my editor. She's great. Also, prestigious company.
>
> Their editorial reputation and quality of their editors. Track record with awards.
>
> Strong editorial relationship and a backlist of work with them.
>
> I feel they have excellent editing and stable staff.
>
> I have a strong relationship with the editor and I would like to keep working with her.
>
> Love the communication, the intensive editing and their work ethic. Been very happy since began working with them rather than my previous publisher.

> Small independent publisher with a very good reputation, eclectic, high-quality list, prepared to take risks and to work with an author to realise a book's potential, provide quite intensive in-house editing. I like dealing with a small team (usually just the one person in this case). Allows for a more personal relationship. They respond to my emails (nearly always within 24 hours): rare in my experience.

Another notable consideration for writers was loyalty, which was also reflected in the responses to participants who had been published by their preferred publisher:

> They have published my books and I have a certain loyalty.

> Existing publisher.

> I have been there for some time. Publishing loyalty should be rewarded.

> I have worked with them on my first two books and hope to keep the relationship going.

Therefore, loyalty might denote some level of satisfaction with the publisher, or perhaps it could signify trust. What is very strongly expressed, however, is the important role of the editor in assisting with communication between the publishing house and the author, post negotiation. The editor is clearly positioned as an intermediary and might be crucial in modulating expectations. While at first their role does not appear to be explicitly connected to contract negotiations, the editor's influence in areas such as 'Delivery and Publication Dates', 'Moral Rights', expectations around sales and marketing performance, and even for un-negotiated small reprints, is highly important. While the aforementioned areas have not been flagged as important to the author, in Q.18a, ongoing communication that positions the author as having some power in decisions made about their work could alleviate the author's feelings of impotency. Such an area, which was raised as relatively important when choosing a preferred publisher, and which the editor could help facilitate, is sales and marketing:

> Harlequin's MIRA imprint appeals to me the most, because they seem to really support their authors with publicity and a long-term view.

> Attention to manuscript, marketing and promotion.

> Ethical. Realistic. Regular royalty/advance payments on time. Initiatives and supportive in placing subsidiary rights and handling international new media. Active help with launching and marketing.

These responses would perhaps explain the high percentage for Penguin Random House (PRH), which is a multinational publisher with a transnational reach. The other qualities of a publishing house that could be seen to support PRH's powerful market position, such as profitability, however, were ranked quite low when writers were asked what they value most in a publishing house (Q.14a).

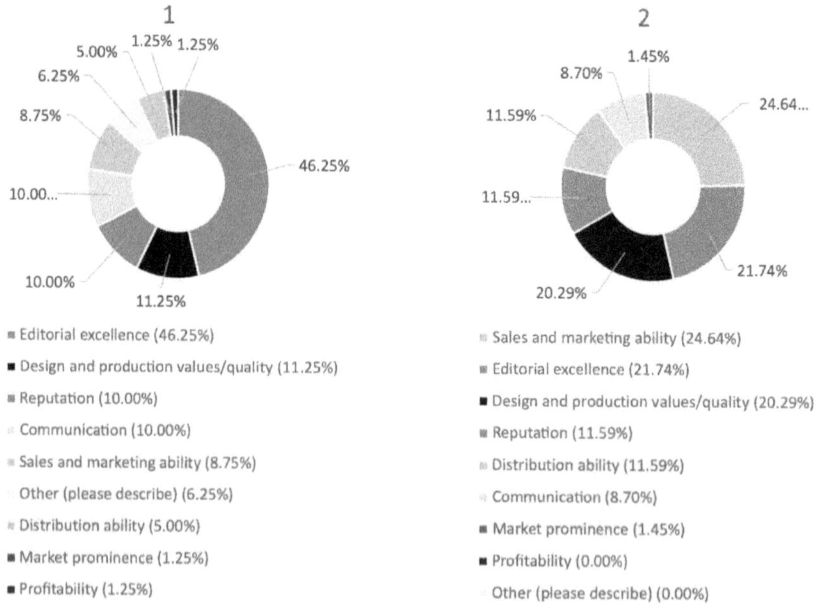

FIGURE 4.25 AS Q14a – What do you value most in a publisher? (number boxes from 1 to 8, with 1 being the highest)

The least valuable aspect of a publishing house, according to the AS, was 'Profitability' (61 per cent of respondents ranked it at No. 8 out of 8 ranked qualities). 'Market Prominence' also scored low (31 per cent placed its value at No. 7). The value of editorial input was further supported, with 46 per cent of authors placing 'Editorial Excellence' at No. 1. Two-thirds of self-published authors also rated 'Editorial Excellence' at No. 1, which is interesting given they would not have had any contact, necessarily, with editors in-house. 'Editorial Excellence' was also ranked high overall at No. 2 (22 per cent), along with 'Sales and Marketing' (25 per cent at No. 2) and 'Design and Production Values' (11 per cent at No. 1 and 21 per cent at No. 2). 'Other' can be seen in the first ranking and was explained as 'Sense of belonging and inclusion in the publishing process', which is a convincing statement substantiating the editor as an important intermediary in the publisher–author relationship.

The data, in this instance, shows an assessment of the preferred publisher that is almost counterintuitive to that publisher's business objectives: What the author *wants* in a publisher is often only achievable via the qualities that the author appears to be least interested in. Further investigation in this area could reveal an interesting dynamic that is potentially played out in contract negotiations and that incorporates the author's pecuniary interests (via their contesting the 'Royalties' and 'Rights and Territories' areas). Authors claim to want the financial reward from their works, and hope to see the works marketed to achieve financial reward, but don't necessarily appreciate that the publisher's market prominence or profitability is integral to this aim. Or rather, the author *is* aware that the publisher's position in the market is important to achieving sales, but the editorial input is *more* important.

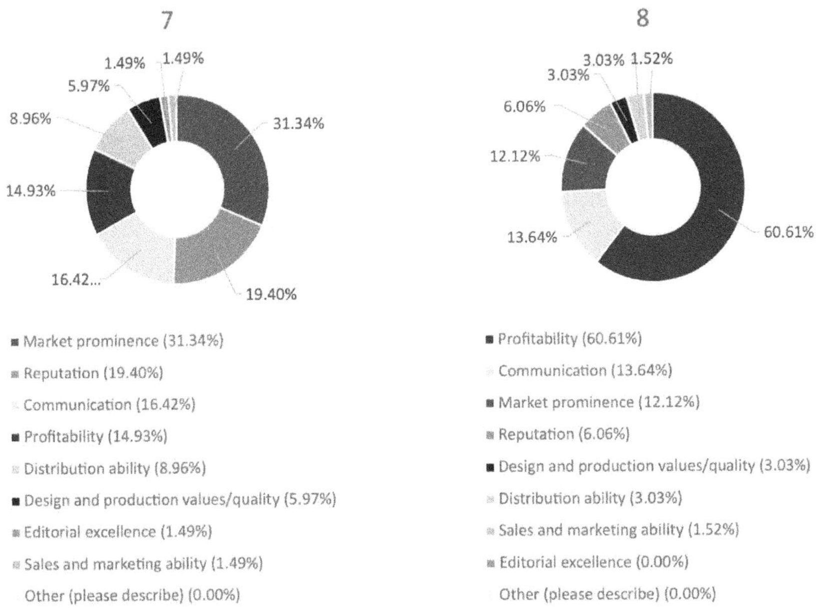

FIGURE 4.26 AS Q14a – What do you value most in a publisher? (number boxes from 1 to 8, with 1 being the highest)

When the publishing professionals were asked what they thought *writers* value most in a publishing house (Q.21a), their responses were evenly spread across the 8 ranked qualities: 'Reputation' and not 'Editorial Excellence', however, was ranked the highest at No. 1 at 24 per cent. 'Editorial Excellence' and 'Sales and Marketing' both came in at No. 1 with 18 per cent each. 'Editorial Excellence' was also ranked quite high at No. 2 (30 per cent). There was a very even spread, in the middle, of the remaining qualities of 'Design and Production Values', 'Distribution Ability', 'Market Prominence' and 'Communication' (between 14 per cent and 18 per cent at No. 5). 'Profitability' was considered the least important with 67 per cent putting it at No. 8. In terms of a noticeable proportion of 'types' of publishers for 'Reputation' or 'Editorial Excellence', none could be identified with responses being quite evenly spread.

Interestingly, when the publishing professionals were asked what the most important qualities of a publishing house are (Q.7a), the answers appeared more closely aligned with the responses in the AS: 'Editorial Excellence' was very clearly ranked at No. 1 by 35 per cent of respondents, with 'Sales and Marketing Ability' following with 18 per cent. The highest No. 2 ranked position was 'Design and Production Values' at 28 per cent, 'Distribution Ability' at 24 per cent, and 'Editorial Excellence' at 20 per cent. 'Profitability', similarly to the AS, was ranked low at No. 8 (35 per cent) along with 'Market Prominence' (35 per cent at No. 8). 'Other' can be seen in the first ranking and garnered responses such as 'It really depends on the author'. Overall, there was less distinction between the ranked categories.

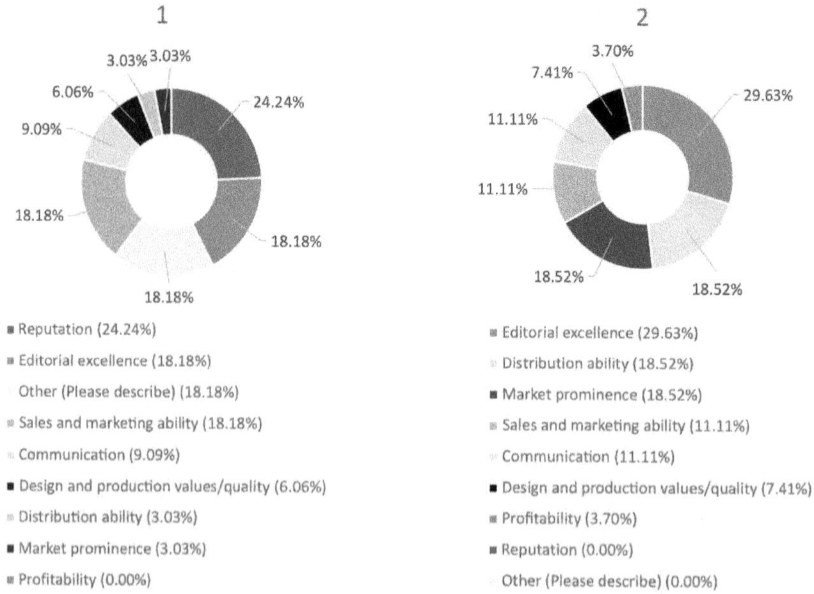

FIGURE 4.27 PPS Q21a – What do you think writers value most in a publishing house? (number boxes from 1 to 8, with 1 being the highest)

This is an intriguing result, given that publishers want, at least from a commercial publisher's perspective, to monetise the cultural product – the intellectual property of the author. Logically, publishers would be less enthusiastic about securing rights to reproduce a work that is unlikely to sell. What is also interesting about this particular section of data is that the publishing professionals appear less certain about what writers value in a publishing house than they do themselves (judging from the response to No. 1 in Q.21a). And while publishers and writers might have very different values overall (the publishers' values being arguably more pecuniary), the emphasis on 'Editorial Excellence' in Q.7a suggests either an ideological shift that challenges our understanding of the positions of the publisher and the writer in the publishing landscape. With 'Communication' in the PPS being one of the least ranked qualities (at No. 6 and 7–28 per cent and 32 per cent, respectively), the publishing professionals perhaps view editorial excellence as representing the *quality* of the editing process in terms of the finished work – not the *experience* of the editorial process, which certainly requires effective communication.

The high proportion of the surveyed publishing professionals representing independent publishing houses might explain the substantial interest in editorial excellence. An independent publisher will often spend more of their resources on the editorial process because their lists are less likely to be influenced by shareholders, who might keep a close watch on time and money spent. The meaning of editorial excellence could also point to the ability to protect the author's expression, as integral to the publisher's own protection of the intellectual property they have secured. Interviews will provide more detailed context to this anomaly.

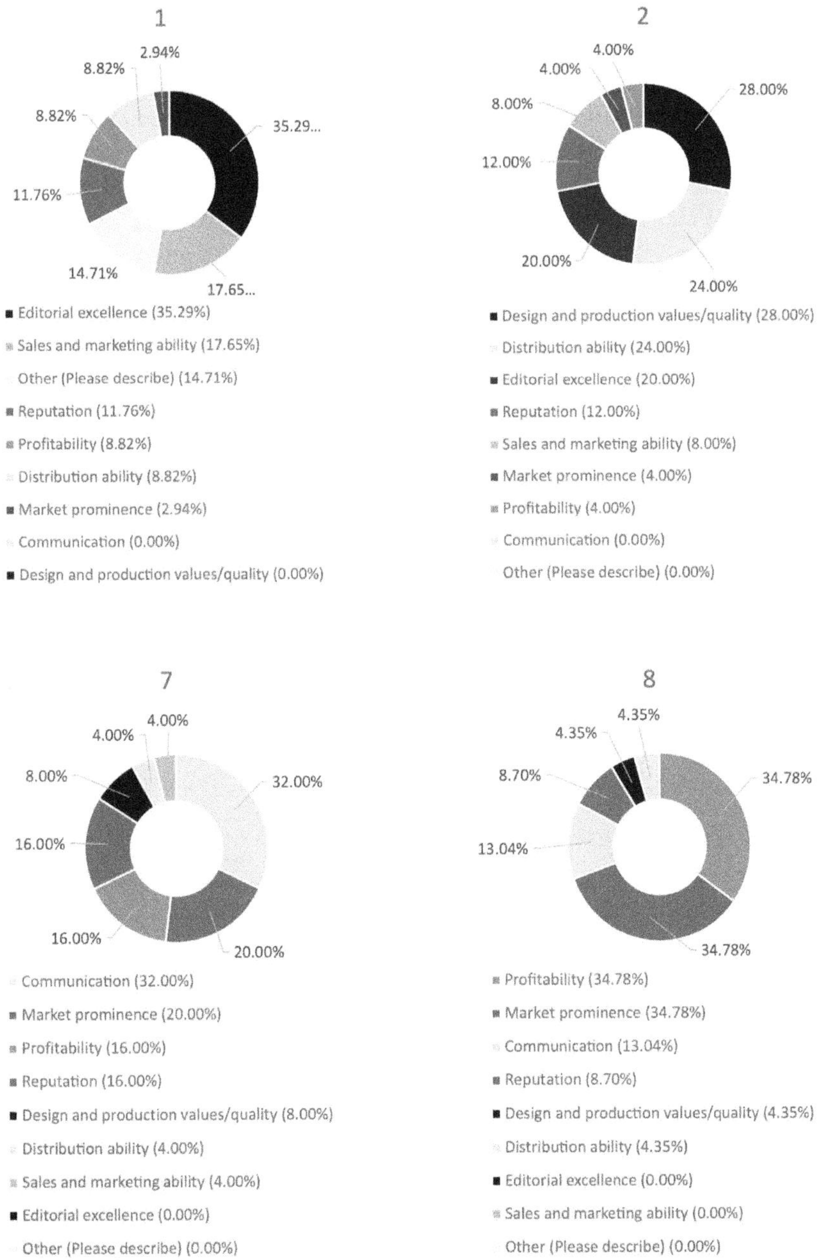

FIGURE 4.28 PPS Q7a – What do you think is the most important quality of a publishing house? (number boxes from 1 to 8, with 1 being the highest)

Lynette Owen says in *Selling Rights*: 'Publishers must be aware of the needs of their customers and concentrate on bringing value to content as justification for their financial reward' (Owen 2010, 29). Is this 'value' the level of editorial excellence that is brought via the book-making process? Or is editorial excellence signifying something else? The surveyed writers ranked 'Creative Expression' very highly when asked what is most important to them (out of the following choices: 'Earning a Living From Writing', 'Having a Reputation as a Great Writer', 'Protecting Your Intellectual Property', 'Having as Many People as Possible Read Your Work', and 'Creative Expression') at Q.24. Almost half of the literary fiction authors (9 authors) rated 'Creative Expression' as the highest value – the most of any other genre. This is unsurprising, given that literary fiction sells less than, say, genre/commercial fiction, which explains why other values such as 'Earning a Living from Writing' would rate lower.

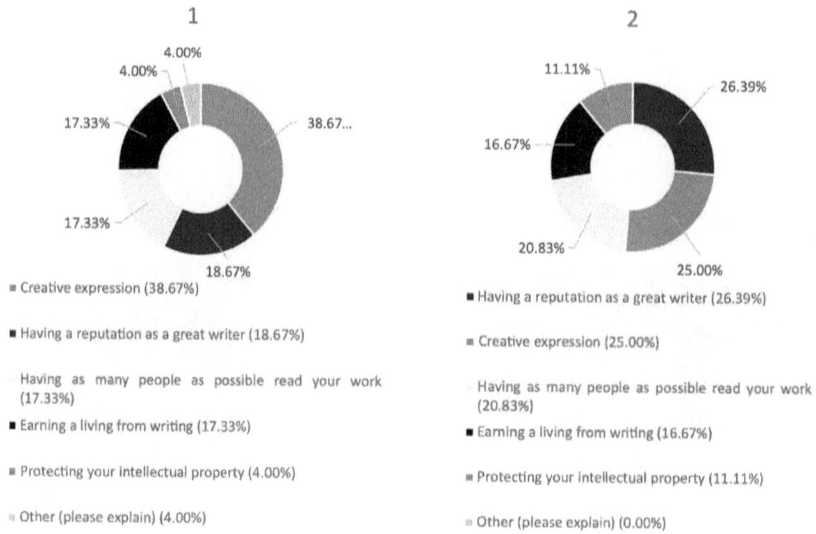

FIGURE 4.29 AS Q24 – As a writer, what is the most important to you? (number boxes from 1 to 5, with 1 being the highest)

Additionally, most adult literary fiction authors also rated 'Having a Reputation as a Great Writer' quite high (higher than writers in other genres). 'Protecting Your Intellectual Property' appeared to be the least important with all respondents, with 41 per cent ranking it at No. 5.

Given the strong response to whether the term of copyright should be changed (AS Q.19), the low ranking of 'Protecting Your Intellectual Property' is an interesting result. However, if given a choice of which would be more important (as was the case in this question), the authors' particular expression is paramount. Deeper insight into what creative expression means for the author, and how they see it manifested in their work will be illuminating, as well as to observe in what way is this expression protected, if at all. Some indication of how important it is to protect creative expression might also reveal a desire to maintain integrity in the work, as codified in the moral rights clauses in copyright law. But in this survey, we witness a see-saw-ing response from authors who seem torn between protecting the personality inherent in the work and their expectations of financial reward.

When asked what they think writers value most (in the same 5 ranked values), the PPS participants' responses (Q.20) were slightly more varied: 'Creative Expression' also ranked highly (29 per cent at No. 1), with most independent publishers placing it in the highest category. Half of the multinationals ranked 'Creative Expression' at No. 1 and half ranked 'Having as Many People as Possible Read Your Work' at No. 1. This might suggest that the multinational publishers surveyed published adult fiction, in line with the responses from literary authors. If so, this would be an expected outcome as opposed to a significant anomaly. 'Protecting Your Intellectual Property' was ranked low (46 per cent at No. 5). The middle rankings were all quite even, with most responses hovering around 20 per cent.

The data reflects that there is some knowledge on the publishing professionals' behalf about what writers value (as was the case, also, in Q.21a). Yet, the publishers' acknowledgement of a writer's desire for creative expression, at least to some degree, does not necessarily form a part of contract negotiation discussions; perhaps because the publishing professional sees creative expression as secondary to an author's pecuniary interests. In the knowledge of how highly writers value their creative expression, the standard contract doesn't seem to allow for these negotiations. Perhaps this is because publishers *and* authors view protecting creative expression as prohibitive to the utilitarian aspects of the contract, and they prefer to broach the maintenance of moral rights in the post negotiation space.

FIGURE 4.30 PPS Q20 – What do you think writers value most? (number boxes from 1 to 5, with 1 being the highest)

Section E – self-publishing

(AS Qs 20–23, PPS Qs 22, 23)

There was an even spread across writers' responses when asked if they had/or had not considered self-publishing (AS Q.20). Reasons for the 45 per cent who had considered self-publishing were as follows: they couldn't find a publisher for their work (22 per cent); they wanted control over the editorial and production process (22 per cent); 20 per cent stated they wanted more financial return; 5 per cent said that they had had a bad experience with a publisher and 4 per cent claimed that a publisher had been interested in their work but negotiations had failed.

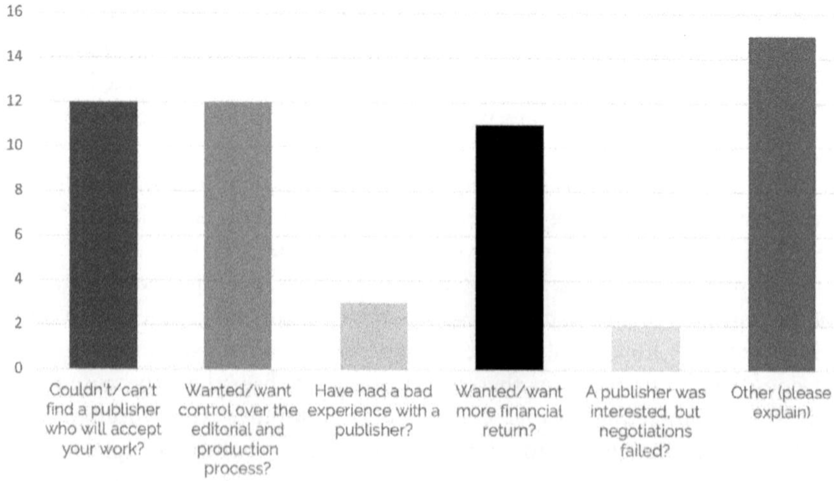

FIGURE 4.31 AS Q21 – If you have ever self-published a book/considered self-publishing a book, is it because you (tick all applicable boxes)

These responses are consistent with other areas of the survey and show authors are still entering into agreements with publishers, even with the option of self-publishing. The fact that *all* self-published authors had only self-published because they 'couldn't find a publisher' supports this proposition. The editorial and production process (also ranked highly) links editorial values with the need to exert control over their particular expression in the work (which would otherwise be facilitated by an in-house editor in a publishing company). Again, financial return is also paramount to authors.

When asked what were the most challenging aspects of self-publishing (AS Q.23a), Sales and Marketing was ranked as the No. 1 challenging aspect (41 per cent) (from 5 ranked aspects). Every self-published author ranked it as No. 1. Editorial was the least challenging (41 per cent at 4 and 35 per cent at 5). This supports the writers' emphasis on the importance of Sales and Marketing in Q.14a.

Forty-two per cent of participants in the PPS claimed that authors' ability to self-publish had not affected the revenue of traditional publishers (Q.22a). Only 7 per cent claimed that it had significantly affected revenue, with 45 per cent claiming it had affected revenue a little, and the rest did not know (7 per cent).

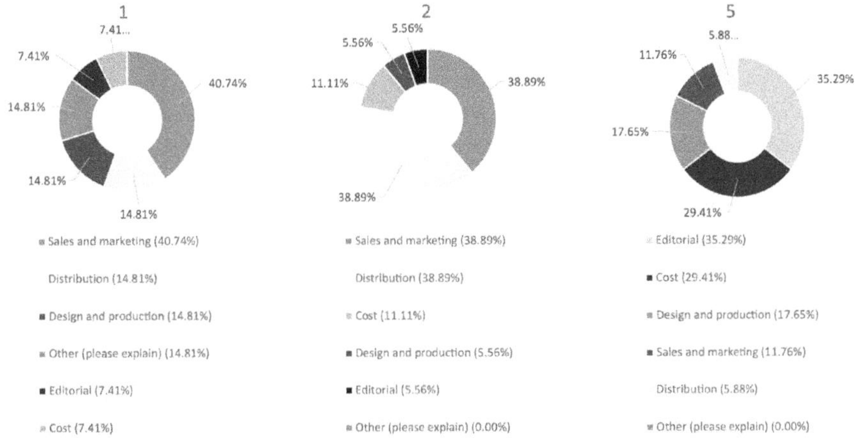

FIGURE 4.32 AS Q23a – If you have ever self-published a book, what did you find the most challenging aspect of the process? (number boxes from 1 to 5, with 1 being the highest)

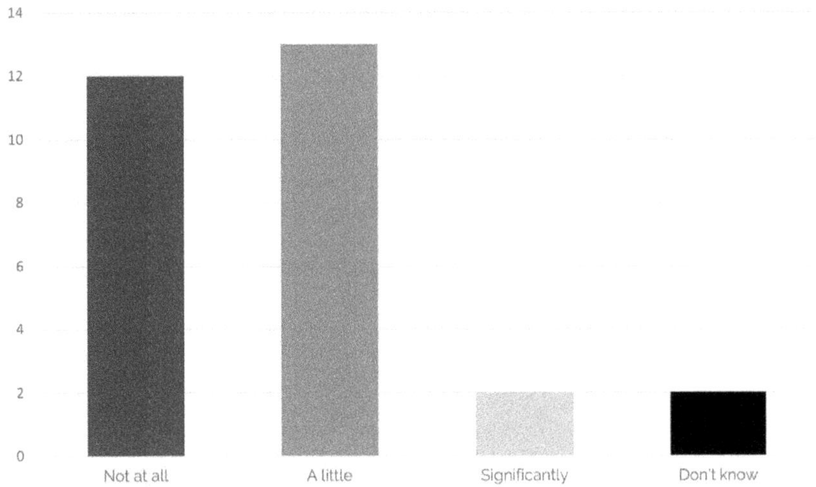

FIGURE 4.33 PPS Q22a – In your opinion, has writers' ability to self-publish affected the revenue of traditional publishers?

Written responses shared the following:

> The big houses have lost market share to small presses and self-publishers. I don't think small presses are competing directly against self-publishers so much as we are competing against big houses. We want our books to look like other professional, widely available

titles. As a small press with distribution, no self-published author can compete with us on distribution and particularly with our relationships with indie bookstores.

Some high-quality writers that we would love to have on our books expect to get more income from sales of their books by self-publishing. This means that we lose a valuable source of sales income in what is a very small market.

It has increased the options for writers and their direct audiences. But in my experience cheap self-published works do not satisfy the market anything like the way books produced by traditional publishing houses do. The revenue is still there for traditional publishing.

In the rare cases that a self-published author makes a splash/some cash, they usually then go on to get a book deal with a traditional publisher.

Writers have more choice. Even writers with a publishing list are opting to self-publish so that they have more control. At this stage though, these people don't have much choice in terms of distribution so it's harder for them to get traction in sales.

This needs a more nuanced answer, but in the broader sense, I do not think publishers' income has been affected by self-publishing, but in some categories (especially romance and SF), publishers are losing income through competition with the self-publishing authors in the online space.

Of the respondents, only 14 per cent had published a writer who had also self-published. The rest, 86 per cent, had not (Q.23). Again, it would appear that writers still want to be published via traditional means and are entering into agreements to secure this position.

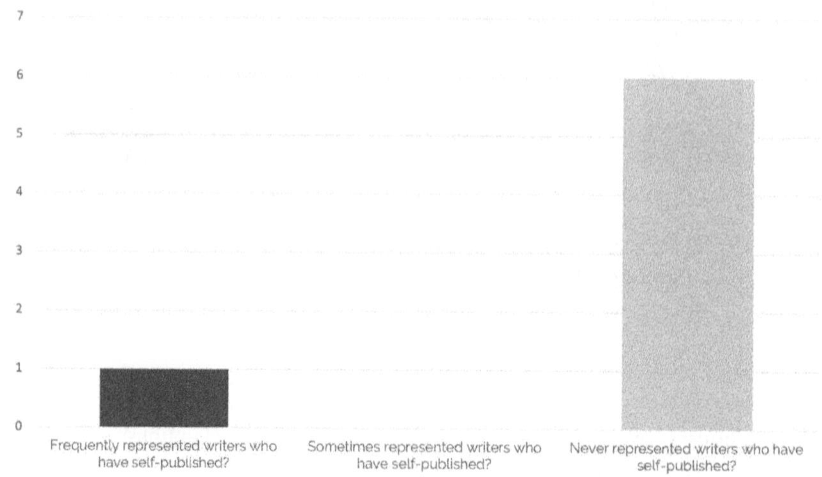

FIGURE 4.34 PPS Q23 – Have you . . .

***

In offering some further information to the survey overall, some AS respondents commented on the lack of income derived from writing:

> I think the degree with which you treat writing as a business has a correlation to your creative expression, but not necessarily to earning a living.

> I guess I am happy just trusting that my publisher has my best interest at heart. I do feel as though this industry is a bit of an odd one, with so many people wanting to be involved in it, but. . . . I have not seen a great deal of financial benefit so far. My first book has been shortlisted, which is great, and my second coming out soon. I hope that a trickle of financial reward will come through soon, as I have only received about $8500 so far and have been doing solid, long, exhausting hours for two years now. This is not realistic for any industry. As a designer and a teacher, it is possible for me to make a good income, but. . . . I would have thought I could sustain some financial benefit from the enormous amount of work I have done . . . and I have a big publisher. I wouldn't really recommend this as a career. You still have to pay your bills, so I'm not sure why the monetary return is so meagre, especially considering that many of the processes of making and distributing books have been streamlined with technology.

Publishing is not usually a lucrative business – for authors or for publishers. The second response, in particular, highlights that market share and size do not always equate to financial return. Being published by a 'big' publisher does not cancel the struggle to make an income from writing, and this knowledge no doubt contributes to authors' concerns with pecuniary interests (as seen in the AS responses). Royalties is an area of the contract in which income can be achieved. Conversely, the earlier statements could equally demonstrate a lack of interest in the pecuniary side of the contract negotiation if authors have no expectations of earning money. It does appear that the authors surveyed have quite clear expectations of how they want their work to be marketed when they license it to a publisher. These expectations are not necessarily in line with what a publisher must do to exploit the licensed work, or the decisions around where the work is situated in the market. Focusing on creative expression as one of the most important considerations might also prohibit the publisher from selling the work in different territories and formats if the author forcefully asserts their right of integrity. Alternately, highlighting creative expression could point to a firm regard for editorial input – that the editor's role in the production/publishing process assists the author to assert their moral rights in the absence of any explicit moral rights clause in the contract. This role is somewhat different to the kind of editorial excellence that mentors the author in their craft. An existing relationship with an in-house editor informs the degree to which an author can contest areas of the publishing house's standard contract, and the survey results suggest that established authors choose their battles when considering their moral rights, knowing that their relationship with their in-house editor will result in support for their work. In practice, this is facilitated by the editor allowing the author to see all edits of the work and corrections at all stages (although the contract would stipulate less involvement); it could result in the author having more input in cover design (again, a level of involvement clearly prohibited in the standard contract analysed), or perhaps the author will have a more direct connection with the publishing house's sales and marketing team, via the editor. From my own perspective, in my time as an in-house editor, I witnessed all of the aforementioned. The written responses to Q. 12 also support these practices. Other comments at the conclusion of the survey flagged a need for transparency in contract negotiations overall:

> I think there is a lot more education of writers needed in this area. Particularly when it's a dubious publisher with a problem contract. I know the ASA helps members, but otherwise people have nowhere to go. I was lucky that with my first contract I had someone really knowledgeable who went through it with me and explained everything. But I have seen many writers (even recently) who have shown me really problematic contracts. And writers who have signed things that left them with no rights at all when the publisher went down the gurgler.

> I think they should be more transparent and we should not be prevented from discussing details with peers if we so desire.

> In my experience with my own publishing contract and speaking to other first-time authors, there seems to be a lack of care from a number of publishers when dealing with new authors. It's a gruelling process to begin and the contracts are complex and perhaps not always slanted in the writer's favour. It would be good to see some changes in this area.

***

The data from the surveys shows that authors, even authors who do not have a comprehensive understanding of the terms of a standard contract, are still entering into agreements with publishers. And they would prefer the publisher to be in the best position to exploit their works for economic benefit. Authors are, however, mostly dissatisfied with these agreements.

Publishers appear content with the agreements and with communication throughout contract negotiations, and in fact seem slightly oblivious to what authors prioritise and value most, except the need for creative expression. Authors present as polarised by the constant pull of their pecuniary interests, which seem hugely significant to them. So much so that pecuniary interests might even outweigh moral rights – or their particular expression of the work – within negotiations. These values are not being effectively communicated to publishers, however. Authors, it could be surmised from the results of this survey, see the contract as a tool that promotes economic value and not symbolic value. While the literature suggests that an author might seek a contract to legitimise their work (Thompson 2012, 43), the survey indicates that, for authors, the individual publisher's strength in the marketplace is more important than the publisher's assessment of the work's value. But surprisingly, authors also don't rate a publishing house's market prominence as a quality they admire.

Other evidence of pecuniary interest can be found in the contentious areas of 'Royalties' and 'Rights and Territories'. We also see that the authors' choices for a preferred publisher indicate things such as 'transnational reach' and 'sales and marketing' ability alongside a strong relationship with their editor. These focuses might be more pronounced because moral rights are assumed in most standard contracts, but perhaps authors' relationships with their editors facilitate the level of communication needed to ensure that integrity in the work is maintained outside of the perception that contracts are utilitarian. For this survey, this editorial relationship presents as having more importance than was anticipated. Not only does the relationship ensure quality in the work, but the editor also acts as the most important mediator post negotiation, where expectations resulting from the signed contract are most vulnerable to being misinterpreted. From the publishers' perspective, editorial excellence does not extend to this post negotiation space; it simply reflects the excellence of the editorial process itself. This particular result can be viewed as a 'breach' in the research, which Hammersley and Atkinson describe as a 'disruption', causing the researcher to rethink their original hypotheses (Hammersley & Atkinson 2007, 52).

Thus, the survey results show that authors underestimate the publishing contract's power to uphold and protect the symbolic value in their work. This symbolic value includes the integrity in the work and the writer's distinct creative expression, supposedly made more relevant by way of the publisher accepting it for publication. This limited perception is particularly evident for new and emerging authors. Many established authors, on the other hand, realise that the contract has a broader capacity, beyond its economic importance. This knowledge comes via their experience and error of judgement. The ASA standard contract certainly alludes to this position through its specific wording – protecting the author at all times – but the improvements and suggestions have not satisfied everything authors wish to gain via their writing and their relationship with publishers. The importance of editorial excellence might explain why authors are tacit and comply with areas of the contract that are problematic for them, at the time of signing. In choosing their battles, authors seem to be focusing on the economic if other areas are more navigable throughout the editing and production process. Again, the high percentage of authors who consider editorial excellence to be the most important quality of a publisher suggests this might be so.

Agents are also acting as mediators, but actual change to the contracts, if it is happening at all, is still not providing satisfactory outcomes for authors. Agents, rather, are being used as 'translators' of the contract: conveying what the terms mean but apparently maintaining the status quo of standard contracts overall. The publishers surveyed are resistant to agents' involvement in the negotiation process, which suggests that the status quo is at least being *challenged*. This certainly presents in the survey in 'Rights Reversion', where agents are seen to have an impact, along with 'Royalties', 'Rights and Territories' and 'Subsidiary Rights'. For example, while boilerplate contracts have often stipulated world rights as a blanket request, agents are encouraging authors to look beyond their relationship with the current publisher in the negotiation and projecting opportunities in their careers. If they don't keep some rights to themselves now, then it will be more difficult for them to take those rights from their publisher later.

Although self-publishing provides a clear pathway for the author to have full control over their works, they have not embraced this option for reasons of sales and marketing, predominantly, which again points to the authors' pecuniary interests. To reiterate, the authors indicate that the qualities of a publishing house that can most facilitate sales and marketing – 'Profitability' and 'Market Prominence' – are not important to them. This illustrates a disconnection that reveals the author's expectations to be impractical, further illuminating their fluctuating between the economic and the ideological.

How authors are negotiating the utilitarian and symbolic spaces in the contract negotiation process in the current landscape tells us that there has been a more pronounced shift towards their pecuniary interests – not necessarily via the construction of the romanticised author as genius and creator. Although creative expression is still paramount to authors in terms of their *overall* values, when it comes to the contract, economic reward trumps their moral rights. Given that authors are mostly dissatisfied with their contract negotiations, a greater interest in self-publishing platforms could be expected if integrity in the work was of the utmost value. But the preference for traditional publishing avenues, as indicated in the AS, suggests that authors are still pursuing contracts with publishers with the means to effectively exploit their works. This development illustrates a new position-taking for the author – not so much derived from challenging the status quo to create a space of possibility (Bourdieu 1996, 221), (the contract does not appear to have altered dramatically or show drastic variation from publisher to publisher) but, rather, from adapting *within* the 'illusio' of the existing publishing field (Bourdieu 1996, 228).

Results from this study indicate that this position-taking is a phenomenon also *within* negotiations – in the pre negotiation space and the post negotiation space – when it might have been expected to occur elsewhere (such as via self-publishing, or within other mediums in a globalised landscape). And the authors' approaches have regard for the current traditional publishing structures, which is slightly different to what Bourdieu describes as an active assertion of their new position 'by imposing new modes of thought and expression which break with current modes of thought and hence are destined to disconcert by their "obscurity" and their "gratuitousness"' (Bourdieu 1996, 233).

Yet the author still avoids or shows a lack of interest and/or understanding when it comes to the specific legal framework of the contract and the ramifications of entering into a legal agreement with a publisher. Perhaps this is why authors appear so irresolute. Publishers, therefore, are still seen to be in a more powerful position, and authors capitulate so they don't jeopardise the contract. The contract also continues to be an inflexible vehicle for negotiations due to its particular wording and evidence of standard clauses. Interpretation of the contract's terms is fraught with misunderstandings (Fried 1981, 50) and the editor's and agent's roles in shepherding the author through this indistinct legal framework are welcomed.

5

THE CONTRACT IN MOTION

An in-depth exploration

The survey responses reiterated the power struggle between authors and publishers, which is unsurprising and well-documented. My next discovery was to identify the exact areas of struggle that caused the dissatisfaction between the parties, and how these affected the relationship between authors and publishers. Given the idiosyncrasies of the publishing contract, it is unlikely that its terms, only, are the point of contention; the surveys indicated deeper social and communicational factors in the post negotiation space. For example, from the survey analysis it was surmised that authors view the contract as a tool that promotes economic value more than symbolic value: while the literature suggests that an author might seek a contract to legitimise their work (Thompson 2012, 43), this research instead suggests that for authors, an individual publisher's strength in the marketplace might be more important than their assessment of the work's literary value. Evidence of pecuniary interest can be found in the contentious areas of 'Royalties' and 'Rights and Territories'. Authors' choices for a preferred publisher include 'transnational reach' and 'sales and marketing' ability. Thus, authors ignore or underestimate the publishing contract's power to uphold and protect the creative expression in their work – something the survey responses revealed that the author cares about very much. This symbolic value informs the choices made about what the work *is* and its market expectations; however, without clear communication, expectations inevitably do not align, and frustration ensues. But the contract itself is not a concern (as per the survey). With the internal workings of the black box partly revealed, the third stage of the research combined these findings with the input and the output by analysing the gathered data and addressing the following questions as part of the interview process:

4 *How are contracts used within the publishing house after signing?*
5 *Is the contract still an effective tool for negotiations in the contemporary book-publishing landscape?*

It is my view that the relational aspects of the publishing contract exist separately to the document itself. The contract sits in its file as a stagnant record of standard terms, until something happens – a surprising sales spike or a failed sales and marketing campaign – when it is dusted off and looked at afresh. But that second glance now holds more scrutiny because something 'changed' to draw everyone's attention to the agreement. Up until this point, the gentleman's

DOI:10.4324/9781003336570-5

handshake suffices: the promise that the publisher will bear the economic risk and the author the creative risk, that each party will work with the other to do what's best for the work. It's a relationship ripe for twists, turns and potential drama. The author might suddenly realise that the financial risk wasn't that risky at all, while their life's work sits redundant in a warehouse, gathering dust and not generating the revenue they had anticipated; the author might have underestimated their novel's sales potential, and suddenly the terms of the contract no longer reflect the actual reward owed; or a cover somehow doesn't signify the content, and an author feels betrayed by the publisher's vision for the title, which wasn't fully expressed at the time of signing.

All of these scenarios can be revisited post contract but not without understanding the existing terms first. This might be why authors attempt to lock in the least negotiable terms early on: the royalties and the rights. In choosing their battles, authors appear (according to the survey) to focus on the economic aspects of the contract *because* other areas are more navigable throughout the editing and production process (such as the look and feel of the book and the editing of their expression). The high percentage of authors who consider editorial excellence to be the most important quality of a publishing house might explain why they are tacit and comply with areas of the contract that are problematic for them. Authors' relationships with their editors facilitate the level of communication needed to ensure that integrity in the work is maintained outside of the contract's utilitarian aims. Not only does the editorial relationship ensure quality in the work, but the editor also acts as the most effective mediator in the post negotiation space, where expectations resulting from the signed contract are most vulnerable to being misinterpreted. The editor also communicates in-house processes from the 'site' of publishing to the author who is on the outside. The editor is the person an author can turn to when they feel the book isn't being adequately publicised or supported. When a book isn't selling, the editor can relay the actual sales. And rights reversion can be raised with the editor if and when the book goes OP. The editor also knows how the manuscript is tracked in terms of delivery dates and quality; they also sell the title to other departments and communicate to design and sales and marketing the decisions about genre and author expectations of cover treatment and format.

With 'Editorial Excellence' defined as very important in the survey, I added some editors/commissioning editors to my pool of interviewees. This allowed for a broader spectrum within the publishing professionals group in direct response to the outcomes of the surveys and helped to further contextualise the social and human angle of this research – the misunderstandings between authors and publishers, and that the contract is not bedrock as contract theory indicates. On the other hand, the gentleman's agreement might also be disproportionately risky for the author. Scholarly work on contracts to date has focused primarily on the agreement itself (Fried 1981; Paterson 2009; Black 2012; Deakin 2006), usually for businesses that provide quantifiable products and services. Even relational contract theory uses examples outside of trade publishing.

The decision to include editors allowed me to incorporate my experience as outlined in the introduction and to involve myself and my personal response in the interview process. My position as a centralised player meant that I could also critically analyse the literature from the perspective of someone who also practices the theoretical propositions. This structure is reflective of how Ellis describes the autoethnographic approach: '[Y]ou might focus on telling your story, then frame it with an analysis of literature, and concentrate on raising questions about that literature or about accepted theoretical notions or on generating new ideas' (Ellis & Bochner 2006, 118). I decided to combine storytelling with the more analytic tools of data and narrative analysis so that I could objectively assess the data as well as relive my own experiences.

Jensen stresses the importance of planning ahead before embarking on qualitative research, stating that the plan is a 'necessary part of that "construction" of the field which most qualitative researchers recognise as their epistemological premise' (Jensen 2002, 237). He identifies three stages to this planning:

1 Strategy – the general plan, establishing the means of communication and points of observation.
2 Tactics – defining the people being interviewed and their particular position in the system.
3 Techniques – the researcher's means of interacting with the people and documenting the process.

The following paragraphs outline my own plan – my approach to the interviews – using Jensen's stages as a guide.

Strategy and tactics

Because the units of analysis for the survey had mostly been gathered via a Google search for all publishing professionals and published authors, or via my personal contact with the participants, I was able to encourage participation by following up with the respondents who were identifiable. All information gained from the hand-picked sample was confidential, but survey respondents had the option of ticking a box at the end of the survey, to be included in the interview process. This last section of the survey also asked for contact details so that the potential interviewee could be emailed or phoned.

I decided initially to cap the interviews at three individuals for each of the following categories: published writer, emerging writer and publishing professional. The reason for the cap was mostly due to the viability of survey respondents who checked 'yes' for a follow-up interview. Some of the willing participants were difficult to access (as a result of proximity and/or time), or not the most suitable for the interview (unpublished authors, for example). The categories included a mix of commercial and literary writers, publishers, agents and rights professionals. As mentioned earlier, editors were added to the pool of interviewees. For reasons of proximity, I also narrowed the list to potential interviewees in Australia only, with a view to ensuring I could speak with the interviewees face-to-face when possible.

Not all survey respondents said that they would be willing to be interviewed (mainly due to time pressures), which narrowed down the pool of interviewees in each of the categories. The next stage in the selection process involved looking at the surveys to see which individual responses reflected the common themes and discoveries that had emerged from the survey overall. These included some existing areas of focus, from the beginning of the research, as well as some new focuses:

What is the power dynamic between authors and publishers?
Do authors view the individual publisher's strength in the marketplace as more important than their assessment of the work's value?
Is the contract a tool of economic value only?
Why are royalties so important for authors?
What does editorial excellence mean for authors? And for publishers?

One exercise that also helped me to refine the themes that had emerged from the survey, and to test whether these themes also reflected the 'parts' that I had constructed, was to develop a list of keywords from the written survey responses. I created two lists – one for authors and one for publishing professionals – using software that collected the words most frequently presented in the survey responses. After eliminating pronouns and conjunctions etc. on an Excel spreadsheet, the keywords emerged. For authors, the top five keywords were support/guidance, sales, negotiate, editing, and rights. These were followed closely by money/earnings, marketing, creativity, and royalties. For publishing professionals, the top five keywords were income/earnings, deal, negotiations, rights/territories, and self-publishing. These were followed closely by royalties, conflict, satisfaction/unhappiness, and processes.

These keywords were integrated into the research questions to trigger further discussion. The keywords also assisted me with my selection process. Ruddock says that for ethnographic research, '[t]he sort of people gathered depends on the research question[s] at hand, and choice of participants is determined by criteria that are appropriate for a specific study, rather than the field in general' (Ruddock 2001, 133). While the sample for the survey was broad and based on a selection of players in the field more generally, the interview selection was far more specific to the results of the survey, and the decision about who to interview was based on the main themes emerging from the data analysis. Thus, the decision, for example, to choose a sample of editors for the interviews was based on the 'breach' of information gained about editorial excellence. Ruddock explains: 'Although research questions are inevitably based to some degree on a priori of assumptions, the ethnographer's goal is to create a flexible observational framework that can register and account for unexpected phenomena' and that 'effective ethnographers allow themselves to be "surprised" by their results' (Ruddock 2001, 128). With flexibility in mind, my selection of interviewees was formed after the surveys and based on the interviewees' ability to elaborate on the survey responses. The individuals were then contacted via email. If they did not respond within two weeks, a follow-up email was sent. If after one more week the potential interviewee had not responded, then no further attempt was made to contact them.

This process generated 10 interviewees: 1 literary agent, 3 publishers, 2 editors and 4 authors. Two of the authors were hybrid – author/commissioning editors. To reiterate, when I refer to 'editor' I am again utilising Freeman's description, which is

> interchangeable between commissioning editor . . . or . . . someone who takes a hands-on editorial role . . . with responsibility for creating a particular list of titles, overseeing writing, design and production, and . . . marketing and sales of each title . . . interchangeable with the role of commissioning editor.
>
> (Freeman 2001, 106)

Techniques

Using these steps as a guide, I created some general questions for each separate interview. These questions were inspired by the interviewees' individual responses to the survey but also incorporated some general questions to the overall survey results. In addition, I added questions about the respondents' reasons for writing/publishing to contextualise their involvement in the industry/creative field and to gauge the reasons for their involvement. This helped me connect the interviewees' responses with my own narrative and to find some parallels between them as well as 'positioning them in the system' more accurately by exploring their individual paths towards their positions. The framework also helped me maintain a degree of objectivity. Anderson states that 'analytic autoethnographers must avoid self-absorbed digression'. But '[t]hey are also constrained from self-absorption by the ethnographic imperative of dialogic engagement with others in the social worlds they seek to understand' (Anderson 2006, 385), and that 'some of the most important and early efforts in autoethnography were undertaken by scholars with clearly analytic goals' (Anderson 2006, 391). Additionally, some structure helps to '[Provide] for better use of the limited time available for an interview; interviewing is more systemic and comprehensive and the issues to be explored are delineated in advance' (Patton 2002, 343). All interviews were either held at the place of employment of the interviewee, at a public meeting place, or via Zoom/Skype, mostly for reasons of convenience for the interviewee. I was mindful of individuals' time constraints and wanted to minimise rescheduling or cancellation where possible. Interviews were recorded on an iPhone (including the Zoom/Skype interviews).

Once all the interviews had been conducted and the data collected, they were transcribed from the iPhone to a Word document. Ruddock points out the limitations of ethnographic research techniques, such as transcriptions' inability to convey nuance in the form of body language, for example. My aim, therefore, was to transcribe the interviews exactly as they were spoken – replete with stutters and pauses, in an attempt to capture the nuance in responses and, in some cases, hesitation around certain questions. Ethnographic research may also have positivist tendencies via the researcher 'detailing' the cultural framework as well as what transpires in the research interviews, 'with a desire to recreate that culture objectively for the reader' (Hammersley 1992, 141). Being explicit about the 'criteria for evaluating transcripts and as honest as possible in reporting data which reflect the position of respondents rather than the researcher' (Hammersley 1992, 141) by way of my exact transcription, however, prevented me from unknowingly manipulating the data.

This is not to suggest that the interview process was rambling and without structure: the survey results enabled a clear framework that proved to be a valuable guide with some surprising value. For example, the surveys offered unexpected information that disrupted the original premise upon which the research was conducted (most notably the meaning of editorial excellence and the emphasis on the pecuniary aspects of the contract). It was important that my methods were flexible enough to incorporate these new findings. Transcribing the responses exactly as I heard them through my recordings had additional advantages: I was confident that the transcriptions were exact, but the stutters and pauses offered an internal language of hesitancy, uncertainty and guardedness that on occasion conveyed more than the spoken words. From the position of someone who had experienced similar scenarios to the ones I posed in the interview questions, I identified this hesitancy and guardedness as symptomatic of the particular positions of each of the participants in the field and of speaking of such things in the workplace (e.g. when company policy was being protected or when an author's behaviour during the editing process needed to be expressed in the most diplomatic way possible).

Jensen and Jankowski state that the ethnographer must learn the rules of the culture in which they position themselves (Jensen et al. 1997, 154) and observe their responsibilities but not miss the 'fundamental requirements for the data collection' (Jensen et al. 1997, 154). The ethnographic approach also 'attempts to explicate the (often unspoken) informal logic of communication and other everyday practices' (Jensen et al. 1997, 156). The original aim for exactness, therefore, opened up further opportunities for me to access a deeper level of meaning from the interviews.

I aimed to maximise my position of knowledge in the research but also constrained my imposition on the research findings by using rigid analytical tools. The research design was deliberately nuanced to counter existing contract research, which is more theoretical and not necessarily suitable to the business of publishing. Barbour and Schostak say that

> The phrase 'research design' sounds powerful, clean, scientific, solid. A bit scary. Really, at times, it can feel like a mess. Employing laboratory-designed methods for research that focusses upon the complex, dynamic, plastic worlds of everyday social and personal life is rather like taking a pile driver to do lace work.
>
> (Barbour & Schostak 2005, 43)

On the contrary, I found the analytical tools (the survey, keywords, contract overview) complemented the interviews well, by testing my initial research questions and revealing further areas of investigation. To reiterate, one of the most intriguing of these was the interpretation of editorial excellence, which prompted me to engage with a selection of editors for my interviews. I entered the interview process with the surveys providing a concrete guide. Other unexpected findings from the surveys, such as the emphasis on the contract's pecuniary value, were successfully contextualised within my own understanding of the field, particularly the field as a more democratised landscape that offers further opportunities for authors. The surveys, therefore, and the steps within my research design, resulted in rich pickings for analysis.

Black box contents: collating and analysing the interviews

Despite the aforementioned advantages, the breadth of information gained from the interviews was initially overwhelming. Every answer to every question seemed to hold vital information relevant to the research questions. I needed a stronger and more identifiable framework to help me organise the information in a way that would make sense to a broader scholarly audience outside of the industry. This framework would also force me to convey what I might take for granted as understood, to the outsider. Collating the many pieces of information was essential to gaining a deeper understanding of the quantitative results of this study (the survey), but the qualitative methods required a disciplined brief. Barbour and Schostak's 'lacework' demanded a tight embroidery hoop.

To break down the interview responses in a coherent and identifiable way, I arranged them so that they corresponded to the 'themes' under investigation. My method for this step was to use 'thematic coding' (Pace 2012; Ellis & Bochner 2006). Ellis describes 'thematic analysis' as 'treating stories as data and using analysis to arrive at themes that illuminate the content and hold within or across stories' (Ellis & Bochner 2006, 116). These themes closely reflected the 'parts' of the survey I had constructed (for ease of cross-referencing) and the keywords I had extracted. From this information, I created the following sub-categories: 'Perceptions of industry values', 'Contract status and copyright', 'Editorial excellence', 'Earnings and royalties', and 'Negotiations'. Each title had a number of areas of investigation via the following legend:

> *Perceptions of industry values [self-publishing, digital and developments, creativity]*
>
> *Contract status and copyright [rights and territories and rights reversion]*
>
> *Editorial excellence [intervention, support, in-house processes, sales and marketing]*
>
> *Earnings and royalties [Money, income, sales]*
>
> *Negotiations [literary agents, power balance, post-negotiation]*

I then grouped the transcribed responses into these themes by highlighting the responses that reflected one of the sub-categories. This made the responses easily identifiable and easy to collect. This system of 'coding' is described by Pace as

> taking the written stories of the researcher or other study participants, and breaking these stories down into discrete incidents – objects, events, actions, ideas and so on – which are then compared for similarities and differences. Significant incidents are assigned labels known as codes.
>
> (Pace 2012, 10)

Once the interviews were coded, I was then able to sort them by collating each response within its most likely code, to build a relationship between each – looking for similarities and linking concepts – as well as how they connected to the core themes (Pace 2012, 12). The analysis was also grouped into the following: 'Publishers' (which included a literary agent), 'Authors', and 'Editors'. The 'Hybrids' (Authors/Publishers/Editors) were separated out. The analysis began with each themed area and then discussed how the individual groups responded to these areas, via an ongoing narrative interspersed with analysis of the content proffered. The reason for this narrative style was to mirror the autoethnographic approach in its most evocative form (within an analytical structure). Pace describes this form of narrative: 'Like other genres of self-narrative, such as memoir, autobiography and creative non-fiction, autoethnography involves storytelling' (Pace 2012, 5). And although my particular approach was more consciously analytical, my arrangement of the interview responses aimed to provide a story whereby 'relationships are dramatized as connected episodes' (Pace 2012). The particular style and choices of the interview analysis captured conversations and struggles within a semi-structured story. Throughout the collation process, I also decided to include as many of the responses as I could. I was very wary of unintentionally manipulating the data: any choice to omit a certain response was a choice to potentially steer the data in a particular direction. I worried that this 'editing' would undermine the integrity of the research in favour of a simpler expression of it. Keeping most of the responses necessitated a solid framework because many conflicted with each other and reflected a highly complicated patchwork that needed contextualisation. The interspersed narrative provides this contextualisation, and the areas of investigation helped to structure the interviews clearly for the reader.

Publishers

Five interviewees brought a publisher's perspective (including one literary agent providing the publishers' and authors' perspectives). Selection of these individuals was based on availability but also to find a cross section of representatives from the field. The chosen publishers' particular responses from the survey also invited further interrogation of the areas that the survey raised as being contentious or disruptive to the research by challenging preconceived theories. The anonymous interviewees are briefly outlined here:

Pub A – Publisher in a small independent publishing company
Pub B – Publisher in a medium-sized independent publishing company
Pub C – Publisher in a large multinational company
Lit D – A literary agent

Authors

Four interviewees brought an author's perspective including the hybrid author/publishing professionals. Selection of these individuals was based on availability but also to find a cross section of representatives from the field. The chosen authors' particular responses from the survey also invited further interrogation of the areas that the survey raised as being contentious or disruptive to the research by challenging preconceived theories. The anonymous interviewees are briefly outlined here:

Auth A – Published author
Auth C – Published author

Hybrids

Hybrid B – Hybrid (author and publisher in a large multinational company)
Hybrid D – Hybrid (author and editor in an independent publisher)

Editors

Three interviewees brought an editor's perspective. Selection of these individuals was based on availability but also to find a cross section of representatives from the field. The anonymous interviewees are briefly outlined here:

Ed A – Editor for a large multinational publisher
Ed B – Editor for a large multinational publisher

Perceptions of industry values

'Perceptions of industry values' as a sub-category encompassed the following areas of investigation: self-publishing, digital, and developments and creativity. These areas allowed me to engage with the interviewees from a broader perspective, not so closely aligned with their particular role in publishing. Doing so also helped to relax the interviewee because they could comment more obliquely on their passion and industry developments without initially investing too much of themselves.

When the editors and publishers were asked what their thoughts were about the profession generally, most affirmed that the people who work in publishing 'work for the love, not the money'. This response reflects the aforementioned 2018 study by *Books+Publishing*, which surveyed 349 people about their employment in the Australian book industry – a survey that built upon their 2013 survey of 263 industry workers. They asked respondents if this was still relevant 'and found that 38 per cent have been asked to accept a lower wage, with the person in charge using this phrase or a similar phrase' (*Books+Publishing*, 2018).

Publishing, as a creative industry, pays lower than other industries. There is a consensus that employees are not paid at all for the hours they spend reading and assessing manuscripts, which is a work-related activity: 'Most full-time workers in the industry (71 per cent) said they read books or manuscripts for work and read them outside of work hours. No-one said they receive income for doing so, but most agreed that it is a work activity (86 per cent). Over one third of respondents said that it is a pleasurable activity (36 per cent) and less than one-third think of it as an educational activity (31 per cent)' (*Books+Publishing*, 2018). To date, not all publishers have entered into an Enterprise Bargaining Agreement (EBA) like that between Penguin Random House (Australia) and its employees in 2019, and the same attitude of 'doing it for the "love of it" and that they should be grateful for getting such a sought-after job' (Millar 2021) perpetuates.

In the interviews, most of the discussions about pay were deceptively light-hearted. It is a particular and common response in publishing to use humour to counter the incongruity of the work–pay disparity. The fact that editors and publishers are paid poorly also provides a comforting sense of camaraderie, of being in the 'same boat'. Unlike the days of the Bodley Head – when the 'reader' was often the publisher, often the CEO, or equivalent of the company – contemporary publishing hierarchies, particularly large conglomerates, position editorial roles further down the chain, at least in terms of pay. Being an Opportunistic CMR (Complete Membership Researcher) (Anderson 2006) gave me privileged access to the 'boat' and the shared double-edged feelings of doing something you love for little pay. This rapport offered immediate ease between me and the interviewees, and a continuation of that humour around publishing in general:

> Pub A: As a publisher I earn this much money: zero cents.
>
> Hybrid B: My work as an author is subsidising my work as a publisher, which is kind of weird.

Despite this last comment, there is a consensus that authors are also not making any money unless they manage to write that elusive blockbuster. This was clear from the survey in this research, but many academics currently also refer to Throsby, Zwar and Longden's 2015 Macquarie University study, which suggests that in Australia the average author income has dropped almost 50 per cent in the past seventeen years (Throsby et al. 2015). This is not confined to Australia only: a 2018 survey of 50,000 UK authors showed that the top 10 per cent of writers earn '70% of total earnings in the profession' (Kretschmer et al. 2019). Similar surveys in other Anglophone countries (Canada and the US) have also been conducted and suggest that author incomes have either stagnated or dropped slightly in the past decade

(The Writers' Union of Canada 2015; the Authors Guild 2018). In this study, interviewee respondents discussed the feeling that writing is more of a 'hobby' than a genuine profession. They did not believe this to be the case but felt that policy, law and a general culture of them 'working for love, not the money' contributed to this perception. Hybrid B explained:

> [I]t's almost like, in Australia . . . it's a nice little hobby. People don't really expect that you should expect to earn a living from your creative pursuits . . . you know, if you actually expect to be paid, in any sort of reasonable way, then you're just expecting too much. It's like when people get you to do something for nothing. And they say, but you enjoy it.

This is obviously problematic when considering how the parties will negotiate the pecuniary aspects of the contract. Both are constricted by a cultural narrative that frames writing as a 'hobby'. Editors and publishers share this common perception via their 'creative' roles, which often have no tangible pecuniary benefits. Many industry professionals reiterated this cultural narrative by way of discussing how they came to work in publishing – not often even knowing that the roles existed, or entering as a secondary choice after first exploring more conventional and better-paid roles.

> Ed A: I had no idea the job existed. When I left home . . . I got a job in a bookstore. And then all through uni I had jobs in different bookstores. And then I ended up a buyer while I was studying something else, and then the sales rep who I had become friends with said 'I'm leaving a job. You should apply for it.' And then I got it and I took it. Then I was a publicist, in-house. I had started to do more stuff in publicity – like that was the same sort of content that we create now. Then started increasingly to do more catalogues and all that kind of content. And then I thought that would be alright and then the job I have now came up and I applied for it and got it. So it was really accidental.
>
> Ed B: I think when I was at uni, because people in my family were authors and editors and publishers, that was like a thing I knew you could do with a love of literature. . . . Opposed to just having a love of literature.

These responses are interesting because they suggest that the professions that revolve around literature and the creation of art are roles that the interviewees working in publishing did not actively choose. There was a need to 'professionalise' the creative role, to raise it on par with the role of artist. Hybrid D also alluded to this:

> I think I decided to become an editor because. . . . I was always a child who loved reading. . . . I always loved grammar and punctuation and learning languages. So I wanted a job that reflected something of those interests and passions, but that had a professional angle to it – so it wasn't just being an artist.

The presence of hybrid participants is no coincidence. Many authors are also editors or teachers because they must support their writing with other paid work (Throsby et al. 2015). It is accepted that creative work is not well remunerated in Australia as it is in some other countries. One author made comparisons to France, where artists are subsidised for their contribution to the cultural fabric of society. Non-hybrid publishers and editors appear to be actively connected to writing and literature as a creative pursuit, but anchor their 'hobby' in a professional setting conducive to a conventional livelihood. They spoke of their role as being indicative of wider conversations around art, with a 'community' and a 'collaborative' aspect, to cement their contribution to the whole as satisfying and important from a cultural and societal perspective:

> Pub B: I always loved this idea of just ideas in any form, and so books, well it's perfect because there are a million different ideas and a million different conversations flowing through these things and so general interest in ideas is perfect for publishing.
>
> Lit D: One of the things I adored about this industry . . . is that even the junior sales manager's assistant is still going to be given manuscripts to read . . . There's always that scope, in some small way, that you can contribute to . . . what the company is passionate about.
>
> Ed B: I continued being an editor because I loved the creative collaboration that is inherent in the role. So all the . . . communal effort it takes to bring a book into the world. And bringing in elements of design and other people's editorial opinions and working to get the best out of an author and brainstorming with them and suggesting things. I really like the sort of village it takes to make a book and the handmade role that an editor has. So it started off as a love of language, but it turned out to be more about the community.

From these responses, important details that contextualise the research emerge: alongside a love of literature/reading, ideas and creativity, is a need to collaborate. As one of the interviewees stated: it's 'about the community'. One other interesting point is that many of these responses referred to the interviewees as having had a sales background – working in bookselling or from sales and marketing – yet many moved from these roles into roles of acquisition and reading as if drawn closer to the source of creativity. Being an editor or publisher is, without doubt, a prized occupation. From my own observation of working in-house, the distinction between the sales and marketing department and the editorial department and how each was perceived in the hierarchy of the publishing house was evident. Despite disparities in pay, editorial is seen to hold more cultural capital than sales – evidence of Bourdieu's 'internal hierarchisation', whereby there exists a 'degree of consecration' in terms of an individual's peers, independent of large-scale economic factors (Bourdieu 1996, 212). And while Bourdieu uses this term to describe authors, it can also be applied to any structured space of social positions (Thompson 2012, 4). There is cultural capital in the role of acquisitions and editing as opposed to the areas of sales and marketing and publicity because one revolves around content and the other money. This positions the editorial team very differently, perhaps even awkwardly, in terms of their rapport with authors.

> Pub B: I would say a general observation is that unless the sums of money start getting large, it's not really talked about that much with the authors. So there's a sort of, a kind of gentleperson-ly kind of agreement that you're engaged in a cultural exercise.
>
> Hybrid D: There is so much artifice around making it appear like we are doing something dreamlike. . . . I was of the mentality that an author shouldn't ask for more money – that they were lucky to be published, and talking about the book sales was somehow a bit grubby. . . . I think it plays into this kind of idea, like, gentility in the publishing industry in that you don't talk about money and the façade of it is about us making art whereas the undercurrent is all commerce.

The keywords of 'gentility', 'dreamlike' and 'art' offer a sense of the work refusing to be anchored by the materiality of contract clauses. Or, more aptly, the writers wanting this positioning and the editors assisting them to do so. Positioning the work 'above' utilitarian considerations consecrates it, along with the artist and the publisher, as being part of a cultural transaction. This process transcends the ordinary and pedestrian concerns around money and exploitation that might 'banalize' (Bourdieu 1996, 247) the work. Instead, by distinguishing the work and the relationship (the author–publisher relationship) as superior, the author and publisher inadvertently apply a much more abstract value on it. This is another example of Bourdieu's 'internal hierarchisation' whereby the degree of consecration is determined by both the author and the 'producers of cultural goods (or merchants of cultural production)' (the publishers) (Bourdieu 1994, 212) To prove this point, the monetary side of the business was referred to as 'grubby' and 'crass'.

The final observation, here, is the reference to gentility and the 'gentleman's agreement' (or 'gentleperson-ly' as the publisher put it). A contract has been signed and a manuscript is in the process of being produced, but, in publishing, from this point, the contract is effectively out of sight, back to the compactus, and a whole new relationship around the book begins. The gentleman's agreement between the publisher and the author – that the publisher will take on the financial risk and the author the creative, with the help of the editor – was referred to in quite a nostalgic way, with an undeniable sense of loyalty and trust between the parties:

> Lit D: Generally it is an industry built on trust and good people who love what they do.
>
> Auth A: I think the process of creating a book is artful in every way. It's also artful in the way the relationships and the ideas are sort of . . . are worked over.
>
> Hybrid B: Some books I think, as the creator, as the author, you do have quite a strong vision on. And some other books are sort of less formed in your own head. Others you do feel you need a bit more of that guidance even with the idea – understanding the vision.
>
> Pub C: It's everything. It's a year of their life. It's . . . nurturing their most precious baby.

The terms such as 'artful', 'creator' and 'vision' allude to something beyond sales and consumerism. Ai-Girl Tan states that '[c]reativity involves processes of being with oneself and the world, doing something meaningful, and interrelating the person with his/her world, nature, and cosmos' (Tan 2013, xviii). This work reiterates the 'meaningfulness' of collaborating in a project that both the publishers/editors and the authors feel is worthwhile. The words used by the interviewees reflect this as the foundational motivation for the creative output. Ed A also discussed the creative side of the process when entering into contract negotiations, and the lack of consideration for the written legal terms of the agreement in favour of the ongoing creative relationship between the publishing house and the author:

> I think with creative people, they almost don't even equate the process with the contract. It's like the contract is just something you have to sign. . . . They just agree. They can't get their head around it at all. They're just not the slightest bit interested. All they want to do is create.

Words used such as 'trust', 'nurturing', 'relationship' and even 'precious baby' add to the altruistic and aspirational expectations inherent in publishing, which are reminiscent of the legacy noted earlier, of the author as 'meaning-maker' (Craig 2011, 16) and 'originator' (Foucault 1997, 124). The responses also raise the danger of undermining this premise – how terrifying it can be to embark on the process of collaboration to developing the work, and the level of trust involved. It is always linked to the 'vision' or 'expression' – the 'precious baby' – which are very much within the moral rights domain. And if '[e]ach idea that emerges reflects uniquely upon the originator's self, his sensory equipment, his mentality, his value systems and his conditioning to the everyday experiences of life' (Rhodes 1961, 308), then there is much at stake within the relationship between the author and the publishing house. Yet the survey responses indicated that authors are not so concerned with their moral rights, which they take as a given in their relationships with publishers, even despite publishers having clear pecuniary interests to survive in a terrain that is constantly evolving, as well as the players within it.

The gentleman's agreement between the author and publisher stems from a period very different to today's industry. From my experience, the juxtaposition of this nostalgic sense of the author–publisher relationship and the contemporary business was always a struggle to reconcile. With all the best intentions, economic factors always presented hurdles that challenged the trust between me and my own authors, and I found it difficult to balance my authors' interests and concerns with the publisher's. But there was always a need to uphold the 'façade' that Hybrid D raised earlier – the pretence that the art is always more important than the money, and that the author can trust the publishing team to bear their particular expression in mind. Unsurprisingly, I found myself slipping back into editor mode during the interviews, when broaching industry pressures with authors. However, some of the authors seemed sympathetic to how publishers are exposed to significant pressure to make money, which will inevitably shape this 'trusting' and 'creative' relationship. Yet, they still expected that their 'vision' would be 'nurtured'. Auth C explained:

> [T]hey're not the bad guys – they're trying to make money too. There's a shift to finding the new next best thing instead of looking at the midlist and thinking, well, how do we help people build careers and are they going to be viable and are they going to keep on making books. I have a lot of sympathy for publishers . . . a lot of publishers go down. What I'm really concerned about is badly informed publishing . . . hurts young writers and smashes, crushes young talent.

Contrastingly, when discussions with the publishing professionals steered towards industry pressures, the aforementioned sense of shared experience allowed me to witness their untethered frustration. For publishers, financial pressure is particularly palpable. I observed Publisher C pivot quickly when discussing the financial side of the business, figuratively throwing the 'precious' baby out with the bathwater.

> [W]e're burning our butts every day. And without going into it, the financial state of the industry at the moment is not good. It takes one bestseller to keep the whole frigging company afloat. . . . So if you don't find that bestseller for them you are in all sorts of trouble. . . . People are really surprised – they think you're looking at fabulous stuff all the time, but you're like 'No, not really'. I mean, you see great stuff every day, but

> just not commercial . . . but, you know, is someone going to spend $35 on a book that they've never heard of the author. I see lots of stories that are kind of slice-of-life, but that's not compelling for the people out there where book buying is a kind of luxury, and they don't want to take a risk. So they buy a big-name author where they have a guarantee, you know.

Yet, almost in the same breath . . .

> (On acquisitions) Ahh, that is definitely the thrill of the job. Yeah, that's the reason you wake up in the morning . . . Just last week I got sent something from an agent and it's like, fantastic.

It's a rollercoaster ride of emotions, oscillating from creativity to cash. But still no one seems to be making any money, including publishers outside of the multinationals. And even the multinationals are struggling in an industry under siege and must balance their 'power of consecration' – of literary quality – with economic and political pressures (Bourdieu 1996, 214).

The 'space of possibles' as Bourdieu describes it, which is to rupture the expectations of what the literary field represents, has not been realised. Neither party has been able to balance market demands, globalisation and digitalisation alongside a stubborn ideology of author as genius and creator. Yet, an

> understanding of the 'external forces' which make each of the partners in a marketplace exchange willing to enter into that exchange is necessary [and]. . . . [t]he construction and perception of 'value', as the element which makes the exchange of books a worthwhile activity in the eyes of both partners, is thus central to a theory of book marketing.
> (Squires 2007, 54)

Existing research that focuses on how little authors earn and how disadvantaged they are in the author–publisher relationship, particularly when negotiating contracts, exacerbates the author-as-creator ideology (Throsby et al. 2015; Kretschmer et al. 2019; The Writers' Union of Canada 2015; the Authors Guild 2018). Discussions about how copyright law could be amended to prevent authors being unfairly disadvantaged perpetuate the 'façade' in the same way that in-house publishers and editors do, which is frustrating. It's a learned behaviour that harks back to a different landscape with concerns that are now changed or redundant. Research around publishing contracts also focuses too narrowly on the terms without exploring the stagnant relationship between the parties – one which doesn't appear to have grown with the industry – and whether it, instead, might be the source of the power imbalance (Giblin & Yuvaraj 2020). In discussing freedom of contract, for example, Rita Matulionyte (who refers to the 2015 Macquarie study) claims that 'the remuneration of Australian authors has been decreasing over the past few decades' and links this back to the existence of 'unfair contracts between authors and publishers' (Matulionyte 2019, 682). Rebecca Giblin and Josh Yuvaraj also conducted an empirical study of publishing contracts sourced from the archive of the Australian Society of Authors, claiming to have found

> serious deficiencies in the agreements generally as well as the specific provisions for returning rights to authors. Many contracts were inconsistent or otherwise poorly

> drafted, key terms were commonly missing altogether, and we demonstrate that critical terms evolved very slowly in response to changed industry realities.
>
> (Giblin & Yuvaraj 2020, 1)

Their solution to the power imbalance is to address reversion rights, which they note 'is a promising avenue' to 'give authors new opportunities to financially benefit from their works and facilitate new investment opportunities' (Giblin & Yuvaraj 2020, 2–3).

This discussion interests me greatly, given that the OP clauses within the contracts I had studied were consistent with the outline that Giblin and Yuvaraj interrogate in their study. As they discuss, ' "Out-of-print" clauses are publishing's best-known and most controversial reversion rights' (Giblin & Yuvaraj 2020, 5). Their proposal is constructive, but it fails to acknowledge the complexities in the ongoing relationship between an author and their publisher. The contract is not referred to until something happens to force the parties to review it. Notwithstanding my hesitation, there is contention in this area, which is worth exploring qualitatively, to gain deeper understanding around why it has seemingly become a battleground for authors.

Contract status and copyright

'Contract status and copyright' as a sub-category encompassed the following areas of investigation: 'Rights and Territories' and 'Rights Reversion'. Reversion, in particular, has been hailed as a solution to author contracts with terms that are deemed to have been inequitable at the time of signing or are no longer satisfactory, given new developments or opportunities for the work. Most boilerplate contracts contain a reversion clause or a small prints clause, which offers reversion when the book no longer becomes commercially viable. In this case, it is up to the author to request that their rights be reverted to them. At a glance, these clauses appear sound and allow the author a way out of the contract if the agreement is not lucrative, but assessing when a book has ceased to become commercially viable is the issue – a fact maintained by Author A who said that '[t]he contract isn't the problem. It's in the administration of the contract. When the time comes'. So while the reversion clause exists and can be called upon, it is not always granted so easily. Giblin and Yuvaraj suggest that a way to improve these administrative difficulties is to have a more explicit reversion clause and, in fact, ' "many publishers will agree" (quoting the ASA) to such mechanisms [reversion clauses] upon request. However, not all authors know to negotiate for "use it or lose it" rights to be included in their contracts, and many simply agree to whatever terms they were originally offered, particularly early in their writing careers' (Giblin & Yuvaraj 2020, 8). This type of mechanism might look like a five-year contract after which the author will have their rights reverted if the publisher has not successfully exploited them – a slightly different form of reversion from the small print clause because it is not open-ended and has a clear time limit. The authors in the interview sample for this study were all published, though of varying experience and length in their respective careers. Raising reversion clause negotiations elicited a particularly passionate response from Auth A, who became very animated and offered a fairly detailed picture of how difficult it had been for them to have their rights reverted in order to self-publish, stumbling a little over their words as they recalled the frustration.

> Getting rights back is a real, real challenge. . . . I've asked for years and never got the rights back. . . . I can't identify anyone by the excuses that I have been given. I say to

> them I would like to self-publish these titles. And they're out of print, but they pretend they're in print. They're 'up for consideration'. They're up for consideration for five years. They force you to go hard ball cos they just make excuses that aren't valid. Then . . . then you've gotta go hard ball and you've gotta say 'that's illegal – you've gotta give me my rights back'. . . . And then, and you can get it wrong. . . . I've got rights back in the past, but then there's. . . . Sometimes they'll give you the print rights back but not the ebook rights. And you want to self-publish, you're going to self-publish as an ebook, which is then print-on-demand. But if they've sold a few of the ebooks, they can keep the ebook in perpetuity.

They reiterated that the contract was not the issue; it was the administration of it. The out-of-print (OP) wording in the contract, which can also be a small print clause, is where the reversion occurs. If the book ceases to sell a certain amount of copies then it becomes less appealing to the publisher, who would be happy to revert the rights back to the author if they feel there is no economic benefit to keeping the book in print. There are many ways publishers can manage to keep a book in print that might create minimal revenue for them but also minimal revenue for the author, thereby avoiding the small print clause and the chance for reversion, which might not seem ideal for an author. It also seems unfathomable why a publisher would want to keep a book in print in this instance. As an example, it could be a book with a short lifespan – such as a timely sports book – that can continue to be sold as an ebook or digital edition at a lower price. Given how rapidly reading tastes can shift and how frontlist books tend to dominate the market, offering new opportunities for older books can keep them alive. However, they might never be as popular as that first edition. Pub B seemed grateful for my understanding of these opportunities when we discussed reversion and therefore appeared comfortable providing a truthful (and frustrated) response:

> An author really has to kick and scream to get rights back from us. Like, we will keep things in print for as long as humanly possible because you just never know, and since that whole digitisation and long-tail principle started up, we still have books that we published a year ago that suddenly pop up there as ebook sales. . . . Or they pop up in a university course, or there's some reason – like maybe the author dies and their whole backlist goes up. They have to make a really good case for getting the rights back. . . . And we say, 'Well, why do you want them back?' If you're going to exploit them with another publisher, then fine. But if you just want them back, what are you going to do with them? You may as well leave them with us.

Hearing both sides of this story from two separate interviews was enlightening and important to this research. It clearly pinpoints how the challenges of the contemporary publishing landscape have affected negotiations in an area that should be fairly straightforward. Both author and publisher want to exploit the work to the best of their abilities. It is frustrating for an author to observe when this does not happen. But the modern-day publisher must have an intuitive approach to this fast-evolving landscape, and that might mean thinking up new ways to reimagine a title that isn't selling well, or waiting for the right moment to strike again with an OP title. Why should a publisher have these potential opportunities taken from them if the author has no other concrete plans for the work? Publisher B made it clear that if there is justification, the publisher is more than happy to revert rights, and can do so easily according to a standard publishing contract:

> it's lovely when you've got a beautiful clause in your contract that says that this is exactly what you can do. But we will do our best to dissuade them.

Therefore, dissuading the author is not refusing to revert the author's rights. The publisher cannot withhold rights unnecessarily, but admittedly they find clever ways to keep the book in print and use the OP clause to do so. Conversely, thinking about how to keep a book in print also presents creative opportunities, which can be canvassed with the author, thereby nurturing the ongoing relationship rather than severing ties unilaterally.

Giblin and Yuvaraj argue that the OP clause should contain 'objective criteria . . . to make it possible for authors to reclaim rights where publishers are no longer meaningfully invested in their book's success' (Giblin & Yuvaraj 2020, 7). I agree that objective criteria for OP by way of dollar amounts versus unit sales would assist, particularly when looking at high-discount sales that would show a higher number of units sold to keep the book at the OP minimum (say, 250 copies). They use a salient example to illustrate the potential success of rebooting a backlist title that has gone OP: Madeleine St. John's *The Women in Black*, which was originally published in 1993 and reissued by Text Publishing as part of their Text Classics series and sold in excess of 100,000 copies. I also argue that this is an example of how well the current OP clause works. Giblin and Yuvaraj indicate that this is precisely how Text came to acquire the rights to the title (Giblin & Yuvaraj 2020, 5). There is also no reason why the former publisher for that author couldn't have created the same opportunities, reimagining the work with fresh publishing eyes. Ed B explained how this works in-house:

> So they pull things out down the track, which were out of print . . . but they're not out of print, they're just sitting there and it's not literally in print. . . . You're not getting the same royalty as if you would for a trade book going out there, but the quantity means you get a really nice amount of money, and if you've just got it sitting there going 'One day somebody will want to publish this again', it's never going to have that opportunity that sitting on a big publisher's list, even if it's not there as a physical book, there are still opportunities.

Pub C also explained how involved the author is in discussions about new editions and opportunities in this vein. However, I did sense that they were selling me an idea that they knew was still not going to produce a huge return for the author:

> [We're] Always looking at the backlist. Especially in digital because it's so easy to do that . . . typically with romance novels because they sell so well in digital. We give them gorgeous new covers – they look like new books, and we put them out and then online retailers want a deal, you know, three for two. And then you have the free chapter of the new book in the back, and so you have all these cross-promotional opportunities [and] We absolutely let them [the authors] know. We'll say 'You know what, we know you haven't seen the sales, but we think we have this opportunity.' . . . We're in the interest of making authors happy.

On the surface it sounds enticing: the cross-promotional opportunities, the gorgeous new covers and the aim to make the author happy. I am well versed in this editorial narrative – of presenting ideas on their creative merit and avoiding the details of the monetary perks because they haven't been realised, at least not yet. As an insider, I can easily read between the lines. I'm also certain that authors go along with this game with a degree of healthy scepticism. But the guise is not entirely disingenuous: the ideas *could* be highly lucrative. The publisher *is* trying to find ways to make money for the publishing company, and the rewards will be passed on to the author. Pub C said:

> I say unless you've got a really strong idea of what you want to do, why wouldn't you just keep it with us?

There is no evidence to suggest that simply changing publishers would make the new digital edition any more attractive to book buyers if the timing is awkward or the style of the work is not trending. The publisher is in the best position to assess this and to be able to action the backlist to exploit new trends. Quite often these exploitative opportunities don't succeed; when that happens, clearly the publisher has failed. If the tempting repackage described earlier doesn't deliver what it promises, the author will inevitably be disappointed and perhaps feel they were 'sold a pup'. This scenario has consequences for the author–publisher relationship, especially if the author wasn't convinced in the first place. Auth C, who is published by a few houses, recalled how they had been burnt by print-on-demand, which is generally associated with small quantities. They explain that while the book can be technically still in print, this might not be so advantageous to the author:

> [T]hey said 'Well why don't we do print on demand for this one?' and I'd never done it before and we talked it through and it sounded like a good idea at the time. . . . Sure the book looks nice, and it is available and it's not, you know, it's not a catastrophe, but it's a disappointment.

There is also the likelihood that a higher quantity of a reissue that is a digital edition or part of a series linked to business development (which is an opportunistic faction of most publishing companies nowadays – linking books with other consumer avenues) will result in a smaller royalty, or a royalty on net receipts. It's probable, though not certain, that the contracts for the Text Classics could echo this royalty. Rights reversion, therefore, does not automatically guarantee supplementary author income, even in the case of a solid 10 per cent royalty on RRP of a print-run of a few thousand.

A European study of authors in the digital age titled the *Remuneration of Authors Report* noted that there was no evidence of 'a direct correlation between the availability of rights reversion provisions and the level of remuneration of authors in a particular country [those countries that have enacted legal protection for authors outside of contracts]' (Guibault and Salamanca 2016 in Matulionyte 2019, 710). The report, backed by statistical analysis, also states that 'while rights reversion clauses also contribute to strengthening the position of authors in their contractual relationship with publishers, they lack the kind of direct up-front impact on remuneration' (Matulionyte 2019, 711). Two reasons were offered for reversion not to have effect: 1) 'since few works are profitable even after they are released in the market, the chances that authors will be able to receive additional revenue from works in relation to which rights are reverted is minimal' (Matulionyte 2019, 711). It is extremely difficult to exploit rights maximally, and authors must be realistic about the market for their book. Pub B acknowledged the limitations the publisher might have regarding overseas rights sales, which they can't always exploit:

> So I was the occasional 'Hey I got you a US deal' or I was the person they would like to beat up because they didn't get any overseas sales and, like 'What's she doing? She dropped the ball'. And like no, I've been working really hard but your book's just not right for . . . overseas.

The publishers' responses indicate that many would be happy to return to the author a right they have tried to exploit but can't. The question, then, is would any other publisher be able to exploit the right if the book is not a good fit for a particular territory? There are simply limitations to how well a book will perform – limitations based on market demand and not publisher performance. Authors' lack of understanding of the market and demands for reversion when the book is doing as well as it can, might affect the author–publisher relationship in the long term. Pub C highlighted one such exchange:

> I've had an author want to leave to go to another publisher – just because she thought she could get a better deal, and so immediately we stopped putting focus on her backlist because we've got plenty of other authors who we're going to give a backlist revamp and promotion to.

This last response reflects the other reason for reversion not to have effect: 2) 'it is a post-contractual corrective measure', which can affect the author–editor relationship. This is of particular importance when you view the contract holistically and not in terms of its 'parts'. It has been firmly established in this research that the author–publisher relationship encompasses a perceived shared vision via a person in-house whom the author can trust with regard to the production of their title and a shared passion and appreciation for books and writing. As I have reiterated in the summary of the survey results, the fact that authors do not see moral rights as an important aspect of contract negotiations indicates that this expectation is being met by other means, most notably in editorial. Rita Matulionyte elaborates: '[F]or authors with limited bargaining power, long-term career prospects are likely to prevail over enforcing certain rights (such as rights reversion clauses) even when they are entitled to do so' (Matulionyte 2019, 709). In this case, limited bargaining power can be seen as a previous poor sales record. Ed A offered some context when asked about rights reversion when a book isn't selling well or selling in minuscule quantities (as a result of the small print-run clause), and whether the author would discuss other options with their editor or go straight to the publisher to request reversion.

> Mine would probably . . . well, some of them would ask me and I would refer them on. And in the case that I can think of with subsidiary rights reversion and something else, they came to me first, and then in another one they just went straight to the publisher for, um, for that. But quite seriously, like, the BD [business development] department at [our publisher] is really, really good.

The interview responses raise important factors that have not been adequately explored to date. Giblin and Yuvaraj raise the limitations of their quantitative study of hundreds of contracts by stating, 'We do not examine the publishing industry norms and practices that can sometimes result in authors recovering their rights outside the circumstances provided for by the contracts' (Giblin & Yuvaraj 2020, 14). But they also assert, 'Accordingly, the insights from this study usefully assist us to evaluate the appropriateness of using publishing contracts as the sole repositories of author rights' (Giblin & Yuvaraj 2020, 12). The contract is the physical and literal repository of author rights, but we can also use the field – its culture and its history – as a repository of specific practices and behaviours that reflect and uphold author rights. Examining the field alongside the actual contract allows us a full view of all struggles, which the literal contract fails to convey.

Catherine Mitchell explains that 'formal contracts and contract law offer only narrow, artificial perspectives on complex phenomena' (Mitchell 2009, 704). Mitchell contextualises the author–publisher relationship in more detail and offers scenarios around why the reversion clause would not (and perhaps should not) be called upon. With regard to its particular wording in the contract clauses studied, I agree with Giblin and Yuvaraj that the expression of this clause differs in boilerplates and is not based on objective criteria. Certainly, this has not been addressed in light of digital developments such as ebooks and print-on-demand. Although digital editions of works have been around for decades, the contract has not changed in line with progress. But I suggest it is deliberately vague to avoid specific terms that cannot allow for later negotiation in this area. Although it is a lot easier to create your own ebook nowadays, many authors still lack the means to exploit the work via a strong sales and marketing plan, which a publisher is in a better position to provide (as Pub C suggested earlier when describing the three-for-two deals with cross-promotional opportunities. Doubtless of whether the plan was successful or not, the publisher still had the means to implement it). Auth C affirmed the fact that a digital edition needs more than its existence to survive in the market. Of course, there are those authors who do have the means, the platform and the knowledge of their market to self-publish successfully (which Auth A has proven), but these authors are few and far between. Auth C spoke about this:

> [A]t that stage they weren't doing them [ebooks], and I said. . . . What are your plans? And they said 'Well, we don't have plans yet' . . . and I said 'Well, I'm not giving them to you then.' And then I just withheld them for a really long time and then I sat down and looked at creating and selling ebooks myself and thought, geez, my life's too short to do this . . . you might know how to do things, like I really know how to clean a bath, but I'd rather pay someone to do it. That's what you see with so many self-published authors. They get terribly fatigued, cos marketing is the opposite of writing. . . . Is that really where you want to put your time?

As Pub C claimed, if an author is selling well, the publisher would be reluctant to let the author go. But that begs the question of why the author would want to go anyway. If the reason is due to sales, then the author might be in a more powerful position to discuss new opportunities for a title with their editorial team and essentially reboot a flagging title via a new edition, rather than exercise a use-it-or-lose-it clause or an OP clause. In actioning the latter, they damage the potentially fruitful ongoing relationship with their publisher, they are not guaranteed more remuneration via a self-publishing platform or a new contract, and they are not promised a new contract by a new publisher anyway. The author already has a publishing contract and an editor in-house working on their behalf (as Eds A and B indicated when discussing backlist and rebooting OP titles). If presented with a viable business opportunity (which would be prepared by the in-house editorial team), the publisher will most likely be willing to action a fresh publication. If not, then the interview responses suggest that the publisher will be willing to let the author go. This scenario requires a discussion/negotiation as opposed to a unilateral action from the author. While the author would be justified in applying their rights, they would risk their relationship with their publisher. The publishing contract lies further on the relational end of the spectrum than other contract types and is therefore more amenable to re-assessment in the post negotiation space, which has the dual effect of strengthening the author–publisher relationship, and which is of great importance to both parties.

This sentiment is backed up by Lit D, who made it clear that when terminating a contract (in the case of a merger or new management, for example), or for rights reversion for a book that has not been fully realised (unpublished), they would rather renegotiate:

> I would never consider pulling a book from the publisher.

On the other hand, Lit D acknowledged times when it is best to walk away from a deal rather than force a situation whereby the vision for the book cannot be agreed upon. In fact, at the time of the interview, Lit D was negotiating terminating two contracts:

> One is a change of direction for the publisher. And one is a breakdown in vision for a book . . . and just delays, long delays, and um, you know promises made about 'Yes!, love the vision, love this, love all of this, great.' Then work together for about a year later and nothing has changed, or sales and marketing don't love the vision any more . . . maybe it is, like, just better in this case to cut your losses and walk.

It is worth noting that many literary agents have come from publishing houses (where they might have been editors, publishers or rights administrators). They therefore have fostered good relationships with the people they previously worked with. At the least, this gives them a realistic understanding of how difficult it is to get a book contracted in the first place, which stresses the importance of the ongoing author–publisher relationship, as Lit D established. In addition, some books need a little more time to attract readers. Success might not be immediately apparent. Authors aren't privy to the hard work that goes into exploiting the work in any way possible, as Hybrid D claimed:

> We put in so much work . . . for them to take that work and then sell it and you not get any part of that. That seems really unfair in terms of the division of labour that goes into a book.

They also raised the limitations of clearly defined reversion rights in contracts, which can hinder a publisher's ability to exploit the book effectively:

> The thing people have asked the most about are . . . [t]he reversion of world rights after two years if we haven't sold into [other territories]. This in both cases was with a very powerful agent, so to keep the agent relationship . . . [we] agreed to it . . . and so we put an addendum on both those contracts saying that the rights will revert. But two years

> isn't really . . . a lot of time for it to sell. Depending on the cycle, it could only be one book fair or one-and-a-half book fairs. . . . It just does make it more complicated for the publishing house, especially if you are using a sub-agent internationally as opposed to using a rights agent in-house.

And for a smaller publisher who can't even compete with mid-large publishers, they seem prepared to completely forego any rights they are not using anyway, as Pub A stipulated:

> We don't want to hang on to rights, cos, you know, we're too small anyway to be able to exploit them. And we're not in the business of trying to be parasites.

Reversion *appears* to empower the author, and it would be completely reasonable to suggest that reversion could allow for a way out of the arguably outrageously long copyright term. Yet there are many factors to consider when choosing to exercise this right. First, there is a contract in place – an agreement that is based on an endorsement of the work and a promise to fulfil the obligations related to it, which include its paratextual expression (its look and feel) as well as its exploitation. In turn, the author promises to deliver the work to the publisher's satisfaction. But these promises are bound to be broken, in which case there is a consent to termination, or to agree to reversion, or other. How can we account for all eventualities and necessary adjustments? These might include the time it takes the publisher to give the book the best chance possible – such as selling it to other territories via the fairs – the investment potential via a business development faction within the publishing house, and the realistic market expectations, which authors (not being professionals in the marketing of books) might not necessarily have express knowledge of. With all the best intentions in the world, all the care and all the marketing available, the title might not sell. And there is also the brutal reality of market expectations to consider: not every book is going to be a bestseller, despite all the blood, sweat and tears that have gone into bringing it forth. Publishers simply won't invest unnecessary time and money into a book that will only sell a few thousand copies. From my own experience, I know how much is invested in each title and the amount of selling that is required to get the book through many different hoops. These are not just hoops within publishing, but hoops for the bookseller to get to the book buyer. Sales history informs the publisher's decision about how much effort will go towards their plan for each title. This study has found that authors and publishers often have very different expectations about the marketing of a work.

Giblin and Yuvaraj also acknowledge that

> [m]any publishers are struggling to continue in the market, competing with a handful of behemoth rivals that enjoy vastly different economies of scale. The economics of independent print publishing in Australia are particularly unforgiving: a 'bestseller' might shift perhaps 7,000 copies, making it hard even to keep the lights on (Tweet by Miranda Luby in Giblin & Yuvaraj 2019). If such publishers were to disappear, it would further reduce competition, thereby making it still more difficult for authors to sustain their craft – and reducing the diversity of voices that get to be heard.
>
> (Giblin & Yuvaraj 2019, 2)

But larger publishers are also feeling the pressure, as evidenced by these interviews, and the work that goes into exploiting each title is not always fully appreciated by the author.

It is not the author's fault, either. Without the benefit of being on the inside – of witnessing and understanding what the editorial team must navigate – they believe their book has been deliberately left to gather dust. It is not in a publishing house's interests to squander the opportunities for a title. Sometimes the market sends a clear message, and there's not much that can be done to prolong the life of a title.

A relationship based on clear communication and transparency is vital to an author's long-term career as well as the success of their titles. This relationship also needs adequate time to establish the author and their books in the market. Claire Squires describes this interplay distinctly in terms of book marketing more generally:

> when a publisher makes an offer for a text, the financial and cultural calculation of value begins with the advance level, but the sum is revised throughout the course of the text's life, as sales are made, as the text progressively acquires readers and readings, and as the mechanisms of canon-making roll into place. Cultural value is consequently mutable, and shifts over time and under the aegis of different agencies. The transformation of text into book and product entails overlapping interpretations, incomplete translations, and a continual shifting of meaning from text to written and consumable object and back again.
>
> (Squires 2007, 57)

Unilaterally severing the author–publisher relationship via a 'clean' rights reversion clause and objective criteria that leaves no room for negotiation undermines the foundations upon which the 'anecdotal' perception of the industry is based – on trust and an ongoing commitment. It also complicates the normal life-cycle of a work relative to its current market position. I argue that authors might action a more explicit reversion clause too hastily because they lack the knowledge of the industry and the market and their work as a commodity within it. Closing the door doesn't necessarily open new doors. Macneil describes how disputes between contractual parties tend to be treated as though performing 'an autopsy on a corpse' and not 'examining an ongoing relationship in which exchange and other motivations create a mutual need for cooperation' (Macneil 1978, in Mitchell 2009, 727). Due to the editor–author relationship being so close, it is necessary to explore it and its function in fostering healthy communication between authors and publishing houses, as well as ironing out any dissatisfactions. Through the interview process, I have sought to examine the editorial team's role much more closely to observe how editors and publishers use the contract in-house, if at all, to realise a book's potential and support authors.

Editorial excellence

It was apparent from the survey that 'Editorial Excellence' encompassed 'working on the page' as one publisher described it (in their interview). Scholars have also discussed the act of editing and the author–editor relationship in relation to creativity and writing. This study is unique in its investigation of the author–editor relationship in relation to contracts and posits that editorial excellence is not simply 'working on the page'. Rather, it encompasses a much wider skill set, as observed earlier (Thompson 2012, 6), and extends to duties that directly impact and challenge contractual terms, often abstractedly, in the post negotiation space. Observing editorial roles in practice, and more objectively within this research, revealed this activity as significant. Editorial excellence, in fact, continues in the post negotiation space as a fundamental stage towards the perceived success of the title. The level of honesty within the editor interviews was on par with the publisher interviews, owing to the editors' comfort in my ability to understand the sub-text of what they said. Sharing my own experiences and a distinct perspective to the results of the survey allowed for an undercurrent of 'insider' knowledge, which has been described as Complete Membership (Anderson 2006). Connecting the information and interspersing it with personal observations and experiences brought another level of understanding and contextualisation to the study – one that ultimately showed me how editorial excellence is not confined to its description in the survey or to how it has been described in scholarly research to date.

Mandy Brett's exposé of the editor's day-to-day life in 'Stet by Me' describes the editor's task as making the book the best it can be, and that it's not about the author; rather, the work should be all about the text. Yet in detailing what that entails, Brett also makes reference to 'my authors' – hinting at the close professional relationship. The book is an extension of the author, particularly when the author and the work are elevated in this way. Romanticising the author as creator is entrenched in the culture of book making, and the editor being the closest person to the author in the book-making process tends to uphold that ideal. It suits the author to have the editor in their court because the editor plays to this ideal. If the contract is a status symbol for the author, then also having a dedicated editor could be seen as icing on the cake.

To get an accurate snapshot of the range of different levels of interaction between authors and editors, I first asked the interview participants what they thought 'editor' means, and about their understanding of the hierarchy of editorial roles on the whole.

> Lit D: Every single publishing company has a different term for the people that work there. There is . . . a non-paper distinction . . . between publisher, acquiring editor and editor. . . . Someone could have a great title but not have the clout to get something through, but one might on paper have a really junior title but actually within the standing of the company have a lot of sway.
>
> Pub B: There is a kind of head responsibility with the publisher of the book. . . . I don't make the production manager actually field . . . queries from the author. . . . As the publisher I'm the responsible party to report to them about their book.

Ed A made it clear that they were more senior to a new editor and had many years' experience working with authors and also viewing contracts. This was not to elevate them to a higher position; they were concerned that their feedback in the interview might be framed as the norm.

> [I am] a commissioning editor. We do the contracts. We do the letters of offer. So we do, basically, what a publisher does. So we look at every element of the contract. From a regular editor's point of view, they wouldn't have a huge amount to do with the contract, except to double-check what the acknowledgement is going to be in the copyright line.

In a large multinational, departments and roles are often more clearly defined. For example, a publisher might have the benefit of a highly experienced rights department to consult about the contract or the territories and rights on offer. This would allow the assistant editor to take on board more of the preliminary administrative editorial roles and the publisher the more intensive work on the text as well as the decisions made about the contract's terms and the vision for the book. Ed B spoke about how a smaller publisher might operate quite differently:

> Depends on the size of the publisher, too, like, smaller publishers, even though the editors might be at junior level, they probably need to be more involved in the contract. Like in previous jobs I've had to do contracts as well. And that is because it was a smaller company.

Pub C, who also works for a large publisher, talked about their role as the person responsible for the book overall, as well as taking on board the major edit. Thus, they are an editor as well as a publisher, so the line is blurred.

> I acquire authors based on the assumption that I will be working with them – I will be their editor to a certain level. So I do a structural edit, and that can be draft after draft after draft. Then I do a line edit in the page – so it's a lot of sort of cutting and shaping, and development, and then it only goes to the editor once it's down to copyedit stuff.

While there was a lot of variation around what an editor does and where they are positioned within the company/publishing house, the overriding sense that they had a direct line to the author, which to some extent excluded other people in-house, was consistent. The authors interviewed had emphasised communication of their creative expression as incredibly important. This was also reflected in the survey. Surprisingly, 'Communication' was not ranked so highly in the author surveys. Authors, therefore, make a very clear distinction between communication in these two areas and don't necessarily see that one contributes to the other. To this extent, there are two ways in which authors are satisfied with their publishing experiences: one is a pecuniary satisfaction of the book selling to expectations or beyond expectations; the other is the satisfaction the author feels when their work has been treated with the care and, sometimes more importantly, the *attention* they believe it deserves. When describing their level of satisfaction with contract negotiations, the authors in the survey expressed the power imbalance between authors and publishing houses, and that the pre negotiation space was dominated by the corporate concerns of the publisher. In that space, the editor is mostly never present, and undoubtedly the reason why authors tend to, wrongfully, separate their editors from such pecuniary considerations. These two levels of satisfaction are also closely aligned with the dual narratives of contracts as 'parallel universes' (*Balmoral Group Limited v Borealis* (UK)), the editor being apparently fully entrenched in the post negotiation space where the 'implicit dimensions of the agreement' (Mitchell 2009, 704), which might be to realise the creative aims of the work, are executed.

As evidence of this position, when asked what editorial excellence means, most authors still clearly targeted the creative side of the process and not the business side of producing the book. Yet editors cannot afford to focus solely on the text in isolation. In the initial chapters of this book, I established that developments in editorial and publishing in general help define a book to its readers. These paratextual considerations are becoming increasingly necessary in a competitive market. Rawson states that '[t]he crucial, initial view that the company's sales reps receive of a book and of the size and composition of the audience for it comes from the sponsoring editor' (Rawson 1983, 273). Most interviewed authors still view editorial excellence as something aspirational, quite separate to sales and marketing, which is in contrast to what transpires in-house. They tend to revisit that romanticised perception of 'nurturing' the written word and of the expression of the 'art' and the 'vision'. Unsurprisingly, larger publishers viewed editorial excellence in highly pragmatic terms, placing the 'excellence' within the infinite number of hours available in contrast to the hours' cap on freelancers or on smaller publishers who employ freelancers at hourly rates. Pub C elaborated:

> I guess it's not having to spend a limited number of hours making sure the book is the best it can be, and that's what we can do – work on that book until it is the very best it can be by the time we publish it. . . . We can just go back and back and back, and that's what we'll do until its where it needs to be.

Ed A also raised the hours cap:

> I think it's a commitment to the book and a willingness to take it through as many, you know, edits as is needed to get the best book out of that manuscript. Make it the best, you know, story that it can possibly be. And if you're working with a freelancer you can have an excellent freelancer, but you've only got this number of hours. So it doesn't matter how excellent they are as an editor – you're not getting editorial excellence.

Time becomes a crucial factor in a book's success. It could be the timing of the publication date – to strike while the subject matter is popular. It might also be time allocated to intense editorial work. Editors can also buy time to have the necessary discussions to encourage authors on board with a particular direction or idea. For the author, time spent communicating the production and editing of the book gives them a sense that the work is important to the publisher because there is no investment boundary to excellence. Susan Greenberg explains from a historical perspective:

> In the long nineteenth century, publishers invested in editing as a form of financial survival, because it saved time and trouble. When the cumulative hours are considered, however, this invested more time, not less, into editorial labour. And time is the essential condition of thought, reflection and judgment, a form of cultural rather than financial survival. If the investment stops being attractive financially or ceases to be perceived as culturally necessary, then editing loses both forms of capital and the survival of the practice cannot be taken for granted.
>
> (Greenberg 2018, 106)

This quote captures the balance of the cultural and the commercial within the practice of editing. Time allocated to editorial tends to only be given true reverence when a book becomes successful (whatever that success is perceived to be). The editor knows this and knows that their role extends to ensuring that everyone is aware of the work's potential. Hence, the editor's involvement can be observed in many more ways than finessing the text. There was a lot of repetition about making the book 'the best that it can be' – a mantra of editors and publishers worldwide. I have often used this expression to assist my editing work:

first, it allows you to separate the work from the person who wrote it. This is a good way of delivering feedback and a critique of the writing without offending the author. Used in this way it reflects the 'craft' or writing and a legitimate desire to hone the author's prose. The editor also knows that they must have the author on their side if the book is going to be successful, and focusing on the published 'book' also allows for other negotiations around the wider vision and how it will be expressed to the readers. For example, there is a slight variation on this expression, which sounds like 'we want the book to do as well as it possibly can', which is linked to its sales and marketing plan. This leads me to the second benefit of using the phrase, as a way of merging the aspirational side of the work with the dirtier business side of publishing. 'The best it can be' is open to interpretation. In whose eyes is it the 'best it can be'? In fact, many publishing professionals can influence the decisions about what is 'best', and the editor juggles these opinions and prescriptions and filters them to the author. The cumulative, creative investment in the work (Greenberg 2018, 106) is, of course, crucial, but the practical necessity of editing is vital to the smooth operations of the publishing house because the editor steers the book towards finality, providing the link between the project's print deadline and the author's expectations. Although creative excellence has been difficult to define in legal terms over the years, there seems to be an agreement, anecdotally, about the end of the project and the expectations of *when* the end is and what it looks like. The 'no cap', therefore, is artificial. The editor juggles this 'end time' with the authors' perception of time being the perceived investment in the work. That investment as time, often undocumented, is in some ways priceless because it plays to the creative expression the author desires and their ability to adequately communicate it. Essentially, if the author and publisher are satisfied, then the book goes to print. If the author is not satisfied, time, as investment and attention, can be a tool used to negotiate the conflicting vision for the book in the post negotiation space.

This 'end' result, therefore, might not be concretely agreed upon. Most publishers and editors seemed sure that they were setting aside their own ideas about how the book should be and ensuring that they were responsible for communicating the author's vision to the reader, and it appears that the author's trust in their editor allows the editor to make those decisions towards a conclusion. Brett says:

> The purpose of writing is to express meaning; the purpose of publishing is to transmit meaning from a single mind to a large number of other minds. . . . The purpose of editing is to ensure the transmission proceeds as far as possible without impediment.
>
> (Brett 2011)

The process sometimes requires careful conduct to get the book to the 'end' with all parties satisfied. Though even if the author concedes to an extent, it is usually the editor who is tasked with allowing them to vent their frustration or express their opinions, which can create a certain level of satisfaction – the mere opportunity to have a say, as Hybrid D explains:

> Hybrid D: So just to make sure that – even if your opinion isn't taken into account eventually – just at least having the peace of mind of having said something, or have it in writing, and to articulate really clearly why you are having a reaction to something. . . . Just to raise the question in a non-combative way. Even if they had said no, it's fine. That's at least on the record that that's something I put in their minds.

Editors and publishers have a very clear plan to support the author, but it's an altruistic plan that becomes distracted by the other pressures placed upon them by the publishing house. The juggle between wanting to materialise the author's vision, yet still ensure the book is financially successful, is fraught. Pub C again expressed the juggle with commercial considerations, but maintained that the author's happiness is paramount:

> [O]ur job – my job in particular, as a publisher – is to make sure the author's happy. . . . Because it is their book. I've been given the privilege of putting it out into the world. I've always felt that way. Many of my authors make big money for the company and, um, I just want their book to be what they want it to be. And of course I bring my expertise and my vision to that.

Revisiting the necessity for communication and the vague phrases that editors and publishers sometimes use to express the publishing house's plan for the book, we see again a variation on 'the best it can be' by way of Pub C using the term 'I just want their book to be what they want it to be'. The struggle for the editor–publisher is constant, and these expressions don't adequately convey to the author just how difficult it is to broach the economic and creative communion with other departments in-house. Authors don't want to know when their creativity might be compromised by money, and the editor reconciles this struggle sometimes awkwardly in their dealings with their authors. But these attempts to temper the blow simply leave the author unaware of the limitations of their work in the market. Ensuring the author is happy inevitably has consequences, as does separating the money side of publishing from the creative side. Even in the best-case scenario whereby the author might have a say in the book's ultimate plan, without adequate information the author still might not fully understand the reasons for the publisher's decisions.

All the publishers interviewed also commented on what happens when the book starts to do well, and the author realises that there are more pecuniary benefits to be gained from the work. In fact, most of the publishing professionals became quite animated during these discussions. Because of the close relationship the editor–publisher has with the author, they are often the first person the author goes to with grievances about being undervalued and underpaid for their success. There can be a sudden shift in the relationship when this happens. Pub B explains:

> [I]t's amazing how quickly authors get interested when advances start getting high. . . . Then you can certainly start to enter a territory where that, where they wake up to the commercial reality of the project.

It is clear editorial departments have had to change the way they operate, to stay viable and to consider the commercial prospects of a book much more than ever before – again having to balance the perception of the industry being built on its cultural merits with consumer expectations. This also obviously affects the choices that are made in-house (in terms of acquisition) but also the decisions about what is achievable for a particular title. Investment is therefore not distributed evenly among titles. But not everything is going to be a Harry Potter. Nobody really can know if a title is going to suddenly sell well. Hybrid D analyses:

> [W]hy shouldn't an author want to make money and why shouldn't a publisher be ambitious for a book in a commercial sense? . . . You are wasting everyone's time and

> money publishing something that doesn't have a specific reason behind it and isn't going to sell. If there is a tiny market for a book and it is meaningful, then fine. But a tiny quiet book about [something insignificant] – there's no moral pull behind it to publish it. . . . You've got an author with unrealistic expectations; you're wasting money printing it and the environmental cost of that. But then, on the flipside of that, sometimes it's those tiny quiet books that win awards. . . . Like, um, there has definitely been a context of not talking about money in publishing, but I think increasingly that has to change because the industry will die.

'The industry will die' admittedly sounds dramatic. But it is a threat that is constantly posed to those working in publishing. This book has established that reading as a pastime is usurped by other entertainment streams (PwC Australia 2011), yet books still manage to find a way of surviving in the highly competitive leisure market; but that is partly due to publishers' ability to acquire content that caters to a larger readership. The quiet book can still be published to add variety to a publisher's list but not without the bigger books that bring in the revenue to make this possible. It is not good business practice to invest a lot of time and money in the quiet book. Pub C explains:

> [Y]ou know there are a lot of authors for whom that [attention] is not possible, too, who we take on at a level. And we say 'Our sales expectations for this author are this – it can go straight to copyediting'. You know, that don't require that high level.

No publisher or editor would say this directly to an author, of course. If they did, the author would certainly consider taking their book elsewhere, yet with the same result. Once again, the perception of time allocated to the title is precious to the author – as a sign of the work's importance and also that it will be given 'the best possible' chance. All publishers, however, are under the same pressures to profit. There are, of course, smaller publishers who might be willing to invest more time to a smaller title, but they would also offer a less attractive advance and might not have the ability to exploit rights to the same extent as a multinational. There are also those occasions when a book's success takes everyone by surprise. Indeed, the publisher is banking on this being the case, but they won't necessarily invest heavily on a whim.

Pub B noted, when the title does suddenly exceed expectations, adequate remuneration for its success arises as an issue. Conversely, when a book doesn't do well, the author questions sales and marketing investment. Lit D talked about trying to lock in a sales and marketing plan in the contract, even with a view to assisting with discussions post negotiation. They were mindful that an emerging author, or an author who has not sold well in the past, will struggle to get support in this area, but an ongoing conversation can be beneficial, at least:

> Publishers are really loathe to lock in marketing into the contract . . . they're often very nervous about making those promises. But anything they can tell you, get in writing, in an email if not the contract, there's room to move there. Particularly in a situation where more than one publisher wants an author, you can then pretty much ask everyone to submit marketing plans, and they do in a bidding scenario . . . they'll submit marketing plans and then you can lock that into the contract.

Again, this statement relates to the big book that generates an auction in which a number of publishers bid for the rights. A smaller book would not automatically receive a comprehensive sales and marketing plan, which would normally fall to the author via their social media activity. This can be a very distracting and exhausting process for authors, who want to focus on their writing. Kim Wilkins reports how

> [t]he ease of building an author platform based on blogs and social media clearly has benefits to an author's career. But the negatives are becoming clearer as the practice of developing platform is normalised: loss of time, distortion of self-image, and the introduction of unprecedented distractions.
>
> (Wilkins 2014, 69)

Those in editorial, however, maintained that they were the champions of the titles they worked on regardless of how big or small the book is; even without a sales and marketing plan from the publishing house, the editor continues to play a role in promoting the book in addition to their work 'on the page'. This was consistent across all responses from the publishing professionals who saw creating 'buzz' around their titles as part of their role despite a lack of editorial or sales and marketing attention apportioned to the book:

> Ed B: There are a lot of documents that are produced in-house by editors that are, you know, selling the book to in-house colleagues and offering all the ways that it can be . . . spoken about to the wider world. . . . So the editor is quite influential in that way . . . to information for memo notes that are taken to the meetings to sell the book. No-one knows the book like the editor, really.
>
> Ed A: Because before you can start selling to a bookstore or the end user or a gatekeeper, the editor is going to sell to the publisher, who then will sell to acquisitions, which is then sales and marketing, then it becomes about selling it outside the company. Everybody's trying to sell it.
>
> Pub C: [T]he publisher is at those meetings where the championing takes place. . . . But it still happens at the coffee machine, at the desk. Books sell by word of mouth. . . . [T]he acquiring editor is responsible for all the documentation, all the briefings about it, all the meeting presentations . . . it is Chinese whispers: I tell you about this book and then I tell sales and marketing, and then they tell the people who work for them, and then they're telling the booksellers and then the booksellers are telling the floorstaff – it's a lot of people down the chain till that message hits the retail sector.

The discussions that take place 'at the coffee machine' are also not quantified in the editor's role. The need to do this for each book is not written into the job description and does not form part of the hours of editorial work that might in fact be observed; it is a culture of support and an unspoken responsibility that the editor undertakes for their part in the book's success – an extension of their 'author care' – and perhaps the reason why many do not consider it an important part of the editorial role. In the current competitive publishing landscape, it is generally expected that authors should create their own author platforms. Wilkins explains how for one of her titles she had 'written nearly 18,000 words of marketing material, which . . . is three to four chapters of a novel, or roughly a month's work of fiction writing. Promotional material serves only the purpose of promoting the novel, not adding to the word count of the next novel' (Wilkins 2014, 70). Any level of encouragement or assistance from an in-house champion, such as an editor, can be a welcome relief for authors.

While Lit D spoke about trying to lock sales and marketing plans into the contract, the type of selling that the publishing professionals describe takes place regardless of any concrete plan. In-house discussions with other departments also help editors gauge where their titles sit in the hierarchy of books being published and how far they can push for attention for them. Authors are never privy to these discussions and pitches, and editors would never think to tell authors that they take place. Even when authors challenge sales and marketing plans, this type of selling activity doesn't rate as being significant, even though it is anecdotally very effective. It is not expressed in the contract, yet it would help the author to better understand their title's position in the market and the efforts of the in-house editorial team to ensure it can succeed in the market. Hybrid D explains:

> I don't think that's articulated, and in the contract that's very abstract. Even the idea of an advance is very abstract if you have not worked in the industry before. But every author thinks they have written the next blockbuster.

Auth A also discussed how authors are not part of these in-house discussions:

> Well, sales and marketing is a giant mystery. I don't assume any ability to judge any of that. I think if a book's good enough it will probably find its way, you know, if the sales and marketing has been done to a good level.

The editor again leaves the author out of the loop. These comments hint at a 'plan' as opposed to a culture of subtle promotion. Another interesting point made in Auth A's comment is the fact that there is an understanding that a big marketing push does not always equate to big sales. Auth A added:

> I've known authors who have had a shitload of marketing and then blamed [the publisher] for not getting enough. You had more than everyone else. Perhaps the book wasn't that great. And the other thing is that we simply cannot judge our own work – at least not for a long, long time. But, like, sometimes I've looked back on books and thought 'Well no wonder it didn't do that well'.

Auth A also described the moment when they ruptured this process and went out on their own to self-publish a title they felt had readers. Some scholars offer sound reasons why publishers as literary intermediaries are perhaps not necessary in the contemporary literary field, which now encompasses a variety of platforms where readers and writers can share content. These platforms, including Amazon's Kindle Direct, bypass the traditional gatekeepers (Davis 2017, 139). But, as identified in the survey, authors have not actively democratised publishing in this way. And those who have tried feel even less inclined to be content with publishing to the mob, and what the mob wants, as Auth A has successfully done:

> I did a book that was rejected by 4 or 5 publishers and then it was up for consideration somewhere and I thought, stuff this I'm not going there. . . . I self-published this book and sold thousands of them. I think it would have sold a lot [more] if a publisher had

> taken it, but . . . but maybe they know [the market] from a corporate direction. Not from the actual readers.

I did note that Auth A acknowledged that they could have sold more books if the title had been taken up by a publisher if the publisher had been interested. It is a significant factor for authors that is worth noting. A non-commercial project, as Auth A claimed, still has readers; it just doesn't have readers on the scale that the publisher needs to justify the economic investment in it. It might also have nothing to do with the content, per se, and more to do with a particular format or genre, such as a short story or a novella (Baker 2015). The new democratised landscape should indicate a 'power shift' (O'Shaugnessy 2016, 91), but the results of the surveys in this research suggest that this is not the case. Auth A's example provides further information about why this is so. Auth A had the experience and the means to self-publish, but this isn't the case for all writers. Authors utilising self-publishing platforms might have less to do with seeking an authoritative assessment of the work's legitimacy, and more to do with support. Most of the author survey responses expressed how difficult it is for authors to find their audience, the exhaustion of producing the book themselves, and the lack of any considerable, measurable success. Auth C notes, however, that it has become easier to make ebooks now, and that they wish they had held onto their rights for a little longer so they could exploit them (rather than the publisher).

> I think I should have kept them a bit longer, and not been so tired and put my head on the desk and said I didn't want to do it. And now the ground's shifted again and it would be easier to do them [now].

But still there is a sense of being part of a team with a publisher, who can provide the expertise in all departments, which is conveyed in the interviews analysis as a fundamental aspect of the publishing experience that cannot be replicated by the author on their own. There is a strong sense of a relationship and community and trust in the publisher that they know the market for the book and have a plan for how to communicate the essence of it to its readers. Unfortunately, the plan is not always articulated to the author – especially when the author is not in close proximity to the team and cannot be part of the meetings in which the title is discussed. These author responses reflect my own experience of being published and how I also acquiesced to the publishing team's decisions – deferring to their experience over my own. Another salient example of where communication fails is in discussions around the cover and the look and 'feel' of the book, which was raised as an area that seemed to be very important to the authors, yet not often something they felt they could discuss successfully with their publisher. Again, this reflects my own experience of agreeing to a cover I would not have chosen. The publishers and editors indicated that decisions about cover were the domain of the publishing house, which supports the authors' claims. Even Pub A, who represents a small publishing house, reiterated that the cover was not a very negotiable part of the book's production. Their response was passionate and presented a 'line in the sand' situation:

> So we tell people what the print-run is expected, but not guaranteed to be. We tell them what the retail price is going to be. We tell them what the format is going to be. . . . We also put in things, like, for instance, the author has the right to obviously comment on design and stuff, but up to a point and the final design decisions rest with

> the publisher because we have had experience. Oh, pains in the neck, you know, who really try to interfere in things that are not in their remit at all. Generally speaking, mostly we have fantastic relationships with, with the authors and illustrators, but occasionally there are people, you know, who . . . are really annoying.

Books are judged by their covers. In bookselling today, the absence of a cover image in a title's metadata can be fatal because it affects the title's searchability. The genre of the work must be clear for it to be positioned correctly in the bookshops and, again, searchable by category. Therefore, the cover image must be created early, and correctly reflect the genre within the booksellers' (and the readers') understanding of it in the 'system'. Authors who have not worked in publishing or bookselling will not necessarily be aware of how the cover image ties in with genre category and metadata. This complex system is also tedious to some authors because it tends to pigeonhole their work, which is a very uncreative thing to do. Most authors like their writing to be seen as original – unlike anything else in the market and appealing for that reason. But, even literary writing is categorised, with specific words to indicate these categories. Pub B also emphasised the importance of keeping details about cover and paratextual elements vague in the contract so that they can remain flexible up to the very last weeks of the book's production:

> In terms of the format, um, we don't put that into the contract. . . . So the author is told what their book is going to look like and feel like, and the setting on the page and all those kinds of things, but . . . we certainly don't put it into the contract for all those reasons that decisions need to change. They also need to trust that you're doing the right thing. If you give them too many rights, they say things like 'I needed it to be a C-format paperback', but in actual fact it's going to look like a pamphlet because you've only written 40,000 words.

Lit D also acknowledged that the publishers do have experience and expertise in this area – further evidence of a level of respect for the publisher as a cultural intermediary.

> I would assume as standard that authors don't have a say in price point. Um, who gets free copies, what's mass market or trade paperback or hard cover. . . . I have seen authors who are irrational about the covers, and you hope that the publisher, you know, is, is, that they're professional, that they know the market that they know the cover is the key marketing tool that the book has, and that's one of the key reasons you go to a publisher. . . . So on balance I would actually defend the publishers right to say, well this is our call.

Most authors talked about the cover as being integral to the sales success of the book, which indicated that they also had a clear idea of its reader but that they had sometimes got it wrong. Hybrid D, however, detailed an experience when the publisher had got the cover wrong and how this had a knock-on effect to sales. Though they conceded that a different cover might not have generated huge sales anyway, they stressed the deep disappointment that they felt about their vision for the book being ignored.

> I felt slighted by it and that I had been misinterpreted or misunderstood. And that my opinion was. . . . I got the sense that this was a big machine that was operating and I was

> outside that machine and not really . . . my opinions didn't really matter that much . . . that was probably the most commercial publisher I've worked with and I really felt that their decisions were being strongly led by their sales and marketing team and not their editorial and publishing team. . . . And the author's opinion in that mix was not important to that sales mode. . . . So I wish I'd said 'This is a really bold cover. I do feel like this is a bit of a disconnect between the tone of the story and this cover. Is that something that you guys have thought about in-house.' Just to raise the question in a non-combative way. Even if they had said no, it's fine. That's at least on the record that that's something I put in their minds.

Hybrid D's memory highlights how quickly things can seem to move in-house in a way that excludes the author. Hybrid D sensed that conversations were taking place, to which they were not invited to contribute. When asked how they would feel if this had happened when they were the editor, Hybrid D explained how they might have handled this scenario differently:

> If I were the editor I would have come back with really specific examples. I would have said 'the things that we've looked at in this section of the market have led us down this path are this this and this. We think it sits really well in terms of tone, in terms of content, and that's what that part of the market seems to really respond to, and we want to give your story the best boost it possibly can have in that market. That's where it's going to be competing. So that's why we've gone with that direction.' So just to have an evidence-based approach.

Here we see another version of that well-versed phrase: 'the best boost it possibly can have'. But this time the editor's dialogue with the author is contextualised within the publishing 'machine'. Hybrid D suggests an 'evidence-based approach', to argue the decisions made. However, from an editor's perspective, they maintained that the author should not have too much to say about the look and feel of the book, as long as the communication about the publisher's plans for it is effective. They also were quite honest about how they might push a project along if they felt that the author was amenable to that as a direct result of their not being aware of operations:

> [Authors] are much more oblivious to scheduling and selling in and how all that works. . . . I think that moving things on is usually the solution . . . and they kind of have to accept for the most part those decisions . . . just because they are not experts in the publishing field, which is different to being an expert in the story field – I think the two are very different things. And I think the editor's job is to be a conduit between those two things, and to be an advocate for the author, but the author often doesn't know enough to be their own advocate. . . . So I think it's probably best that they're not asked about those decisions.

Comparing this statement with Hybrid D's earlier comment about the specifications of the book not being articulated to the author reiterates that editors know that knowledge is power. Transparency about in-house processes would be a radical departure from the status quo. With so many areas of the book to manage – marketing, design, editing – it would be potentially catastrophic to allow the author inside to see what transpires, and to have a say in every aspect. When I asked Hybrid D if they thought it is unfair that the author is not included in those conversations, they said:

> I don't know if I would use the word fair, but I think it is cleaner and less problematic for an author not to be involved in every round of decisions.

Having worked in-house, Lit D also understands that when an author is allowed too much decision-making, the book-making process can be slowed – sometimes even derailed. Their response showed that taking on board an author's ideas is important but that the author does not have the contact with other publishing professionals 'inside' who have the skills and knowledge to make decisions about areas of publishing that authors don't possess:

> I'd love to build in more collaboration and consultation . . . but I would actually accept the publisher's right to make that call at the end of the day. . . . I wouldn't defend the publisher's right to do that with the text of the work. I know authors can be as irrational about their text, but at the end of the day that's theirs.

The last part of Lit D's response, here, swings towards another area of intervention that requires a sound knowledge of the market, but also a deft touch in negotiations, and again a level of trust between author and editor–publisher. Anecdotally I have been aware of, and have also experienced myself, that level of trust extending to creating part of the work or recreating it in such a transformative way as to fundamentally change it. With genre categories, audience and booksellers to consider, crafting the prose is not simply a case of fixing typos and finessing expression. It requires intensive redrafting to hone the text to reflect the focus of the book in a way that the reader will recognise it. In the same way that the editor takes on board much of the stress around 'how the sausage is made' (Greenberg 2018, 5) and keeps that information from the author, the author often keeps from the reader exactly how much intervention might have taken place at the initial editorial stages. In this way, editing is a silent practice, and the relationship between the author and editor also guarded. In many cases, it is a fraught relationship – working on the page – that the author does not welcome, and presents another reason to believe that editorial excellence encompasses more than the act of crafting the prose. Editorial excellence could be how the editor negotiates the author's vision to the rest of the company in order to consecrate it in the work. This was accurately reflected by Ed A:

> I was really interested to hear that they [authors] rate it [editorial excellence] highly. Because some people really value that and other people just think they've done all the work that they need to do and it's deeply irritating to them that you'd want to do more to it. . . . With published authors, this might not be something that they want to talk about. They certainly will with you [the editor] . . . but they certainly are not going to . . . be going around saying 'Well actually a significant amount of work was done in conjunction with my editor'. They're the brand.

So while the editor should not be too heavy handed with the work, sometimes a little more editing is needed and the line between what is too much and what is enough is blurred. If the author is happy with this level of editing, then that is generally considered acceptable, however. Lit D suggested that intervention can be expected, but that it must not be enacted without full consent, which can pose a problem if the contract specifically says 'consent':

> [M]ost publishing contracts say 'consultation', which is not the same as consent. And that's something I always try to negotiate in. Very few publishing contracts have that as standard as consent.

And Hybrid B spoke of the need to balance the input from both parties, and that this can be an ongoing discussion that, again, focuses on what is best for the book:

> It shouldn't be a power thing. It should be about what is best for this book. And sometimes the author has some great ideas for that. But sometimes the publisher's got good ideas for that, too. Because they're able to see it objectively.

What is best for the book encompasses so many things an outsider has no way of knowing, unless it is communicated to them by an insider. We see, however, that insiders are reluctant to do this for reasons of efficiency and often for the book's ultimate success. The interview responses convey that for authors and publishing professionals editorial excellence is distinctively connected to the romantic impression of authors and their works being unique – the process also an artful extension of the creator. This process requires a nurturing and trusting relationship between the writer and the publisher, whereby communication is vital to the success of the project. Success is not necessarily defined as economic, however (i.e. in book sales). Hybrid D's particular scenario detailing the cover treatment of their title discloses that not all editors possess the communication skills required to achieve satisfaction for all parties. Hybrid D's described approach to solving the problem they encountered demonstrated an improved capacity to balance the author's desires with the publisher's – something that can come with professional experience. No doubt, if an author is actively supported, understood and encouraged to contribute to the publishing process, they will inevitably feel satisfied with their experience and that the publication is successful despite the degree of financial return. Effective collaboration, then, would also result in a sense that the author–publisher relationship is more balanced.

It comes as no surprise that editors with experience in project management were highlighted as advantageous for authors. Steering the book through the stages of editing and production, with the support of a well-oiled publishing house's workflow, offered authors some degree of comfort and reassurance. Despite there being many opportunities for self-publishing, the interviews supported the survey results and indicated that self-publishing is still not an ideal option for authors who seek not only the production values of a publishing house but also the community and sounding board that an in-house editorial team provides. Matulionyte observes that '[w]hile authors have more options to self-publish or pursue alternative dissemination methods, most authors still desire the reputation, editorial skills and marketing budgets that large publishers can provide' (Matulionyte 2019, 688). Additionally, and in some ways very closely related to the editor's particular skills in project management, is the benefit of time management. The advantage of time is multifaceted: unlike freelance editors, who charge by the hour, in-house editors can keep working on a book until it is ready – and decide when this is. Although the authors did not raise this as beneficial, the resistance to self-publishing indicates that they are aware of the infinite value of in-house editing assistance and the hours dedicated to it. From another perspective, time is also a valuable gift when it can be borrowed to control the pace of a project or to execute a timely plan that is likely to ensure a book's success. An example of this might be the ability to move a book to a more advantageous publishing date. Editors are therefore the most powerful people in-house to create precious time when needed for development and excellence or to explore opportunities that arise in-house by using time to wait and assess. In this capacity, editors are an effective and essential point of contact for authors. Interestingly, the authors surveyed didn't appear to be so cognisant of editorial excellence being concretely linked to time.

To control time in the post negotiation space, editors must possess a great degree of diplomacy. As well as triaging time, the editor triages their title within the whole publishing list. It is here that the editor can also exercise skill in juggling where their author situates their title in the market alongside the publisher's view of its position. A skilled and experienced editor uses diplomacy to navigate a satisfactory outcome in this often-fraught negotiation, which can also lead to significant changes to the author–publisher agreement. Editorial diplomacy can influence the contract's terms and, in some instances, cause terms to change or cease altogether. Effective communication is paramount to allowing this flexibility and indicates the reason why many authors prefer established and larger publishers. That is not to say that these publishers always deliver what the authors might expect, but their perceived experience and capital can be seen to represent the values of editorial excellence in its broadest sense, which, of course, is highly attractive to authors who consider their works to be skilful and worthy of considerable attention.

Earnings and royalties

The survey results indicated that royalties is a very contentious area of publishing negotiations, so the interviews set out to discover why this is so. It became apparent during the interviews that initial royalties in a publishing agreement are considered inadequate when a book suddenly becomes a bestseller, whatever that might be. The definition of 'bestseller' is subjective, and its subjectivity creates problems about royalties and revenue from the start of negotiations. Also, if you consider what a 'lot' of money is, how is this amount quantified? What is it in relation to what is being earned to keep the publishing house afloat, and what the author expects as remuneration for their creative efforts?

Royalties are generally standard across all contracts, but as was established in the previous area of investigation – editorial excellence – when sales exceed expectations, authors suddenly realise that they are not happy with the royalty in the boilerplate contract, even though they had agreed to it at the time of signing. Their belief is that if the book does well, then they should be adequately remunerated for it – and rightly so. But in terms of the book's sales, proportionately, to the company's list overall, the sales might not be that significant. Or perhaps it is that, in a domestic market particularly, strong sales simply aren't that significant compared to other countries. Still, rising royalties presented as a very contentious area distinctive of royalties more generally. Before digging a little deeper into rising royalties specifically, I asked the interviewees why they thought royalties would be a contentious area generally. Lit D had a negative response to the current royalties in boilerplate contracts, which they said had shifted over time to include fine print that degraded the base royalty:

> I would say 10 per cent of recommended retail price is base standard in Australia, but there are lots of fine print that degrade that . . . the inferior version of that clause for

> authors in every aspect of that fine print. And they've put that forward in their standard and that really they're not being very negotiable on it. So while on paper it looks like they're offering the same 10 per cent that everybody else is, in reality they're offering the lowest royalties in Australia. And they're using, I think, their market power to do that.

However, Lit D also spoke about many publishing companies that had fair boilerplates and that

> at the end of the day we're talking about tiny amounts of money for the company for that, it just goes to show the respect that they show authors.

Pub A discussed that authors don't understand how the royalties work, particularly around the area of discounted stock. Authors don't always understand that in order to get a large, firm sale (to somewhere like Australia Post, for example), the discount to the retailer is going to be much higher to confirm that sale. The publisher isn't getting a significant amount of money for the book either, hence having to drop the royalty, but everyone is getting a little more, which is always good:

> I think a lot of people are very concerned about . . . a high discount, like, you're going to get a lower royalty because we're going to less price . . . sometimes it's like seventy per cent what they take . . . so I think people are, fixated on that because they think of it as their reward for their work and the sales.

Many of the interviewees quickly came to what is most upsetting about the royalties – that there is often no rising royalty when sales continue exponentially outside of a discounted sale, beyond the initial print-run. A rising royalty is set in the contract as a small increase dependent on sales of the title. In other words, if the book doesn't sell then you do not reach the point where you would receive a rising royalty. Not all contracts will include a rising royalty, but most offer at least a 2.5 per cent increase for subsequent print-runs. Many of the authors interviewed had signed more than a few contracts and were a bit more experienced when it came to negotiating a rising royalty. Auth A said:

> You've gotta have a rising royalty. That's not in the boilerplate. And that's essential because if you have a runaway success, then you deserve to participate in the profit as well.

Royalties are almost always based on the recommended retail price of the titles, though some authors, anecdotally, have spoken of contracts that have the royalty against net receipts. As Pub A explained, net receipts are often associated with high discount sales – when a publisher is able to secure a firm sale at a very low retail price. This can at first present as a fantastic deal because the author and publisher are essentially selling many copies of the title, but if the author has signed a contract that has a royalty set at net receipts and not recommended retail price, then the mass distribution loses its appeal very quickly. Hybrid D elaborated on why they think the author should be more concerned about their royalty on high-discount sales.

> I would say the two things I get asked most about – it's the advance and it's the international rights split . . . what they should be interested in is high discount clauses. . . .

> That's the thing that's going to have the biggest influence on their earning capacity, I think.

Pub B also had a very optimistic view of rising royalties and saw it as an author's right to share in the profits:

> The more they can see that you become more profitable, why not escalate the royalty rate from 10 per cent to 12.5 after a certain amount of copies sold whether that be 20 thousand or whatever the publishing house's general principle is. . . . I think for some projects that is the right thing to do. Um, because it's (the author) saying, you know, we, we understand from the publisher's perspective, that you're taking on all the risk, the print costs, the advance, and all the overheads that go into the creation of a book. . . . But when that's all covered, then . . .

This comment, however, highlights that it is not appropriate for all projects. So only those that are generating a significant profit for the publisher will be considered. Second, Pub B speaks on behalf of authors who *do* acknowledge that the publisher has taken on a significant risk. Some of the aforementioned comments indicate that a vast proportion of authors don't fully understand how royalties work, or how much money is invested in a project that does not see a return – a view not solely confined to authors. Giblin and Yuvaraj, for example, describe advances as something that is given to the author by way of a payment and that it should not be owed back to the publisher if the first print-run is not exhausted, the book goes OP, and the rights are reverted. They support and quote a study by Shapiro and Caute who

> found that five publishers [out of 60] require[ed] authors to repay unearned parts of their advances to exercise out-of-print rights, and three of them to buy back all plant (such as moulds and engravings) made for the work at half their original cost.
>
> (Shapiro & Caute, 898 in Giblin & Yuvaraj 2019)

The advance, however, is not payment for the purchase of the manuscript; it is the payment of part of the royalty of the first print-run. If the book doesn't exhaust its first print-run, the publisher is out of pocket. As Ed B said, 'It's not like anyone really pays advances back, really'. Caute also describes how one of the publishers in their study 'invariably strikes out this clause, which begs the question of why it is there in the first place' (Caute in Giblin & Yuvaraj 2019). But eliminating this clause from the contract would also eliminate the evidence that this payment is a gesture of goodwill and an indication of how the publisher has positioned the work in the market and how invested they are in the project. Without the clause, ambiguity would essentially stymie post negotiations and fail to provide concrete expectations around the project by way of the level of investment.

Stating that it would be unfair to ask for payment of the files if the author wishes to take the book to another publisher after reversion is also not realistic. The publisher has contracted the work because they believe they can exploit it, but the market is never dependable; readers' tastes change over time. The publisher, therefore, is taking a risk with no guaranteed return. Even for digital editions, a lot of editing, design, and sales and marketing is invested in each title – the costs of which are mostly never recovered by a publisher. This is further proof of publishing houses being dependent on a few key titles, and the ratio noted by Caute and

Shapiro generous in the author's favour. Pub C spoke of the sum of the advance that is paid nowadays to secure big-name authors or big books and how publishers often lose money when these books don't perform.

> Well we typically have an acquisitions meeting where we say what we think the book's going to sell, look at all the different editions, and we calculate it on that. And if . . . the other publishers are paying . . . well over the amount that Bookscan would tell you a person of this celebrity with this kind of story would sell, then it's been doubled. Because they need a big, say, blockbuster or whatever.

The issue, then, when considering royalties, is when the author feels that they *have* sold many copies but cannot see a sufficient return. As Pub B indicated in the 'Editorial excellence' area of investigation, when the author suddenly 'wakes up to the commercial reality of the project' (if it starts to sell), then the return for them, on sales, can become an issue. Authors often don't consider the very small return that publishers also gain from the title, however. Pub B also acknowledged that some publishers are being pretty mean with their royalties:

> A lot of people now are doing net receipts, which I think is really awful. Um, we're not doing that. I'm seeing six per cent of net, you know, it turns into a cent. Like, really bad stuff out there.

But they also relayed a time when an author had become 'enraged' about the return on royalties and that they had renegotiated the contract to keep the author happy:

> I had an author [get quite frustrated] because they didn't understand an overseas deal, that the sum, which was quite large for this deal, was a) set against the original advance, so it had to earn against the original advance, and b) that they were only getting 60 per cent of it, not higher. And when they broke it down they became enraged . . . whilst I negotiated in good faith with them at this point, and I did actually meet them in the middle with their demands because we wanted to keep them happy, we wanted to work with them again. . . . I was peevish because, understand your contract.

While Pub B was obviously annoyed by the change, their relationship with the author was far more important than this specific percentage in the royalties, for reasons that they saw longevity in the author's work, which meant more content for their list and potentially more sales. This is a clear example of post negotiation at the relational end of the spectrum, and, from my perspective as an insider, exactly how publishing is more likely to operate (as opposed to strictly enforcing terms not agreeable to authors). This scenario presents post negotiation with a valued author, and it could be argued that a different author might not negotiate the same flexibility of contract. However, for an author whose titles have underperformed, publishers might revert rights back to the author, or negotiate more appealing terms for a subsequent edition instead. Hybrid B gave a specific example of post negotiation, when they negotiated a rising royalty as an addendum to the head contract.

> One author I know never got a rising royalty on one of her books that's done extremely well. And she wanted to retro-fit that contract. The publisher said no, but . . . they

> have amended the contract so that she gets a riser when the paperback comes out. . . . I mean, you can't really retro-fit a contract for a book that's already in print. It's a bit hard. But they did for the paperback. That wasn't easy, but they did agree to that.

Pub C also mentioned the possibility of a refresher advance, which is not in a standard contract clause in a boilerplate contract:

> What we do do, if a book is doing really well, or it is up for a film, or wins a major prize, or if there's a new edition coming out, we give a refresher advance often. That's not unheard of.

The negotiations described earlier were actioned on behalf of the author by the editorial team – with the publisher speaking to the appropriate in-house decision-makers. With an experienced editorial team, however, these considerations can often be accounted for in the preliminary stages of the book's acquisition. The editors interviewed contextualised this a bit further by explaining how they act in-house to ensure that the author gets the best deal possible. This might involve tweaking the costings, to ensure the margin on the book is higher, meaning the company is more likely to offer a higher advance. On the advance, Ed A said:

> Everyone wants to improve it. People always want more money. . . . And they'll always want a rising royalty. Even though there's no way they are going to sell 15,000 of the book, they'll always want a rising royalty at, like, 15–20,000 or something.

And on negotiating the advance, Ed B said:

> We don't really get to say 'Sure, have that'. We pass it on and say 'This is what they're asking for', and they say 'No, no, no'. And then I go back and say no, or . . . fiddle the costs to try and make it work. For a slightly larger advance, or something. . . . Cos what they don't remember in all of this is that the editor wants this book as much as they want it on the list. And like we wouldn't have bothered if we didn't like their work and didn't want it on the list.

Once again, this supports my contention that the editor's role in navigating the in-house hurdles on behalf of an author is vital and part of what is considered editorial excellence. Because the costing of a title might happen before the contract is signed, the editor's foresight can make or break the deal. In the instance of a book about to be reprinted or reissued, the editor's expertise in costing a title effectively can also result in changes to existing contracts. But how often are the in-house negotiations communicated to the author? Authors are understandably oblivious when they are on the outside of the publishing house. Even when they have some knowledge of in-house processes, as I also did when I wrote my own book, they might not be invited to participate in discussions about their own title, which was also my own experience.

There is a difference between agreeing to the terms with an understanding of in-house procedures and agreeing to terms without this knowledge. The latter puts the author at a distinct disadvantage and explains why they might be shocked or disappointed with the financial return on their title. The rising royalty was mentioned again in the above statement from Ed

B, but they also highlighted that the riser only kicks in when sales reach a certain amount, which might never happen. And the higher the print-run, the more likely it will be a high-discount firm sale – especially with an author who does not usually sell thousands of copies of books. Hybrid B expresses this frustration from a writer's perspective:

> So I have found with the big publishers that they will get, get away with what they can. And that's what's also been interesting with this whole thing recently with selling to Big W and selling to the big DDS, authors just . . . no publisher is going to point out to you 'Oh, by the way when this sells you will get 12c at the DDS as opposed to $1.25 when it's sold elsewhere.

This could be an area where objective criteria would be advantageous to the author – if they can lock in a riser at a lower print-run, they are more likely to see a higher financial return. But that could come at a cost to the publisher. Pub C elaborates on how publishers are affected by risers, even with well-known and best-selling authors:

> The really strong authors who can command what they like, or authors with an agent will typically have a rising royalty anyway, so if a book hits 20,000 up it goes. Which actually really goes against the interests of keeping that book alive longer. . . . Because the longer the life of the book is, the smaller the print-run. So you'd be looking at print-runs of under a thousand. And so if you have a royalty that's suddenly jumping up, so a standard of 7.5 if it jumps up to 10 or more, it makes the book unviable. And I have sat in meetings where we've said, 'We are not going to print that book because the royalty's too high and we can't make profit.' So the book dies. So I'd much rather have 7.5 per cent of something than 10 per cent of nothing.

Pub A also pointed out the pressures that a higher royalty would have on a smaller publishing company:

> [T]he ASA is wonderful . . . but sometimes I think some of the rates that are quoted . . . are completely unrealistic. They are for big press.

Even for 'big press', a rising royalty on a book that has exceeded its sales threshold might have exhausted its time in the market. Some books simply don't continue to sell strongly, and when this happens the royalty is disadvantageous to the publisher. If the book sells then the sales should compensate; books don't always sell well, however, and the publisher still relies on a few big ones or strong sales of the backlist to keep the midlist (which are the books that sell solidly or for a short time). There is also some disagreement between what an author thinks *is* a lot of sales and what a publisher defines this as. The recent Australian Society of Authors' 'Advances and Royalties' survey conveys that almost 50 per cent of author respondents to that survey were not paid a rising royalty, but the study does not outline whether those authors are referring to actual wording in the contract or the fact that they simply haven't sold enough copies to warrant a rising royalty (ASA 2020). In any case, it is arguable that rising royalties should be standard in publishing contracts, but defining and agreeing on what the riser should be, and at what point, is not as simple as a blanket clause. To illustrate the point, Pub B said previously 'whether that be 20 thousand or whatever the publishing house's general principle is', which alludes to the fact that the general principle is defined by the publishing house's economic capital in the field, and that this might be taken into consideration when assessing what a large print-run would be and when a riser could be negotiated. Twenty thousand copies could be a good print-run for a multinational; this would be unsustainable for a smaller publisher, who would consider even half of that print-run to be significant. Without a database such as Bookscan (which is too expensive for a small publisher to afford), there is no secure way of determining a solid sales history to use as a comparison for the title currently being assessed. An author's expectations, therefore, are likely to be even less realistic. A flexible contract would enable the publisher and the author to gauge year by year what is fair *post* contract. For example, Auth C explained how they negotiated an addendum to their head contract when sales of one of their titles increased significantly.

> I didn't check for the rising royalty clause on the contract and then, um, rising royalty would go on normal sales but not on high discount sales. And I was like 'Ah!, this isn't in the contract!' and one of the books was on the [sales package], which meant that they printed 100,000 copies of it, and I was outraged. So [the publisher] went back into that and negotiated a rising royalty on high discount sales.

The response from Auth C raises high discount, in this case 100,000. This would be an anomaly in Australia. Auth C also noted that the return can be insignificant for both the author and publisher:

> And the discount was so enormous, too, that you were only getting a few cents a book . . . it's more the principle.

As explained earlier, Giblin and Yuvaraj used sales of the Text Classics title, Madeleine St. John's *The Women in Black*, to argue that reversion has the potential to refresh a title that might otherwise be sitting in a publisher's collection of OP titles. What this example does not discuss, however, is the likelihood that this title could be a high-discount sale, which would not remunerate the author in a way that reflects the significant print quantity. Yet, still, Auth C was able to negotiate an addendum to another head contract when high-discount sales presented as an opportunity, which highlights the ability to reassess the book's position in the market post negotiation:

> And so we had an addendum . . . with this particular title because it had been in print for five years, and then after five years, because it had been established in schools, they all of a sudden out of the blue did this huge high-discount sale. And I said 'that's not fair' . . . and they said 'But oh it's an easy print-run'. And I said 'but those are guaranteed sales. You don't have to do a high-discount sale on that.'

The only way contention around royalties can be eliminated is via an industry standard 10 per cent of RRP as well as objective criteria for rising royalties at standard print-runs. Most publishers do this anyway, albeit providing a rising royalty for quite high print-runs. However, the low royalty on high-discount sales is a tricky area. While the author doesn't benefit as much as they could from these sales, the publisher also needs these sales to stay afloat, or even to keep the book in print. This is not something enforced by the publisher; it is something that is a retail factor enforced by the DDS and other business-development-type sales via businesses and organisations sometimes outside of publishing or via book clubs. If the publisher doesn't meet the demands of the DDS or provide a discount for a bulk purchase, then the deal falls through and there is no sale and the book stays out of print (OP). No overarching copyright law or objective criteria in contracts is likely to prevent how reading trends affect book sales.

Other jurisdictions have proposed to assist authors and publishers to reassess royalties post negotiation. Germany's 'bestseller' clause has been posited as a potentially effective post-contractual measure: 'In Germany, the so called "bestseller" clause allows authors to ask for a modification of the contract if the remuneration agreed upon is not proportionate to the income generated from the use of the work' (Matulionyte 2019, 700). This clause is codified in the German Copyright Act, s 32c to assist authors and publishers post negotiation. The clause does not 'lead to the termination of the contract or a change of the right holder but instead, result in the adjustment of the contract' (Matulionyte 2019, 712), however, because it is acknowledged that publishing is a business whereby 'It is essentially impossible to, in advance, predict the success of the work' (Matulionyte 2019, 702–703). Yet, this bestseller clause has failed to provide documented advantages because it would appear that negotiation post contract is effective in addressing royalty adjustments.

It could be surmised, therefore, that the problematic term 'bestseller' is something that can be determined retrospectively dependent on the mutual consent of the title's success. Choosing negotiation over a codified rule has its advantages: Matulionyte proposes that authors seeking to use the law to adjust their contract risk 'being "blacklisted" by other publishers, which could negatively affect their future career prospects' (Matulionyte 2019, 713). The disturbing undertone to this statement is that the publisher is manipulative and that if the author doesn't accept the terms of the contract, then their reputation will be irrevocably tarnished. Or the author's expectations are unreasonable. Without the knowledge of how readers' tastes translate to sales, without access to data that informs the decisions that are made in-house about each title, and without effective communication from editors and publishers about the house's plan for their title, authors have no way of understanding that the royalty could be realistic. The author also does not always understand what is at stake for the publisher – especially if the author is outside of the in-house conversations that take place. Access to sales data is also costly and copyright protected, and sharing knowledge of other titles' successes, or admitting that a work will not gain traction with readers from the outset and has been contracted to bring diversity to the list, is information that is not likely to be well received by an author. Perhaps this is why editors don't discuss these points.

It might therefore be useful to consider the German bestseller clause in light of the author's and publisher's differing views on what solid sales might be, and to see if it at least provides an effective forum for broader industry discussions in the post negotiation space. In a domestic market, solid sales can be quite small but proportionate to the level of investment and interest in the arts in general. Low author incomes are by no means an isolated phenomenon in the creative industries. A 2017 study of professional artists in Australia found that between the 2014–2015 period, 'artists earned average gross incomes of $48,400, comprising $18,800 in creative income, $13,900 in arts-related income, and $15,700 in non-arts income' (Throsby & Petetskaya 2017, 9). The distribution of these incomes fell mostly to the lower end, with 60 per cent of artists making less than $10,000 per year from their creative pursuits. Those who wished to spend more time on their creative work were prevented due to economic pressures via a lack of work opportunities in the creative industries and inadequate financial return for their work. However, collection agency payments had doubled since 2009 (Throsby & Petetskaya 2017, 11). Contracts might not be as devastating to author incomes as other factors. It seems unlikely that unilateral and significant changes to publishing contracts have resulted in significant increases to author incomes. The underutilisation of the German bestseller clause suggests this – by way of not being able to provide sufficient evidence in favour of the change, as well as suggesting that authors and publishers are using the existing contract and amending it. The next part of the interview analysis, therefore, focuses on the negotiation itself, also discussing in a little more detail how publishers and editors respond to literary agents' roles in negotiations. As mediators between the publishing house and the author, the agent potentially has the capacity to provide the aforementioned knowledge of in-house processes and decision-making.

Negotiations

This area of investigation continues to interrogate the survey responses and the post negotiation space to reveal what activities take place separate to the contract as a physical document, and explore in depth what the contract means for the author. The survey responses indicated that emerging or un-agented authors sign contracts without any pre negotiation, worrying that challenging their contract might sabotage the agreement with the publisher. For those authors who tried to challenge the contract's terms, their experience was that the boilerplate was rigid. The publisher is more likely to be conservative around royalties and possessive about rights, to minimise losses. This is because they have taken the financial risk. The author takes on the creative risk, but that risk can be controlled by the author and is not impacted by the market in the same way. However, it has been shown via the interviews that publishers are able to revisit the terms of the contract in the post negotiation space, if the book exceeds sales expectations. But *only* if the book exceeds expectations, and they would rather create an addendum to the head contract than lock themselves into unrealistic terms in the first instance – playing it by ear so to speak.

Although the market is unpredictable, publishing houses still, arguably, have the expertise and the experience to be able to make a more accurate assessment. Auth A expressed this in the 'Editorial excellence' area of investigation stating that the publishing company understands the market from a corporate perspective, which is sometimes quite different from a reader's perspective. The power balance, therefore, is less to do with power and more to do with misunderstandings. This study shows that authors and publishers both respond intuitively to the work as a creative expression, and publishers are happy to support this expression by endorsing it, via a contract. But the endorsement won't necessarily come with financial rewards for the author, particularly if the style of the work hasn't proven to be lucrative in the market – the 'quiet' book, as Hybrid D explained earlier.

Editors are undoubtedly the closest 'in-house' people to the work, understanding its merit and potential from all perspectives, and they can, therefore, facilitate the most appealing terms for the author. The preparatory work undertaken by the editor includes costings and other administrative paperwork, which tells the company what the manuscript is about and its likely success. Editors also embark on subtle marketing throughout the publishing house, which can have a surprisingly positive outcome for the work. Editors are also the first people to alert the company to opportunities for both the author and publisher to generate more revenue from projects that might be sitting OP. Most of these post negotiations are instigated without the editor or publisher looking at the contract. Rather, the contract is revisited only when the pecuniary terms are obviously imbalanced. In accordance with contracts at the relational end of the spectrum, publishers are often happy to renegotiate or to find other ways to reward the author for a title's success. The author does not know the extent of in-house editors' efforts, which take place often before a letter of offer. They also don't know if a publisher could or would add an addendum to a head contract, so there is a degree of suspicion at the time of signing. Some authors also simply don't think about the terms at all. Pub C provided a snapshot of the varied responses:

> Some people are like 'Just give me the piece of paper' and it is signed. Other people get really quite anxious about it and at that point go and try and find an agent, if they haven't got one, to help them with it, or, you know, even just a lawyer to help them through all the technicalities of the document.

Their response to an agent's intervention, however, was mixed:

> I find [it] so frustrating. It's like 'You got your own foot in the door; why are you giving away 10–15 per cent.' And of course the agents snap it up. 'I'll be your agent. Deal done, and now give me my 15 per cent.' That happens quite a bit. It's annoying. But the bulk of what we see does come in from an agent . . . with some of the big agents we have a sort of standard template contracted, so . . . They then take on all those discussions with the author.

Unless the agent is facilitating the relationship with the publisher from the beginning, it makes sense for the publisher to query why the author would secure an agent at contract stage. This is especially so if the contract negotiation is not a part of an auction scenario, and the terms are likely to be standard. Agents, now, are just as difficult to obtain as a publishing agreement, and authors often see agents as the person who is unfalteringly on their side. It's likely that an agent will make an author feel special when a publisher won't – especially when deciding on advance and royalties. That is not to say that an agent is highly successful in negotiating these aspects of the contract, however. The survey results made this quite clear, with authors indicating an agent was helpful albeit mostly in assisting them to get their 'foot in the door'. Lit D reiterated the importance of maintaining relationships with publishers and editors in-house with a view to being in a position to offer a publisher a promising manuscript:

> [It's] [h]ighly important . . . working out who loves what, who has the standing within the company to get what they love through, and then knowing when they are free or when [is] a good time to pitch to them.

Pub B also spoke quite highly of the agents that they deal with, but they also raised that not all agents are good communicators with their authors:

> All the agents that we deal with are very high-level negotiators. . . . They're not always very good at explaining things to the author, and we end up having to supplement that explanation, so . . . sometimes it's like 'Okay, deal done. Moving on'. And then the author's left trusting that they've got the best deal that they can get, but they still don't understand the various aspects of the contract.

So while it might seem that the agent should be an effective mediator between the author and the publishing house, this is not always the case. Pub A also gave an example of a particular area where it might be assumed that authors have some knowledge when they don't. They indicated that they work hard to ensure that their authors understand the terms of the contract fully before signing, giving an example of how they explain the Public Lending Rights (PLR) proportions. Public Lending Rights (PLR) and Educational Lending Rights (ELR) payments are made to authors annually to replace lost revenue from the work being freely accessible at a library or school.

> We put down a very good thing for copyright agency money because a lot of the time it's very unfair . . . we also specifically state, when there's an author and an illustrator, what PLR and, and ELR percentage then would look like. Because a lot of people don't understand that, and they don't understand the difference with copyright agency and stuff and so we try to explain what each one is.

While PLR and ELR percentages are unable to be negotiated post contract, we have seen in the royalties area of negotiation that contracts are not as rigid as authors believe. If justified, the contract's terms can be revisited and fairer terms established dependent on the benefits to both author and publisher. In the first instance, it is the editor–publisher who acts as the mediator for these discussions. If not, then the communication could come from the agent. However, from the statements above, the agent might not be as strong a negotiator as expected. Perhaps because they are also an outsider to the publishing house, albeit with a closer relationship than the author. Once again, the author is at a disadvantage when the terms of the contract are not explained to them and the realities of the market and the position of the publisher within that market are also not clear. Even when terms are explained, authors – especially emerging or first-time authors – are not practised in negotiating aspects of the contract and are not overly familiar with publishing norms.

Auth C challenged their publisher regularly and encouraged other authors to do the same. Their activity in the post negotiation space resulted, in at least one instance, to a significant change in one of their contracts. The pre-existing ideas and norms, therefore, can be challenged by the players within the culture of publishing (Ruddock 2001, 117). Each time a post negotiation is enacted by an experienced author such as Auth C, it can create a precedent that creates possibilities for new players (Bourdieu 1996, 214). This is a good argument for why it is important for contracts to be flexible and include less objective criteria: the more flexible the contract as a physical document, the more effective the ongoing conversations between the parties. Auth C described their relationship with their publisher as being integral:

> [T]hey've been open to renegotiating things that I've been really unhappy with at later periods. . . . Usually I once a year look at my list and request to see how much is in stock and when they were last reprinted . . . we usually have those conversations once or twice a year.

Hybrid D also stressed that a productive author–publisher relationship is contingent on the author feeling comfortable to express their opinions but to also be reasonable:

> What I've tended to find over the years is that an author will have a strong initial reaction – good or bad – and if it's a negative one then often they'll come back the next day

> with more specific feedback and a more considered response . . . usually you can drill down into the particular aspects that they're responding to.

Post negotiations can be prompted by industry changes, which can also alter the original vision for the book – and the marketing for it. These changes are usually unexpected. Requests for changes because the author didn't understand their contract were not as accepted. Pub B stated:

> [T]here is a certain kind of coldness when people try and negotiate after the fact and they say 'Well I didn't understand', and, well, you signed a legal agreement. I'm sure when you bought your house you went through the paperwork quite closely.

Publishing companies are obviously not banks. It must be remembered that it was also Pub B who changed the terms of the contract for an author to maintain an ongoing professional relationship with them. If the ongoing relationship with the author is more important than a specific term in the contract, which the author doesn't like retrospectively, it appears that the publisher will change it. The business of publishing is built on a joint respect and passion for writing and books. This is a cultural commodity which, despite every means possible to control, is not quantifiable. And when authors and publishers often have differing market expectations for their books, it can be an upsetting and fraught experience for both parties. Pub B also raised their experience of unreasonable behaviour from agents and authors, who they felt had lacked a realistic understanding of the market for their book, or whose expectations were unrealistic. Yet they maintained that, in publishing generally, there is a 'fairness' principle that any reputable publisher will abide by.

> [I]n terms of fairness; in terms of management of rights and responsibilities, I haven't seen much scurrilous behaviour in publishing. I've seen some awfully nasty behaviour from authors and agents. You know, lifting copies off publishers, saying they are underselling the work and, you know, demanding rights back. And absolutely ignoring the market reality. You know, fever of egotism; I've seen that. And I've seen it more than once. . . . Then there's the 'Someone just simply didn't pay me stuff'. But that's usually because that publisher has gone under. . . . I think we're really fair. I think we have a fairness principle. And the kindness principle, actually, running through our company philosophy – it's very important that we are fair and current. Otherwise, what are we?

All publishers interviewed maintained that they believed that the contracts that they negotiated were fair. But this sense of fairness is from the perspective of the industry as a cultural practice with unspoken codes and ideals. On the relational end of the spectrum, it is very much an industry that would encourage discussions outside of norms other businesses might adopt. Pub B also spoke of the chance to revisit negotiations when a contract expires, though this would of course not necessarily be as straightforward if the publisher has the full term of copyright:

> I think if you are negotiating an extension of an agreement or if the agreement expires like if you are under a ten-year agreement, then that's the point to renegotiate your terms. But otherwise we would be very unlikely to renegotiate an agreement. . . . The

> idea is that you're supposed to carefully consider the commercial possibilities of your project at contract time.

The author is not aware of the codes and ideals, however. They might therefore employ an agent who could have more success because of their awareness of the culture of publishing. The difficulty of negotiating with authors who had agents was also raised as problematic, not just because the agent might also have an unrealistic view of the book's position in the market but also that the agent can potentially prevent effective communication between the author and their in-house editorial team. This was contextualised by Ed A when asked how much communication was affected when agents were present, especially when the editor had been working with the author, only, to develop a manuscript pre-contract:

> No. Like it goes dark . . . when you've had extensive communication with the author . . . and you've shaped it and you've got it to a point where you can take it to acquisitions. Then they say yes, and then it vanishes from the author, and out of the author's control and into the agent's hands. And then the agent either doesn't understand that all this work has been done . . . [a]nd threatens to take it somewhere else. . . . Because they [the agent] want to make their money. And they don't care about the author's relationship [with the editor]. . . . I think it's really tough on the author because I think the agent then is looking at . . . the benefit of that one-time action, because it's going into their hip pocket and they encourage people [publishers] bidding for that. But they disregard that the editor will be on the side of the author, and would be hoping to publish with that author who they really like. . . . And that's it, then. You can never do that again with an author. And I have had situations where, once that's happened they're never going to get that support again.

This type of response adds further context to the surveys. Publishers and editors feel that agents are important to authors if they have an existing relationship and help the author 'get their foot in the door', but the agent who steps in after a letter of offer has been sent is not looked on favourably at all, and can be very detrimental to the author's relationship with the publishing house because they don't understand that the editor has exhausted all the possibilities already for that work's success. Hybrid D gave a perspective of agents from a smaller publisher, whereby the agent/publisher relationship has been beneficial, but again from the point of developing an author before a letter of offer is sent:

> And especially with a small publisher, you might not get offered that much from a literary agent and so you always want to be nurturing that relationship and that does play a part in the decisions that stand outside of that particular book deal. It's more of an overarching issue rather than the merits of each individual case.

Obviously, similar to different editors, there can be differing levels of engagement, and experience, with agents. An agent who has strong industry connections and a good grasp of how publishing companies work to sustain themselves might be in a stronger position to facilitate deals that, while not necessarily hugely lucrative, can prove to be long-lasting and financially beneficial to both parties over time. The editors interviewed discussed how agents who demand large advances and who lack the understanding of the temperature of the market can negatively influence an author's career prospects. When a book that has been purchased with a large advance fails to perform, it can be difficult for an author to get their next book contracted, as Ed A and Ed B explain:

> Ed A: I think that authors who aren't thinking about this aspect of contract aren't thinking about how it looks to have a book with a huge advance on it that has lost the company money, when actually their sales have not, have not been disreputable sales. Like, they've done okay, but we've paid out so much for the book, that it looks like it's lost money.
>
> Ed B: [I]t does happen, and when, even though, when you look at it from the outside it was highly successful. It still means that there is a bit of hesitation on the next project.

So while the size of the advance offers the author and agent some immediate benefit, in the long-term, if the book doesn't meet expectations, it can be devastating for the author's career longevity. A recent study by the Australian Society of Authors also highlighted the 'high-risk nature of publishing and the double-edged sword of advances, given that if you don't earn out your advance, you are often unlikely to attract a subsequent publishing offer' (ASA 2020).

Exploitation of a title in the subsidiary rights section of the contract can also present some unanticipated problems, particularly when emerging and first-time authors are not aware of how their work will be reimagined in film and TV rights, for example. Subsidiary rights can, initially, seem like an exciting opportunity for the work, with the potential to reach new audiences and generate some more income for the author. But unless carefully managed, the treatment of the work can lead to the author feeling that it has been mistreated and that their moral rights have been infringed. Lit D raised the incidence of authors simply not realising what might happen until it's too late but then integrating that knowledge into future contract negotiations.

> Until an author gets very big and realises they can control more things, they're more just delighted that translation is happening. And until they're burnt by something, they're generally happy to go with that. An author might be absolutely fine with all of their editions overseas, but the Polish edition might have the most appalling cover . . . and then they're like, oh, okay, didn't realise. Then, in every contract going forward they might actually specify it can't be a certain publisher, or it can't be a certain type of cover.

Negotiations with authors who have published enough books to have a deeper understanding of publishing will more likely be successful, but large advances and more satisfactory terms for the author might not be in the publisher's best interests. Publishers will almost always draft contracts to their own benefit. Boilerplates, for example, don't just indicate a framework of negotiations that have come before – they also frame the terms in a way that ensures the publisher is more likely to benefit from the agreement in the long term. Emerging authors also tend to sweat the small stuff. Auth C describes how many emerging authors tend to worry over clauses that are relatively fair or that can't be enforced anyway:

> [T]hey get their knickers in a twist about clauses where you think, why are you so upset about that because that clause is not legally enforceable and why do we allow publishing houses to put it in?

Auth C raises a very interesting issue with authors focusing on aspects of the contract that have perhaps become embedded in the boilerplate – the patchwork of historical incidents in the publishing house – that aren't even enforceable. This is evidence of the dual narrative of the contract: the official narrative and the ongoing discussion, but also how the contract functions as an artefact that is 'consciously produced or transformed by human activity under the influence of the physical and/or cultural environment' (Suchman 2003, 98). While publishers seem to be au fait with this duality and incremental development, the author is not. Hybrid D elaborated on this point, too, and talked about their experience, as an author, receiving their first publishing contract:

> I have a law degree and I don't think I read a single clause. I was just so over the moon. I felt so validated as a human. I felt like I could die happy now that I had got this book contract. And actually, interestingly, I gave it to my boyfriend at the time to read – to ask him if I could use that character in a different novel, and he went over the contract and he said 'Do you know, I don't think this contract is legally binding. I don't think it's actually a legal contract' . . . [H]e was a contract lawyer and he was like very confused by the contract and was like he didn't think it was valid at all.

They also spoke about their publishing house's response to the contract as a formal document and that it was a conversation based on trust rather than a legal mandate:

> So at our last strategy retreat we had a session on publishing contracts, and they said the same thing. The director and the publishing director said: 'This contract probably wouldn't stand up in a court of law. It's actually just . . . we write at the top "agreement"'.

Hybrid D also said of another occasion where an author had challenged the contract:

> [T]he publishing director just came in and said to the author 'We're not changing any of this. Trust me, we're good people. Just sign it – it'll be all fine.' And [the author] did.

In empirical studies of contracts in business management, it has been revealed that the existence of a contract in fact denotes a lack of trust (Smitka 1994, 91). In many business transactions, long-term relationships and reputation are of the utmost importance, and trust is given precedence over contractual details. But what is that trust based on? Is it what's 'best' for the book? If so, then the author–editor relationship is ever important to straddle the more personal trust required to have honest communication with the author compared with formalising trust in a more objective and business-like way. Hybrid D considers:

> I feel like rather than referring back to the contract, it would be more about what can you say to stroke the ego of the author. . . . I think it would be more like interpersonal strategy rather than leaning on the contract.

What party to the contract would abandon their own interests for the benefit of the other? Perpetuation of the boilerplate continues as a standard or a starting point. Contracts can stipulate consequences for breaches and non-performance. Many have also argued that boilerplate frameworks and carefully drafted clauses help the parties to understand expectations and create boundaries which minimise the potential for litigation (see Deakin 2006) With publishing having its own norms and particular practices, the degree of formalisation is often based on eventualities that have transpired but also a degree of calculated risk as a hopeful measure. Focusing on where agreements have failed ignores the successful negotiations that might have occurred and potentially 'distort[ing] conclusions about the role played by formal contracts and contract law in functioning business relationships' (Mitchell 2009, 684).

Despite the fairness principle at play and the trust inherent in the gentleman's agreement, authors are still wary of publishers and try to change the contract after signing if it is unfavourable. Most publishing professionals maintained that authors had to prove themselves in the market, first, before they could bargain the boilerplate terms successfully. Ed B admitted to offering a standard boilerplate:

> [I]t's only for a new author that you would give them the boilerplate, that this is the standard.

Pub C spoke of keeping established authors happy:

> [O]nce an author develops a reputation, we're going to do what they like because we're often in a highly competitive situation where we're going to try to keep that author. Also, if the author's been on the backlist for a long time, you're going to think is it worth the bother of that? There's a whole range of things that come into play.

And in response to how authors who are just starting out might feel about the attention they receive in contrast to an established author:

> [W]ho is the author? How willing are we to bend to get this particular author? You know, so, if it's a first-time author where there's not a lot of competition, we would stick to our standard royalty rates.

Lit D also elaborated on the boilerplate framework as described earlier:

> I don't think you could talk about a standard if there was not enough people in the industry that are kind of performing to these norms.

This statement also supports the principles that Pub B stipulated and that the boilerplate, while being a conglomeration of historical incidents and reflective of industry developments, has mostly been constructed with a view to helping the book succeed in the market, and without infringing on the author's moral rights. Lit D also spoke more broadly of the boilerplate:

> I find every single publishing contract in Australia in some way deviates from what is deemed the standard . . . but there's enough other publishers who use a certain term that you could call standard even if a publisher, you know, nine times out of ten, doing standard or what is better, they could still have a quirk where they don't comply. And that, in some cases is negotiable and sometimes it isn't. So, yes, broadly speaking, there are more good guys than bad.

Yet, evidence of ad hoc additions to boilerplate contracts 'suffer[ing] from "cut-and-paste" syndrome, whereby clauses from different eras were sewn together, join lines betrayed by inconsistent fonts or language' (Giblin & Yuvaraj 2020, 26) are not uncommon. Ed A also explains how the patchwork emerges in the case of multiple contracts for one author, for example:

> There has always been changes because it's sometimes that the [author's] previous book dates from a different period of time. And the standard contract has changed so many times. . . . And then the renegotiations on that contract in terms of audio, and various percentages for subsidiary rights – all of that just changes. . . . I've never *not* touched a boilerplate [contract or letter of offer].

The patchwork effect is concerning for an author who doesn't have the benefit of seeing the history of negotiations that bind one clause to another. These negotiations are like stitches that convey the changing landscape. While this is interesting, it is often the publisher doing the sewing, not the author. However, the upside for the author is that the patchwork construction in fact weakens the contract's framework so that it is highly negotiable. Mouzas and Furmston elaborate on how the boilerplate acts as a flexible framework:

> Umbrella agreements are not concerned with immediate contractual decisions and are in fact 'framework contracts' that provide a set of clauses which regulate the conclusion of future contracts. For this reason, umbrella agreements are contracts that do not predetermine future selection processes. Instead, they create the framework within which future selection processes may take place.
>
> (Mouzas & Furmston 2008, 39)

Auth C also suggests that it is up to the author to be aware of how industry developments affect the redrafting of contracts – something they often don't keep abreast of – to effectively negotiate within this framework:

> The contracts are shifting all the time and the ground is shifting all the time. . . . You need to interrogate your practice . . . and also to interrogate your relationship to your contracts, too. Like, is it worth having a fight? What is worth having a fight over? And, in terms of making mistakes on the contract, it's also about what has changed – it's not really about the contract; it's about what has shifted. I mean, high discount sales are core business for publishers in a way they didn't used to be.

Hybrid D elaborated on authors who seek advice from professionals who don't necessarily understand what's at stake for publishers. Their example indicates that authors have been advised to ask for the warrants and indemnities clause of the contract to be taken out, but this would leave the publisher highly vulnerable to litigation:

> I had authors take it to the ASA and come back . . . with like 5 pages of feedback. . . . I had to sit with the author and go through line by line and negotiate. And there was a set of clauses I could negotiate and the ones I wasn't allowed to budge on. . . . One of

> the things these authors had been told to ask about was warrants and indemnities. They wanted to change our warranties section and we were like, no.

The existence of organisations such as the ASA and also some legal professionals was raised with mixed responses. There was a general acceptance of the ASA as a reasonable service for authors, and which provided realistic expectations of what is achievable in contract negotiations. But many publishers expressed concern that legal consultants do not necessarily have the industry knowledge needed to assist authors to make reasonable requests – and that this sometimes put authors on the back foot in the pre negotiation space. Pub B explained:

> The problem there is that their lawyer is often not a lawyer who understands book contracts. They might understand general principles, but they do come back with some pretty hair-raising advice and strange questions that it's just a waste of everyone's time. I would actually prefer that they go to a proper book body – someone like the ASA as opposed to a lawyer who specialises in property or something . . . the skills aren't really that transferrable.

***

A contract negotiation is based on a relational premise as well as the trust instilled in the gentleman's handshake as a cultural practice within the industry. As artefacts, contracts convey the conventions upon which agreements are formed, and 'merit study because of what they reveal about the lives and times of their makers and users' (Suchman 2003, 98). But this research asserts that the gentleman's handshake is a cultural practice that the parties rely upon too heavily; in light of many authors' lack of knowledge of in-house processes and of how developments have altered the publishing industry, how can the terms of the agreement be equitable? The author's position as an outsider is exacerbated by publishing's growth as a commercial business; the nostalgic perpetuation of the intimate author–publisher relationship has been vigorously challenged in the global and digital landscape. If we view the contract as a cultural artefact, however, the evidence of patchwork amendments to emerging and 'live' boilerplates belie this romantic image. Viewed critically, they present like small scars – evidence of mistrust. Alternatively, and in a more positive light, the amendments are like stitches that form a subtle but strong bind. This might seem abstract, and I'm sure many authors would claim it isn't true; it would be wrong to dismiss the experiences authors have had when their contracts have been enforced against their desires. When this happens it is mostly due to industry challenges that impose expectations on the work, which does not necessarily reflect the reasonable relationship between the author and the publishing house. Authors don't always fully understand the whole suite of rights and opportunities for a title until they are enacted. Pub B articulated this fact: 'I think that when an author considers copyright they think of a book and they forget about a length of time'. The length of time is the length of copyright, which is also the length of the relationship with the publisher, which is susceptible to industry changes and therefore integral to the success of both the book and the author. It is appropriate that the relationship is given adequate time to adapt to these changes for lasting satisfaction to happen.

6

THE POST NEGOTIATION SPACE

The research outlined in this book was born out of the experience of negotiating my own book contract. As an in-house editor myself, I believed that publishers and editors do everything they can to ensure each book they edit is successful – from the perspectives of both the business and the craft of writing. Observing the publisher's decisions and actions from an author's perspective raised a dilemma for me: not in the author–publisher power imbalance alone but in the underlying reasons for that imbalance. I sought to discover what happens in that time between the contract signing and the finished book, to define more accurately what was taking place.

From this place of investigation, I observed that

1. the expression of copyright law within publishing contracts is beholden to significant historical influences, mostly dominated by publishers' needs but also reflecting a romantic view of the author that enshrines their creative genius;
2. these influences create conflicting perceptions of contract negotiations for authors and publishers;
3. globalisation and digitalisation have given authors greater flexibility and power to publish their works on their own terms;
4. despite this new power, authors still see the publishing contract as the ultimate endorsement of their work;
5. authors are not fully satisfied with the terms of their contracts.

The way in which my own contract negotiation transpired, and the subsequent research, revealed far more interesting and complex answers than was anticipated. In conclusion, I turn to those initial questions to reveal and discuss the findings.

Research questions revisited

1. *What does the book-publishing contract represent for the contemporary author and publisher? Does it have symbolic, legal and/or economic significance?*

DOI:10.4324/9781003336570-6

My research confirmed that for the contemporary publisher the contract has legal and economic significance. Historical developments in publishing and law since the end of the nineteenth century and beginning of the twentieth century underpin these focuses, the expression of which are perpetuated in the present day. However, this expression does not necessarily reflect the contemporary field.

A romantic view of authors as original creators, as per the landmark case *Donaldson v Becket* (1774), persists, at least anecdotally. Readers, writers and publishers make distinctions between literary works versus commercial works; they distinguish genre fiction from general fiction and blockbuster authors from emerging and literary authors. This was witnessed in the categorisation of reading tastes in the survey responses to AS Q.4 and PPS Q.5, for example, with respondents able to position their work, and publishers their lists, in one or more of the broad genre categories. While some readers prefer to be challenged, others wish to be entertained. Readers are also generally aware of the 'charismatic illusion' (Bourdieu 1994, 76) of the author, which is created via reading tastes.

Unlike readers and authors, publishers are in the business of observing these phenomena and acquiring and producing texts that fall within broad reading categories and their subgenres. It is the publisher's skill to observe trends and to balance lists with a selection of titles that will cater to the market while also competing with other entertainment choices, which erode their expected revenue. Publishers are constantly on the lookout for the next big thing, but the elusive bestseller is notoriously difficult to define and identify; most books, in fact, fail to sell out their first print-runs. Despite the unpredictable return on investment, publishers are still mostly characterised as dominant players in the author–publisher relationship because their decisions are often seen to be strictly guided by market demands. From a publisher's perspective, the contract is a tool that helps them lock in the exploitative potential of a work, which hopefully goes towards their financial return. This position was evident from the interviews with publishers, with statements such as:

> I see lots of stories that are kind of slice-of-life, but that's not compelling for the people out there where book buying is a kind of luxury, and they don't want to take a risk. So they buy a big-name author where they have a guarantee, you know.

The pecuniary position is often challenged by the publisher's own desire to curate diverse lists of writing that might also be non-commercial. The distinction, then, between the publisher as an individual and the publisher as a business becomes blurred when other qualities of a publishing house outside of its profitability emerge as important. The survey responses to AS Q.14a and PPS Q.7a reflected a clear shared value outside of the pecuniary: 'Editorial Excellence' was ranked No. 1 by 46 per cent of authors and 35 per cent of publishing professionals. Contrastingly, 'Profitability' was ranked the lowest quality of a publishing house with 35 per cent of publishing professionals and 61 per cent of authors placing it last at No. 8. In AS Q.24 authors ranked 'Creative Expression' as being most important to them (39 per cent) – a view shared by the publishing professionals, 29 per cent of which placed 'Creative Expression' as important to writers (significantly more than the other categories).

Creative expression was also supported. Both publishers and authors used specific, vivid terminology such as 'vision', 'artful' and 'precious' to describe writing and creating books. From these results, I deduce that while publishing houses as businesses focus on economic imperatives, the editors and publishers as individuals within these businesses sometimes have separate agendas. I have observed that publishing professionals struggle with this position; they are clearly supportive of writers and writing craft, but they must also make choices that create revenue for the publishing house. It is often the latter to which the publisher as individual eventually capitulates, as evidenced by Hybrid D who claimed:

> [T]here has definitely been a context of not talking about money in publishing, but I think increasingly that has to change because [otherwise] the industry will die.

For the author, the romantic ideal persists because the contract symbolises an endorsement of the work as an extension of its creator (as genius). Many authors surveyed, especially emerging authors, had little-to-no understanding of the specific clauses and/or of what contract terms mean. Over half of the authors surveyed (54 per cent) were not familiar with the Australian Society of Authors (ASA) standard contract template, which is very supportive of authors' rights. Nine per cent of authors did not answer Q.16a about which areas of the contract would be most important to them, stating that they either hadn't experienced an author contract or that they hadn't thought about the terms. To reiterate, some of the survey responses also highlighted trust with the publisher that the contract would be fair:

> I really don't understand a great deal about this industry. I may be naive, but I just trust that I am getting a fair deal.

> As an emerging author . . . I am still at a stage where any contract is a good thing. I am yet to be affected by, or experience, these particular areas.

Other authors who said that they challenged the contract's terms in their own publishing negotiations eventually agreed to the terms in the publisher's boilerplate because they did not want to jeopardise the agreement.

> My contract was the only one I was ever going to receive, at that moment in my career, and I felt as though I was unable to ask for more. . . . I felt as though asking for more money would seem ungrateful somehow, and jeopardise my contract.

The survey results also revealed that despite authors not being satisfied with their contracts overall (19 per cent unsatisfied and 23 per cent only moderately satisfied), they were still entering into agreements with publishing houses (57 per cent of authors claimed their negotiations resulted in contract signing 'all of the time' and 39 per cent 'most of the time). These results clearly show that the contract has significant meaning for the author – enough that they might put aside their wishes so as not to lose the deal. The contract was also observed as being emblematic of the relationship between the author and the publisher, steeped in trust as per the gentleman's agreement, and authors often took for granted that the publisher would 'do the right thing' by them.

Minimal-to-no revenue, however, is a source of frustration for authors in the period after the contract is signed. It is in this space that authors begin to question the contract's terms outside of its symbolic value and discover that it fails to meet their expectations. While a work might garner great reviews, or be revered by the publisher and readers, it might not sell well. Authors in this scenario begin to wonder about the publisher's investment in the sales and marketing plan. Both the surveys and interviews in my study revealed that authors want publishing companies to support their work via a strong marketing campaign, with the aim of getting the book to its readers and making sales. This was particularly evident in the written answers to AS Q.18, which asked why authors have a preferred publisher:

> [T]hey seem to really support their authors with publicity and a long-term view.
>
> [M]arketing and promotion.
>
> Active help with launching and marketing.

The literary agents also raised the need for a sales and marketing strategy, even suggesting that it should be locked into the contract where possible. In AS Q.14a, 'Sales and Marketing' was also rated particularly high (25 per cent at No. 2) out of 9 ranked qualities in a publishing house. Authors mostly want to be published by a publisher with transnational reach and market prominence despite these qualities being of lesser importance to them than 'Editorial Excellence', 'Creative Expression' and the inherent value that the work possesses from an artistic and cultural perspective.

Therein lies a perpetual confusion over whether the author is rewarded for their creative genius or sweat of the brow (the former with not unreasonable expectations of financial reward). Entwined in this confusion is the contract itself, which persists as the ultimate endorsement of the work – but an endorsement as it was perceived back at the turn of the century, not in this new, highly diverse and democratic publishing landscape beholden to market demands. While publishers as individuals within the publishing house struggle to balance the economic with the creative, this study reveals that authors, too, are unable to successfully reconcile creative endeavour with economic interests.

While the cultural backdrop of apparently irreconcilable economic and creative struggle is familiar, the various viewpoints through which the contract may be regarded is not. What happens at the time of signing the contractual document is only a small part of the struggle. Additionally, we continue to believe that the contract is a rigid document when malleability is more common than has been documented. Observing the contract through the lens of 'cultural artefact', with its facets of symbolism, law and economics, is a perspective more reflective of the industry.

The post negotiation space

When viewing the contract through the theoretical lens of 'cultural artefact', it is possible to more accurately assess how it is received and used from the authors' and publishers' distinct perspectives, why conflicting perceptions of contract negotiations exist and, more importantly, why they persist. Viewing the contract as an artefact also reveals incremental industry developments. Although relational contract theory speaks about contracts' dual aspects encompassing the real and the imaginary, nobody has until now thought to apply this theory to *publishing* contracts specifically. It is, however, the most appropriate way to describe how these agreements operate.

The contract's dual properties are confusing and often fail to meet authors' expectations: if authors believe that the contract symbolises quality in the work and an endorsement of it by people who the author considers gatekeepers of quality, authors naturally make assumptions about that assessment resulting in financial reward. Yet it is the market that determines whether an author will make money or not, not the contract. The author and publisher are never able to fully consolidate and then express all the things that the contract represents because each has a separate understanding of it and its importance relevant to their individual positions. Existing contract theory has established that 'terms' can only be understood from the respective parties' personal understandings of the culture and field in which the terms are created. The chasm between the publishers' and authors' understandings of the publishing field and publishing negotiations and agreements is underexplored.

To assess this chasm, I created the term 'post negotiation space'. Amendments, even unilateral severance, are possible when we observe the contract as a fluid instrument. Its flexibility is also promising if we view it more positively and with an understanding of the reasons underlying clauses as they have emerged. Ad hoc additions to boilerplate templates are evidence of publishers' pecuniary interest. For example, most boilerplates will ask for as many rights as possible, and the emphasis on territories and subsidiary rights often encompasses existing and future digital editions. These adjustments maximise exploitation, but while they might at first seem opportunistic on the publisher's behalf, the clauses also show us that the degree of amendment is dictated by the landscape. This is not a limitation imposed by publishers as selectors and gatekeepers of literary works; it is a limitation created by readers, trends, globalisation and technological developments. Attempts to change the contract to provide the expected revenue without reflecting on these influences won't necessarily provide a remedy for authors. The 'gentleman's agreement', therefore, is misunderstood from the outset because it is still framed by the understandings and expectations of publishers, who possess more knowledge of these industry influences to which the contract almost always complies.

However, as with Bourdieu's breach of the 'illusio' (Bourdieu 1996, 221), players in the field find ways to adapt and grow around existing frameworks. The fact that publishing contracts fall more to the relational end of the spectrum means they can facilitate the bending and navigating that takes place in the 'space of possibles' (Bourdieu 1996, 228). Subsequently, the opportunities for authors to abandon traditional publishing avenues have transferred more indirectly to the post negotiation space – and we witness authors effecting change from within instead of looking out towards alternative publishing opportunities (such as self-publishing). Authors are not embracing these opportunities; rather, they are attempting to customise existing, traditional publishing models.

Witnessing and hearing about the way new clauses and addendums have been stitched into the ad hoc contract patchwork shows that the contract, as a malleable instrument, is not tethered to an existing, rigid structure at all. I therefore find two reasons *against* reform: first, observance of the foundation of contract law, being a framework whereby rules are 'create[d], modif[ied], and extinguish[ed]' (Hart 1994, 92), allows the flexibility needed in an industry 'in a constant state of flux' (Mannion & Stinson 2016, introduction); second, and perhaps more contentiously, I argue that the current 'cut-and-paste' method of contract development helps us to see what has gone before. The artefact's paper trail is a valuable meta-narrative within the larger historical narrative. Though messy and fragmented, it shows us where we have been and where we might go next.

From this vantage point, I shifted from what contracts *mean* to authors and publishers, to how they are implemented in publishing practice. This area of investigation took the historical analysis and revealed how it influences decisions against the backdrop of the shifting landscape. The data provided a rich contextual study around the following questions:

2 *How are the utilitarian and ideological spaces in book-publishing contracts negotiated?*
3 *What can the negotiation process tell us about relationships of power in book publishing?*

My research highlighted how the dual aspects of the contract – its utilitarian and ideological spaces – are synthesised, using black box theory as a structural tool to explain the process. Reframing black box theory within a publishing context constructively conveyed the area under investigation as being untapped and containing information that might be valuable to other researchers as well as industry professionals. The analogy was effective to define the spaces within the negotiation process and a solid structure for analysis. This structure illustrated the different stages of the methodology and highlighted the pre negotiation space (which can be regarded as the space that reflects the contract as a sanctioning document) and the post negotiation space (which is what transpires). Within this framework, I brought my own perspective (from my experience as an editor as well as an author of a published book) via an autoethnographic 'narrative voice', which I supported with rigorous analytical tools via the survey and coding of the in-depth interviews.

Question 2 assumed that publishing contracts do not have satisfactory outcomes for all parties, and this was reiterated in the survey responses. Many authors do not scrutinise the terms of their contracts until problems arise (e.g. when financial return for the title is not forthcoming). Because of this, there exists a skewed view of the contract which ignores how beneficial the contract could be, more generally, in business relationships. Viewed through the lens of failure, the contract inevitably pits the publisher as having the most power in the author–publisher relationship because they tend to promote their in-house boilerplates. When the document is criticised, it becomes an extension of the publisher; conversely, when authors are satisfied with their contracts, it is rarely in relation to the publisher as an individual in the relationship. In fact, when authors express satisfaction with their publisher they never link their level of satisfaction to the contract alone. The relationship, therefore, is of great importance. Studying the post negotiation space provided insight not only into the author–publisher relationship but also into the status of the contract within the publishing profession. Macneil said: 'A set of blueprints and specifications, however detailed, and a newly built house are simply not the same thing' (Macneil 1978, 863). I discovered via this study that the author–publisher relationship was more balanced than expected, a highly important factor in the author's sense of satisfaction.

Recalibrating the perceived imbalance

Publishing contracts are not easily obtained. In the interviews, Lit D observed that they are reluctant to terminate their authors' contracts even if the authors find them unsatisfactory. They claimed they would rather work around a clause that the author is not happy with and that could be renegotiated at a later stage. To reiterate, some of the publisher responses from the interviews also suggested that they would be willing to create addendums to contracts after they are signed, and had done so on occasion:

> [W]hilst I negotiated in good faith with them at this point, and I did actually meet them in the middle with their demands because we wanted to keep them happy, we wanted to work with them again.

> I mean, you can't really retro-fit a contract for a book that's already in print. It's a bit hard. But they did for the paperback. That wasn't easy, but they did agree to that.

But the circumstances for altering contracts must be anomalous to the expectations of the book's success, or to publishing practice generally. Authors can reason with their publishers when conditions change, but publishers are unlikely to be flexible with contract terms if the author did not understand those initial terms upon signing. It is a misconception that publishers refuse to make changes because they are opportunistic. Providing authors understand the publisher's vision for their works and are realistic about its prospects, publishers appear open to ongoing discussions. Additionally, if an author does not have reasonable expectations, and if the book is not selling well, the publisher is likely to revert rights back to the author – particularly if the author has something they can do with the book or somewhere else to send it:

> [A]fter three years we can go back to them and say "Do you want to keep doing it? Or would you like to take these rights back?" We don't want to hang on to rights, cos, you know, we're too small anyway to be able to exploit them.

This is an important distinction: if circumstances change outside the original terms set into the contract, such as an unexpected success, publishers will exercise a 'fairness principle', which aims to maintain the relationship with the author by way of rewarding them for that success. The change in circumstances is the defining element. Publishers are not willing to negotiate post contract if the author changes their mind because they did not understand the initial terms. Authors' inability to earn a sufficient living from their writing (Throsby et al. 2015) has been presented as the consequence of such contentious contract negotiations (Giblin & Yuvaraj 2020). Responses from international authors in this survey also illustrate this struggle. However, I contend that author incomes are not necessarily negatively affected by publishing contracts.

After collating and analysing the survey responses and interviews, I observed that the contract is often incorrectly conflated with a drop in author incomes. Instead, market indicators affect author incomes more than the minutiae of contract clauses. One author response from the surveys was particularly enlightening:

> I do feel as though this industry is a bit of an odd one, with so many people wanting to be involved in it, but. . . . I have not seen a great deal of financial benefit so far. My first book has been shortlisted, which is great, and my second coming out soon. I hope that a trickle of financial reward will come through soon, as I have only received about $8500 so far and have been doing solid, long, exhausting hours for two years now. This is not realistic for any industry.

In the study, contention in the areas of 'Royalties', and 'Rights and Territories', highlights the conflation because these are the areas that generate the desired revenue. In PPS Q.13a, 38 per cent of publishing professionals ranked 'Royalties' as the No. 1 author query in contract negotiations. Thirty-one per cent of publishing professionals also ranked 'Rights and Territories' at No. 2. These figures were supported by the response to AS Q.10a in which 16 per cent of authors claimed that 'Royalties' was the most problematic area of the contract, followed closely by 'Rights and Territories' at 13 per cent and 'Subsidiary Rights' at 9 per cent. These findings reiterate the perceived power imbalance associated with communication around money and decisions about how the book can generate it. The responses to the question regarding the term of copyright (AS Q.19a) were also enlightening for this reason:

many of the written responses focused on authors' writing as a form of property and 68 per cent claimed that the term of copyright should not be changed. However, only 10 per cent of authors placed 'Copyright Provisions' as the No. 1 area of importance in AS Q.16a. It could be surmised, then, that the term of copyright is not as important as the author's remuneration, even when the publisher licenses the author's work for the duration of the term.

On the basis of these findings, I argue that a perceived power imbalance between authors and publishers is incorrectly associated with the contract. First, the Macquarie study, which is often cited to argue this point, but which was not executed with this focus in mind, shows that authors' incomes are mostly derived from CAL payments and ELR/PLR payments, *not* from royalties from sales (Throsby et al. 2015, 22). The pressure of finding bestsellers, bearing in mind that this is an elastic term, is perhaps difficult for smaller publishers that can't compete with large multinationals. But the same can be said for multinationals, too. Independent publishers are not competing with the multinationals in this way, anyway; rather, they are competing to secure talent, which is being siphoned to the bigger publishers with transnational reach and sales and marketing clout. Authors who have Harry Potter-style success in their sights won't immediately consider a smaller publisher, for obvious reasons. While multinational publishers are still the top pick for most authors, those surveyed who had sought out a smaller publisher found more satisfaction in contract negotiations because they had more communication with these publishers. Smaller publishers also have more favourable terms for authors (sometimes to their own detriment). But communication and favourable contract terms will not necessarily translate to financial reward. Neither does securing a publishing contract from a larger publisher. Publishers and editors don't accept texts based on literary merit alone; they have to think of the book on all levels. Those considerations create a less 'artistic' notion of the work, which affects its position in the cultural field when money becomes a concern. If a title doesn't sell well, it's probably because it's not right for the market at that moment in time. Or perhaps it is a 'quiet' book that the publisher knows will never sell well because of its niche readership. That does not mean it wasn't supported within the parameters of what the publisher deemed its audience to be – as Auth A noted: a small audience doesn't mean *no* audience; it's just not a large audience.

The term 'bestseller', then (or 'better-than-expected' seller), is one that can only be definitively applied retrospectively and by mutual agreement between author and publisher. In the post negotiation space, indicators of success can be reassessed and the contract amended if the parties agree that the current contract no longer reflects a fair remuneration for the author. Thus, while reading tastes tend to shift incrementally, a contract can be changed relatively quickly. The fault, therefore, is not in the contract. Notwithstanding, while clauses that support authors' rights (such as reversion clauses) exist in current boilerplates, it is not a simple process to action those rights. As one of the authors in this study noted: it's in the 'administration of the contract' where problems arise. Therefore, the post negotiation space can perhaps also be a negative space for the author if they don't have strong negotiation skills to highlight those clauses. Without solid reasons for instigating reversion, for example, the request will likely be refused.

To answer question 3 then (What can the negotiation process tell us about relationships of power in book publishing?), I propose there is not a power imbalance in the way the literature or perceptions from the players in the field describe. If the power imbalance is deemed financial, then there is no power imbalance. Creative industries generally are not supported in the English-speaking territories through law, market or culturally. If creative professionals aren't making any money, neither are the professionals who facilitate the works' production, marketing or distribution. Publishers are struggling to remain economically viable (multinationals included) and must balance the business side of their profession with the need to create consumer products of cultural value. If it is a power imbalance based on knowledge, then the author is most certainly the weaker negotiator. Yet, if authors expanded their knowledge of the 'business' of publishing and the current industry conditions (or already possess it), they would possibly be steered towards the publisher's view of their work anyway. It appears that knowledge of the industry does bring authors and publishers closer, helping them to successfully negotiate possibilities for published titles.

I would have expected that the contract (and the relationship with the publisher) would hold less importance when authors can self-publish and reach audiences via many other platforms, but this study confirmed that the contract's significance persists. Less than half of the authors surveyed said that they had self-published or considered self-publishing (45 per cent). The No. 1 reason to self-publish was also because authors had found it difficult to find traditional publishing opportunities – often towards the biggest publishing houses that employ professionals with the experience and skill to produce books (AS Q.12a). Interestingly, 41 per cent of authors positioned editing as the least-challenging aspect of self-publishing (AS Q.23a) even though 'Editorial Excellence' is seen as the most important quality of a publishing house. The authors positioned 'Sales and Marketing', instead, as the most challenging aspect of self-publishing (41 per cent at No. 1).

To this extent, authors understand that finding readers and getting the work to those readers is an onerous task. A publishing contract's symbolic importance for the author is closely tied to their assessment of the work's cultural capital. If the publisher's assessment of the work's value is not the same, then satisfaction is unlikely. The work's value is reflected in all aspects of the book, not just the writing: from a pecuniary perspective it is reflected in the sum of the advance, the breakdown of the royalties scheme, the initial print-run and the paratextual elements of the text and physical book and how much might be invested in it – editorially, in marketing, and in production. Knowledge of the market and the publishing process allows an accurate assessment of the book's position alongside its competitors. In this respect, power is not necessarily tipped in favour of the publisher via the contract. Instead, the power is in the knowledge that the publisher holds – of the market and publishing, in general, as a business and a process. This power is also a selling point when a publisher wants to attract an author. For publishers to enforce contractual terms in current standard boilerplate contracts above existing relationships with authors, therefore, is simply not good practice – particularly if the work fills a niche or the author shows promise and longevity for future works. A post negotiation space exists in publishing practice and is an adequate forum for addressing how publishing developments influence contract clauses and how the parties can work together towards success and satisfaction. The power imbalance between authors and publishers is one of knowledge, whereby the publisher often has more insight into market realities.

Here, also, the editor emerges as an unexpected and often underrated conduit, not only between the author and their readers but also between the author and the publishing house. My interpretation of the data extracted from the self-publishing questions, in particular, is that editorial excellence encompasses more than working on the page; it is closely linked with many more areas of publishing expertise that can have a direct effect on authors' livelihoods. One of those areas of expertise is bringing the author's and publisher's visions together. This book posits that editors' roles are not being recognised and utilised in a way that can potentially offer a remedy to the perceived author–publisher power imbalance. Editors are highly effective in the post negotiation space, where their communication with authors outside of the contract – the cultural artefact – can facilitate satisfying outcomes for all parties.

The book editor

The editors, or publishers as editors, facilitate the utilitarian and ideological spaces in publishing post negotiation because they are the closest people to the text and to the author. Their role also encompasses many more tasks outside of the editing process as described to date. Mackenzie vividly describes this position as 'the pivotal figure in the production process, at the centre of a triangle' (Mackenzie 2011, 48). She elaborates:

> *Author*: It's my book!
> *Publisher*: I'm paying the bills!
> *Reader*: Don't forget me! I'm the purpose of the whole exercise!
> For the author you are an assistant; for the publisher you are a quality controller; for the reader you are an advocate. So you're always subject to a three-way stretch, balancing competing demands.
>
> (Mackenzie 2011, 48)

Triage is where the experienced editor's skill transcends the restricted description editorial work has been confined to. While pre negotiation takes place based on an educated prediction of a title's success, the post negotiation space is the most dynamic area because it exercises the knowledge of the publishing house in a very practical way. This becomes the 'what actually transpires' part of the contract's dual nature. Each of the editors interviewed for this study alluded to their job requiring exceptional communication and people skills in addition to editing. In describing how an editor prepares the paperwork, Ed B explained how they

> fiddle the costs to try and make it work. For a slightly larger advance, or something . . .' cos what they [the author] don't remember in all of this is that the editor wants this book as much as they want it on the list. And like we wouldn't have bothered if we didn't like their work and didn't want it on the list.

Not only does this extra editorial work potentially generate more income for the author, it illustrates the editor's dedication and their belief in the work at the early stages. Pub C also described this undocumented support by describing the 'championing' that takes place in-house via the editor's communication of the project to other departments:

> [T]he acquiring editor is responsible for all the documentation, all the briefings about it, all the meeting presentations . . . it is Chinese whispers: I tell you about this book and then I tell sales and marketing, and then they tell the people who work for them, and then they're telling the booksellers and then the booksellers are telling the floorstaff – it's a lot of people down the chain till that message hits the retail sector.

To those in-house, it is understood that the editor's role includes these nuanced activities. Publishing staff know this extra work is vital to a book's success; it is not always known to those outside of publishing processes. In that respect, it remains a part of the 'secret' side of editing – the networking and the cajoling, the tweaking and manoeuvring. Without the benefit of understanding the editor's role within these negotiations, we automatically default to a historical understanding of contracts and book publishing in which the editor is seen to work on the text alone. This narrative underutilises the editorial role. In assessing the role of the editor afresh, the fourth research question is answered:

4 *How are contracts used within the publishing house after signing?*

This research reveals that the contract is only periodically, if rarely, looked at after it is signed. Publishers and editors, therefore, don't always use contracts to guide their work unless it might offer concrete details about dates, specs or delivery. Mostly, editors strengthen relationships and steer the text towards publication with the author's expression and the publisher's aims as tandem guides. While the editor's work with authors on their text has been extensively discussed in academic literature, an editor's key position as the conduit between the author and the publishing house – and the editor's particular tasks of straddling the commercial and the cultural, keeping the author informed and satisfied with the book's production, and creating opportunities for titles and authors – is discussed in this book with insight. While editors remain behind the scenes, my access to that space, as a Complete Membership Researcher (CMR) (Anderson 2006), was unique and advantageous to achieving such insight.

There are some familiar examples of author–editor relationships where the editor is as recognisable as the author: the notorious relationship between Gordon Lish and Raymond Carver, for example, or Max Perkins and F. Scott Fitzgerald. Perkins and Fitzgerald remained lifelong friends, but Lish was criticised after Carver's death and the release of Carver's original works, which reveal the heavy-handed cutting Lish imposed on the text. However, the editor's work on a title is mostly a silent affair, which takes place backstage, in the wings. As one of the editors in this study noted, no author is going to put their hand up and say that their editor had a major part in the success of the text (whether that is expressed in good sales or great reviews). Even authors who openly name and praise their editors tend to shroud the editorial role in mystery, as an unexplainable phenomenon within the publishing process:

> Looking back over my experiences of being edited, apart from a few striking moments, I find I can't elucidate what those experiences have taught me. They have nourished me, that is certain, but the details have entered so far into my depths as a writer that when I look for them, all I can hear is their echo, like the lotus-leaf imprint left on the surface of the water after a whale dives deep.
>
> (Wood 2014)

This statement is beautiful, poetic and appreciative, but acknowledges the editorial contribution very indirectly – an 'echo' as Charlotte Wood describes it. It also claims that the grind of the editorial work is linked to the creative output and the formation of words and ideas. Wood highlights qualities such as 'generosity', 'humility' and 'imaginative courage' to reinforce this idea. What about business savvy, strategy (for the list and for those meetings) and knowledge of domestic and overseas book markets? Where is the talk of the hustle and persuasion that takes place in-house? This side of editing isn't quite as appealing, perhaps, but probably not conveyed to authors by their editors, either. Yet, it is very necessary, as

Mackenzie highlights: 'Editors should always keep the dollar in mind. Don't kid yourself that you're a dedicated literary artist with a soul too refined for sordid commerce. If your books don't sell, you're out of a job' (Mackenzie 2011, 19). Scholarly commentary only occasionally characterises the editor's role as being more business focused (Thompson 2012) and possessing marketing knowledge in the competitive landscape, but the ways in which this business knowledge is applied have not been fully explored from the perspective of the publishing house's agreement with the author, and certainly not revealed to the author as clearly.

The editorial profession is much more complex than the classic image of the passionate reader, who sits poised with pen in hand honing and crafting the words 'on the page', or slicing and dicing as Niles threatened to do in the final scenes of *Little Women* described in this book's introduction. My research reveals that in the post negotiation space the editor–publisher facilitates the most pleasing terms for the author, and in many instances creates opportunities for books which might not even be evident in the contract's clauses. I believe this to be part of the skillset of an excellent editor.

The survey highlighted 'Editorial Excellence' as the most desired quality of a publishing house (PPS Q.7a 35 per cent at No. 1 and AS Q14a 46 per cent at No. 1). While agents have become the main spokespeople for the authors at the point of negotiating the contract terms, agents do not necessarily continue this championing after signing, in the post negotiation space. The publishers and editors interviewed claimed that the agent's presence in negotiations in fact sometimes complicated the process, especially when the editor has taken the time to do the groundwork before acquisitions, as Ed B explained:

> Because they [the agent] want to make their money. And they don't care about the author's relationship [with the editor]. . . . I think it's really tough on the author because I think the agent then is looking at . . . the benefit of that one-time action, because it's going into their hip pocket and they encourage people [publishers] bidding for that. But they disregard that the editor will be on the side of the author, and would be hoping to publish with that author who they really like. . . . And that's it, then. You can never do that again with an author. And I have had situations where, once that's happened they're never going to get that support again.

In the surveys, having a literary agent was seen as only moderately important (AS Q.14a). In the post negotiation space, it is often the editor who takes the baton from the literary agent and continues to champion the author within the publishing house. What happens in-house from this point is an unintentional secret side of the business, and the editor is complicit in not disclosing their activities to the author. The interviews provided some reasons, with editors claiming that authors cannot know as much about how to market their books as publishers and editors:

> [T]hey are not experts in the publishing field, which is different to being an expert in the story field – I think the two are very different things.

Authors are so close to their work they may not see it objectively, which can lead to unrealistic expectations. If authors are the best people to take charge of their writing, publishing professionals are the best people to help get the book to its readers via some stipulations in the contract. For example, many boilerplates maintain full control of the price, print-run, format and cover concepts, stating author 'consultation', which is very different to author 'consent'. Evidence of consultation filters down through to the production process, though in a much more nuanced way based on actual practice: the editor knows that from the author's perspective the value of the work is often disproportionate to the market demand for it. It's a constant negotiation whereby the editor uses specific 'language' to appease all parties in a sometimes-hopeless situation. 'The best it can be' is a vague and frustrating phrase, twisted and spun to sound appealing. For the author, who is conscious of this role play, it's a torture. The author has no access to inside processes and databases, and takes no part in the myriad conversations about the book. This position renders the author vulnerable, but it also does not make the publisher–editor necessarily opportunistic or unreasonable. To get the title through as many hoops in-house as they can (the program and acquisitions meetings especially), editors can streamline the process by blocking the author's input. The author is often their own worst enemy in this negotiation because they can complicate the process with demands and questions, so the editor's ability to only convey what is necessary becomes a way of protecting the author's relationship with the publishing house. Publishing professionals have intrinsic knowledge of how successful a title will likely be in a global market (hence their insistence, often, for world rights); authors don't necessarily have this knowledge.

While the contract, as a physical document, is an endorsement and an agreement, the editor's performance as an extension of it, post contract, is much more complicated and arcane. The post negotiation space until now has been a whole other mysterious world with many angles to explore. It requires a balance of understanding writing craft, and a good dose of experience, wisdom and business knowledge. None of the aforementioned has anything to do with the contract, in fact. And all of the aforementioned is subject to change, and does change, this research has revealed, if the need arises. But the need must be fair within the current landscape. Perpetuating the historical narrative of the 'craft' of writing and the editor's role as the 'mender and repairer' undermines the myriad ways the editor supports the work. This research opens the black box to reveal those inner workings and concludes that the post negotiation space is vital and highly flexible, but that the author is usually completely absent in the negotiations. For all their powers of communication and excellent facilitation, publishers and editors have kept the black box tightly closed to authors. If authors are dissatisfied with their contracts, it is because they have not utilised their editor to full advantage and in some ways cannot. This is because many authors simply do not know what editors do if editors cannot tell them. And in the case of author–editors, as I once was, the feeling of being shut out of the process was alienating but perhaps necessary in order for the project to get to print.

The greatest chance an author has of finding satisfaction in the publishing process is not always via changes to the contract, then; it is via a deeper understanding of what editors and publishers do, and why. In turn, understanding the publishers' position should allow the publisher to better support the author. The publisher–editor is the person who can facilitate a forum for this understanding to take place and help the author to see that the investment in their title/s is as significant as the industry will allow. The collaborative effort required for this deeper level of satisfaction is dependent on a relationship that transcends the physical contract as document. The relationship, in fact, renders the contract almost notional when trust and a fairness principle are evident, provided the author fully understands the publishing landscape and the true and realistic potential for their work within it. The emphasis on 'Editorial Excellence' in the surveys is backed by the interview responses. Within the publishing process, editorial excellence includes support and encouragement, which is just as important to authors as financial success.

Acknowledging and highlighting this perspective of editorial excellence could potentially alleviate the current conflict around fostering creative output and market demands by using the contract as a forum to discuss the expectations of the parties involved. Changing the contract or copyright law might not recalibrate the perceived author–publisher power imbalance, but other solutions in addition to the emphasis on editorial could prove fruitful. These are discussed in answer to the final research question:

5 *Is the contract still an effective tool for negotiations in the contemporary book-publishing landscape?*

Publishing contracts are not the problem

Publishing contracts are not the problem; rather, publishing contracts are important social and cultural artefacts that signify the relationship between an author and the publishing house and provide a necessary and useful framework for that relationship. This framework is further supported, if somewhat tangentially, by the editor who is the crucial link between the in-house publishing process and the author outside. As an artefact, the contract is symbolic of the historically formulated relational agreement; it can also be observed as a technical patchwork of industry developments. From this perspective, the patchwork is fascinating rather than suppressive and reveals the problem with author incomes as not solely stemming from the publishing houses but from a systemic lack of support for arts and artistic and cultural products. The lack of support is beyond publishing houses' power to correct without government intervention.

I propose that the way to explore, improve and expand upon publishing contracts and their application is not necessarily via a rigid legal document with highly objective criteria that is alien to the entrenched cultural practices of the publishing industry. Rather, I encourage writers, industry professionals and scholars to observe the cultural practices upon which this document has been formed and to study publishing contract negotiations through a relational lens conducive to a contemporary landscape.

Whatever is deemed unfair in a contract probably *is* unfair if the parties' expectations exceed what the industry can withstand. Even in the highly dynamic world of book publishing and the constant challenges it faces – the author–publisher relationship, made stronger by the cottage-industry idiosyncratic behaviour between authors and editors in particular – shared principles of fairness and a collective endeavour remain. These have not changed, but the external pressures have created a chasm between what happens in-house and the author's position. It is this chasm that prohibits communication. While publishing practice has perhaps placed more emphasis, now, on the pecuniary aspect of the 'agreement', the other enduring social phenomena that come from this transaction – that of trust, creative expression, shared passion and personalised mediation – remain significant and possible because of the artefact's malleable architecture.

I utilised relational contract theory to assess what is possible in the secondary framework, and I discovered that prescribing strict rules works against the culture of the publishing industry because publishing contracts fall to the relational end of the discrete–relational contract spectrum. Therefore, the best way to tackle contract negotiations is for authors to be given the tools to help them understand publishing as a business and its attendant processes, to realise their work's true value in the market. If authors are more involved in the publishing process, they will see the hurdles editors navigate to get the publishing house to support the book, and they will understand the market reality of their book – on the house's list and the bookselling industry more broadly. I believe this access to information can correct the power imbalance between authors and publishers and result in productive connections and communication with in-house staff.

The onus is on in-house staff to explain to authors why certain choices are made and avoid perpetuating the author-centric ideal when it is no longer relevant. The author-as-genius narrative continues to dominate publishing – the 'art', the 'precious baby', the 'creative expression' is how the interviewees described the 'work'. This language obstructs direct communication about the work's likely success. These honest in-house deliberations are withheld from authors, yet they are vital to successful post-contract discussions (which might include, for independent publishers as one example, realistic expectations about how long it takes – and what it takes – to exploit overseas rights). If authors have the option of asking for their rights to be reverted after only two to three years, they may not have given their publisher a reasonable chance to sell the book into other territories. Communication, realism and flexibility are more possible within a strong, existing relationship. Creative expression is important, and this book does not suggest that it should be superseded by commercial imperatives; it is short-sighted to apply practices from businesses that do not reflect the complexities of producing and selling cultural products. However, if creative expression is predicted to affect a book's likelihood of commercial success, the author must understand why, and take responsibility for accepting or ignoring the publisher's assessment.

Notwithstanding this, preventative 'ex ante' measures, which pre-empt problems before they arise, can be instilled at the time of signing and might also be beneficial. These types of measures have already been implemented in some European countries and are referred to as Rules on Contract Formation. (Guibault & Hugenholtz 2002) According to a 2002 report from the University of Amsterdam, the Rules on Contract Formation bill has proven to be the most successful way to remunerate authors and foster existing and future author–publisher relationships. This is because authors, at the outset, are provided with the necessary information, in consultation with industry professionals, to assist them with their negotiations. This balance of power results in 'immediate legal pressure on the publisher to clearly define the scope of the transfer and pre-empt all-encompassing rights transfer provisions' (Matulionyte 2019, 717).

The ASA is an Australian organisation that already provides this information to authors, as do agents, but the onus is on the author to ask and pay for the information they seek. Therein lies the perpetual problem of the author not even knowing what to ask as well as not wanting to sabotage a publishing contract by instigating an interrogation of it that the publisher is not expecting or that might complicate the book's production. A blanket procedure like the one described in Europe insists that publishers follow guidelines expected of them and they should therefore not be surprised by the questions and requests from the author pre contract. Such guidelines, however, might increase administration costs for publishers, who would need to spend more time explaining the contract and the reasons why certain clauses in the boilerplate have been conceived, not to mention the impacts on the book's schedule. Publishers would also need to vigorously justify why these clauses should be retained, which would also allow authors sufficient time to understand the agreement and the consequences of accepting certain clauses – not from a legal perspective only but also from a publisher's perspective, as they try to find ways to ensure their business remains viable. This won't eliminate the need for ongoing mediation from the editorial team throughout the production and editing process, which could facilitate this level of understanding just as effectively; if the terms are understood from the outset, authors' concerns could be focused on what is achievable rather than chasing the parts of the contract that are simply not negotiable because there would be no reward at all for the publisher.

Communication is paramount because changing copyright laws won't create more income and control for authors if the market doesn't desire, or is not ready for, the work. Reversion clauses exist in most boilerplates, though some clauses are not explicit; rather, they are embedded in small print-run clauses. The reversion clauses suggest that the publisher is willing to break the term of copyright if the book is no longer financially viable. The small-print clauses, however, make it fairly unlikely that the author would be able to action the reversion clause unless the book is legitimately out of print (OP). For example, the publisher could continue to sell the title as a print-on-demand book, which might only sell a few copies per year and would not be a lucrative proposition for an author with only a few titles published. But severing ties with a publisher with in-house editorial staff, as well as a current contract, means being thrown back into the acquisitions process to start all over again, and perhaps fail if there is no plan or means to self-publish. The surveys in this study revealed that authors do not consider reversion an important part of the contract: only 3 per cent of authors placed it as the most important area, and only three publishing professionals marked it as an area that had caused difficulty in contract negotiations. It is possible that authors are not aware that reversion enables them to take the work to another publisher, but the survey results also indicated that authors show that they often have a preferred publisher and would stay with that publisher. Authors aren't just interested in making money, they want other things from their publishers.

Through the data collection, I have emphasised the multi-faceted quality of editorial excellence, and editors as having the agency to recalibrate power imbalances in publishing practice. I ask this question: If there were no editors, what would happen? Susan Greenberg explores this question by investigating the underlying reasons for why editing might have been transferred to a digital process and highlights that 'skilled human intervention is expensive, and the invisibility of editing makes its "added value" hard to quantify' (Greenberg 2010, 13). The editor's gatekeeping role has certainly been challenged by digital developments, particularly those that give users the power to select, adapt and construct texts in an 'active' way (Greenberg 2010, 13). Self-publishing is a good example and includes larger platforms such as Amazon or Tablo as well as blogs and shared writing sites like Wattpad. However, not all authors have fully embraced these opportunities. Greenberg presents a good reason for this by stating that '[e]diting, like "experienced" writing, is a way of regulating the user's attention by creating a sense-making pattern' (Greenberg 2010, 15). Yet this explanation still tends to focus on the editor's role in producing, selecting, shaping and linking the text alone (Greenberg 2010, 9).

My research supports Greenberg's concerns but moves deeper into the editor's role as a potent agent in the post negotiation space. For authors wishing to experience satisfactory relationships with their publishing house, the time and care that the editor invests in the project is crucial. Excellence has been described in one way by the publishers surveyed as having no 'cap' on the hours of editing involved, which is very different to a freelance editing experience, where time and money have an endpoint:

> We can just go back and back and back, and that's what we'll do until it's where it needs to be.

Time is a highly important value: it includes the time that the editor manages in-house by triaging all the various aspects of the process and exercising diplomacy when championing the book. Time also includes listening to the author. As one interview respondent conveyed:

> So just to make sure that – even if your opinion isn't taken into account eventually – just at least having the piece [sic] of mind of having said something, or have it in writing, and to articulate really clearly why you are having a reaction to something.

Time, therefore, fosters relationships that can potentially withstand the pressures and changeability of the industry and support the author for the long term.

Thinking back on the introduction, I imagine a different scene from *Little Women*. In this scene, I picture Alcott and her publisher as they discuss the next book or the next contract. There is no desk between them. Alcott is uncertain about her future, but her publisher is encouraging. He has a plan and a vision for her next title, and he wants to see her succeed. If she succeeds, so does he. Perhaps this imaginary scene is as much a fiction and a fantasy as the movie version I critiqued, but I believe that it more likely reflects a real scenario.

Conclusion

As a consequence of this study, the editor–publisher role and its relationship to author satisfaction should be investigated further. This can be achieved by reframing how we describe editors. Editors have been relegated to an industry group confined to 'working on the page', which is perpetuated because it maintains the author as the creator, and the editor as their 'midwife' – a relationship with which both parties are familiar. But while the narrative reveres the author, it keeps them at arm's length, excluded from the inner workings and emphasising the chasm between authors and in-house staff. I have lifted the lid on the black box and interrogated its contents, observing contractual obligations and demystifying and deconstructing the role of the editor in the post negotiation space. I propose further exploration of this box.

Attention has been drawn to contracts as the source of difficulty in author–publisher relationships, but I reveal this position as reactive. Economic imperatives are not always authors' main goals for their writing – other motivators are indicated in the survey question AS Q.24 and in subsequent interview responses. This is not to say that authors do not care if they are not well remunerated for their work; on the contrary, authors see the contract as potentially the only tool they can use to gain more income from sales of their books. The contract, however, is unlikely to generate the financial success authors seek (with or without objective criteria) or the career satisfaction. Authors will be more satisfied if their work is steered through the editorial process with the attention they feel it deserves, and a sales and marketing plan that is in step with their expectations. Editors can facilitate all this providing they have an ongoing relationship with their authors and the time to invest in their authors' works and career longevity post contract. Enforcing strict parameters via the contract is an inflexible remedy that undermines the positive work that editors can achieve.

I argue that our current understanding of publishing contracts and of publishing contract negotiations has been stymied by historical understandings of what authors and publishers represent, as well as what we expect of contracts via our understanding of how they are used in other industries. In untangling these representations, I observed a striking difference between the theory and perception of contract negotiations and what transpires. To better articulate the latter, I devised a term I call the 'post negotiation space' – an innovation that has proven to be instrumental to this research. The post negotiation space should not be confined to publishing alone, either; all creative industries – the fine arts and dramatic arts, as well as musicians and designers – find themselves navigating a complex web of creative expression, pecuniary interests and the economic reality dictated by trends and market demands. The post negotiation space is a theory that should be applied not just to contract interpretation and execution; it should be embedded as cultural practice that facilitates success and satisfaction. For publishing, delineating the post negotiation space as a genuine stage in the contractual process brings the parties to the contract together to strengthen their work and its success and reveal the potential for, and indeed existence of, collaboration. Publishers and publishing houses want authors to succeed; it does not make sense for publishers to undermine the potential success of authors who provide them with the work that keeps the publishing house in business. Publishers are therefore invested in forging long-term relationships in the hope that their authors earn money – for themselves and for the publisher. The post negotiation space is where this relationship is tested and sometimes recast; it is where the contract as a malleable artefact, and not a physical document, becomes an extension of the space – a forum for discussion and renegotiation. The post negotiation space is the only way that the parties can work together effectively in this problematic field. It is a workaround, yes, but a necessary means to an end. Perhaps it is also a blessing in disguise, too: if we have become so adept at renavigating terms that are no longer fair and effective, then anything is possible; I would argue that trying to enforce strict objective criteria to protect authors essentially shuts down this forum for discussion and renegotiation.

Policy is, in fact, a continuing burden for the creative industries when governments do not value creative output as they do other businesses. I would encourage further studies that actively employ relational contract theory and contract as artefact within a post negotiation space with a view to documenting even more specifically the results of improved communication and collaboration in this space. This could be achieved via further qualitative research in any industry that is dynamic and unique, and that is subject to renegotiation post contract. The music industry, as one example, has proven resilient in spite of the many copyright obstacles presented to creators and owners of works. Musicians and artists also must be allowed to explore their agreements post contract if the original document no longer serves the business relationship adequately. Likewise, those in the legal profession can utilise this research to reimagine the contract as an artefact, with a view to navigating conflict more successfully. For these industries, the people, practices and relationships hold the key information – not the contract as document. For this book, and for publishing, that emphasis on relationships and people has shown to be clearly manifested in the ability of the editor.

While this book has examined 'editorial excellence' and discovered that it encompasses a large portfolio of skills (such as supporting and developing writers and writing, publishing and readers, and providing further opportunities for titles when circumstances change), continued research to support this discovery will further our understanding of editors as adaptable figures whose creative *and* business-focused interventions add undeniable value to book publishing. We cannot continue to perpetuate romantic notions of the editor's role and ignore the complex balance of tasks they perform. Award wages for full-time in-house editors with significant experience is insufficient (Millar 2021) to sustain a professional position that requires so many specialised skills and that has so great an influence on author satisfaction and publishing success. We need to acknowledge this work and importance – not just in increased wages but also in more exposure. Editors play a crucial role in the book-making process; they also possess the ability to effect change in the post negotiation space.

BIBLIOGRAPHY

Books

Alcott, LM 1868, *Little Women*, Penguin Viking edn. 1989, London.

Alexander, I 2010, *Copyright and the Public Interest in the Nineteenth Century*, Hart Publishing, Oregon.

Australian Society of Authors 2001, *Australian Book Contracts*, Keesing Press, Strawberry Hills.

Barbour, RS & Schostak, J 2005, 'Interviewing and Focus Groups' in Somekh, B & Lewin, C (eds.), *Research Methods in the Social Sciences*, Sage Publications, London, pp. 41–49.

Black, O 2012, *Agreements: A Philosophical and Legal Study*, Cambridge University Press, London.

Bode, K & Dixon, R 2009, 'Introduction' in Bode, K & Dixon, R (eds.), *Resourceful Reading: The New Empiricism, eResearch and Australian Literary Culture*, Sydney University Press, Sydney, pp. 1–27.

Bourdieu, P 1984, *Distinction*, Routledge, London and New York.

Bourdieu, P 1994, *The Field of Cultural Production*, Columbia University Press, Columbia.

Bourdieu, P 1996, *The Rules of Art*, Polity Press, Cambridge.

Brannen, J 2004, 'Working Qualitatively and Quantitatively' in Seale, C et al. (eds.), *Qualitative Research Practice*, SAGE, London, pp. 282–296.

Buckingham, L 2013, *Copyright and Publishers (B147)*, Australian Copyright Council, Strawberry Hills, NSW.

Butler, D & Holland, G 2017, *Entertainment Law*, Federation Press, Annandale.

Cantatore, F 2014, *Authors, Copyright, and Publishing in the Digital Era*, IGI Global Publishing, Hershey.

Carter, D 2016, 'General Fiction, Genre Fiction and Literary Fiction Publishing 2000–13' in Mannion, A & Stinson, E (eds.), *The Return of Print?*, Monash University Publishing, Melbourne, pp. 1–26.

Chartier, R 1994, 'Figures of the Author' in Sherman, B et al. (eds.), *Of Authors and Origins: Essays on Copyright Law*, Oxford University Press, Oxford, pp. 7–22.

Clark, G & Phillips, A 2014, *Inside Book Publishing*, 5th edn., Routledge, London and New York.

Commins, D 1978, *What Is an Editor? Saxe Commins at Work*, University of Chicago Press, Chicago.

Couper, S 2016, 'Bookish Girls: Gender and Leadership in Australian Trade Publishing' in Mannion, A & Stinson, E (eds.), *The Return of Print?*, Monash University Publishing, Melbourne, pp. 27–47.

Craig, C 2011, *Copyright, Communication and Culture*, Edward Elgar, Gloucestershire.

Curtain, J 1993, 'Book Publishing' in Cunningham, S & Turner, G (eds.), *The Media in Australia: Industries, Texts, Audiences*, Allen & Unwin, Sydney, pp. 102–118.

Davis, M 2017, 'Who Are the New Literary Gatekeepers? Literary Mediation and Post-digital Publishing' in Mannion, A et al. (eds.), *Publishing Means Business*, Monash University Publishing, Melbourne, pp. 125–146.

Deakin, S 2006, 'Learning About Contracts: Trust, Cooperation and Contract Law' in Bachmann, R & Zaheer, A (eds.), *Handbook of Trust Research*, Edward Elgar, Cheltenham, pp. 218–234.

De Vaus, DA 2002, *Surveys in Social Research*, 5th ed., Allen & Unwin, Sydney.

Doust, K 2009, *The Crafty Minx*, Murdoch Books, Sydney.

Elbert, S 1987, *A Hunger for Home: Louisa May Alcott's Place in American Culture*, Rutger's University Press, New Brunswick.

Ellis, C & Bochner, AP 2006, 'Communication as Autoethnography' in Shepherd, GJ et al. (eds.), *Communication as Autoethnography: Perspectives on Theory*, SAGE Publications, Thousand Oaks, CA, pp. 110–122.

Epstein, J 2001, *Book Business: Publishing Past, Present and Future*, W.W. Norton & Company Inc., New York.

Fink, A 1995, *How to Sample in Surveys*, SAGE Publications, Thousand Oaks.

Fink, A 2003, *The Survey Handbook*, 2nd ed., SAGE Publications, Thousand Oaks.

Foucault, M 1997, 'What Is an Author?' in Bouchard, DF et al. (eds.), *Language, Counter-memory, Practice*, Cornell University Press, New York, pp. 113–138.

Freeman, R 2001, 'Writer-Publisher Relationships' in Cope, B & Freeman, R (eds.), *Digital Rights Management and Content Development*, Common Ground, Altona, pp. 105–124.

Fried, C 1981, *Contract as Promise*, Oxford University Press, Oxford.

Glass, L 2004, *Authors Inc.: Literary Celebrity in the Modern United States 1880–1980*, New York University Press, New York and London.

Greco, AN 2005, *The Book Publishing Industry*, 2nd ed., Routledge, New York.

Greenberg, S 2018, *A Poetics of Editing*, Palgrave Macmillan, Basingstoke.

Gross, G 1993, *Editors on Editing: What Writers Need to Know About What Editors Do*, Grove Press, New York.

Hammersley, M 1992, *What's Wrong With Ethnography?*, Routledge, London.

Hammersley, M & Atkinson, P 2007, *Ethnography: Principles in Practice*, 3rd ed., Routledge, London and New York.

Hart, HLA 1994, *The Concept of Law*, 2nd ed., Clarendon Press, Oxford.

Jensen, K 2002, 'The Qualitative Research Process' in Jensen, K (ed.), *A Handbook of Media and Communication Research: Qualitative and Quantitative Methodologies*, Routledge, London and New York, pp. 235–253.

Jensen, KB & Jankowski, NW (eds.) 1997, *A Handbook of Qualitative Methodologies for Mass Communication Research*, Routledge, London and New York.

Jones, H & Benson, C 2011, *Publishing Law*, 4th ed., Routledge, London and New York.

Juby, S 2005, 'Editor to Author: Some Personal Reflections on Getting Published' in Lorimer, R et al. (eds.), *Publishing Studies: Book Publishing 1*, Canadian Centre for Studies in Publishing, Vancouver.

Kells, S 2015, *Penguin and the Lane Brothers: The Untold Story of a Publishing Revolution*, Black Inc., Melbourne.

Leib, EJ 2013, 'What Is the Relational Theory of Consumer Form Contract?' in Braucher, J et al. (eds.), *Revisiting the Contracts Scholarship of Stewart Macaulay: On the Empirical and the Lyrical*, Hart Publishing, Oregon, pp. 259–288.

Lincolne, P 2012, *Meet Me at Mike's: 26 Crafty Projects and Things to Make*, Hardie Grant Books, Melbourne.

Mackenzie, J 2011, *The Editor's Companion*, Cambridge University Press, Melbourne.

Madison, CA 1974, *Irving to Irving: Author-publisher Relations, 1800–1974*, Bowker, New York.

Mannion, A & Stinson, E 2016, 'Introduction' in *The Return of Print?*, Monash University Publishing, Melbourne.

Myerson, J & Shealy, D (eds.) with Stern, MB (associate ed.), Alcott, LM 1995, *The Selected Letters of Louisa May Alcott*, The University of Georgia Press, Athens and London.

O'Shaugnessy, T 2016, 'Deck Chairs and Life Rafts' in Mannion, A & Stinson, E (eds.), *The Return of Print?*, Monash University Publishing, Melbourne, pp. 89–114.

Owen, L 2010, *Selling Rights*, Routledge, London.

Paterson, JM & Robertson, A 2009, *Principles of Contract Law*, 3rd ed., Thomson Reuters, Rozelle.
Patton, MQ 2002, *Qualitative Research Evaluation Methods*, 3rd ed., SAGE, London.
Rawson, H 1983, 'The Editor's Role in Marketing' in Carter, RA (ed.), *Trade Book Marketing*, R. R. Bowker, New York, pp. 273–283.
Rose, M 1994, 'The Author as Proprietor: *Donaldson v Becket* and the Genealogy of Modern Authorship' in Sherman, B et al. (eds.), *Of Authors and Origins: Essays on Copyright Law*, Oxford University Press, Oxford, pp. 51–85.
Rosenthal Kwall, R 2010, *The Soul of Creativity: Forging a Moral Rights Law for the United States*, Stanford University Press, Stanford.
Ruddock, A 2001, *Understanding Audiences: Theory and Method*, SAGE, London.
Sainsbury, M 2003, *Moral Rights and Their Application in Australia*, The Federation Press, Alexandria.
Seeber, M & Balkwill, R 2007, *Managing Intellectual Property in the Book Publishing Industry*, Creative Industries – WIPO Booklet 1, viewed February 2018, <www.wipo.int/publications/en/details.jsp?id=255>.
Simensky, M, Selz, TD, Lind, RC, Burnett, B, Palmer, CA & Dougherty, FJ 2003, *Entertainment Law*, 3rd ed., LexisNexis, New York.
Smitka, MJ 1994, 'Contracting without Contracts: How the Japanese Manage Organizational Transactions' in Sitkin, S & Bies, R (eds.), *The Legalistic Organization*, SAGE, Thousand Oaks, pp. 91–108.
Squires, C 2007, *Marketing Literature: The Making of Contemporary Writing in Britain*, Palgrave Macmillan, London.
St. John, M 2012, *The Women in Black*, Text Publishing, Melbourne.
Tan, A (ed.) 2013, *Creativity, Talent and Excellence*, Springer, Singapore.
Thompson, JB 2005, *Books in the Digital Age*, Polity Press, Cambridge.
Thompson, JB 2012, *Merchants of Culture*, 2nd ed., Polity Press, Cambridge.
Throsby, D 2017, 'Commerce or Culture? Australian Book Industry Policy in the Twenty-first Century' in Mannion, A et al. (eds.), *Publishing Means Business*, Monash University Publishing, Melbourne, pp. 1–21.
Torremans, PLC (ed.) 2004, *Copyright and Human Rights*, Kluwer Law International, New York.

Journals

Akerlof, GA 1970, 'The Market for Lemons: Qualitative Uncertainty and the Market Mechanism', *Quarterly Journal of Economics*, vol. 84, pp. 488–501.
Anderson, L 2006, 'Analytic Autoethnography', *Journal of Contemporary Ethnography*, vol. 35, pp. 373–395.
Barnett, R 2011, 'Contract Is Not Promise; Contract Is Consent', *Georgetown University Law Center*, pp. 1–21.
Bode, K 2010, 'Publishing and Australian Literature: Crisis, Decline or Transformation?', *Cultural Studies Review*, vol. 16, pp. 24–48.
Brett, M 2011, 'Stet by Me: Thoughts on Editing Fiction', *Meanjin*, vol. 70, viewed 11 June 2019 <http://meanjin.com.au/essays/stet-by-me-thoughts-on-editing-fiction/>.
Cantatore, F 2011, 'Negotiating a Changing Landscape: Authors, Copyright and the Digital Evolution', PhD Thesis, Bond University, Gold Coast.
Deakin, S & Michie, J 1997, 'Contract Law, Trust Relations, and Incentives for Co-operation: A Comparative Study', *Cambridge Journal of Economics*, vol. 21, pp. 121–125.
Driscoll, B & Rehberg Sedo, D 2020, 'The Transnational Reception of Bestselling Books Between Canada and Australia', *Global Media and Communication*, vol. 16, pp. 243–258.
Ellis, C, Adams, TE & Bochner AP 2011, 'Autoethnography: An Overview', *Forum: Qualitative Social Research*, vol. 12, viewed 30 May 2019 <www.qualitative-research.net/index.php/fqs/article/view/1589>.
Fried, C 2007, 'The Convergence of Contract and Promise', *Harvard Law Review*, vol. 120, pp. 2–19.

Giblin, R 2018, 'Reclaiming Lost Culture and Getting Authors Paid', *The Columbia Journal of Law and the Arts*, vol. 41, pp. 369–411.

Giblin, R & Yuvaraj, J 2019, 'Why Were Commonwealth Reversionary Rights Abolished (and What Can We Learn Where They Remain)?' *European Intellectual Property Review*, vol. 41, pp. 232–240.

Giblin, R & Yuvaraj, J 2020, 'Are Contracts Enough? An Empirical Study of Author Rights in Australian Publishing Agreements', *Melbourne University Law Review*, vol. 44, pp. 1–30.

Gigerenzer, G 2020, 'How to Explain Behavior?', *Topics in Cognitive Science*, vol. 12, pp. 1363–1381.

Ginsburg, J 1990, 'Moral Rights in a Common Law System', *Entertainment Law Review*, vol. 1, pp. 121–130.

Glover, S 2016, 'Getting on the Same Page', *Overland*, vol. 223, viewed September 2019 <http://overland.org.au/previous-issues/issue-223/feature-stuart-glover/>.

Green, JM, Tolentino, G & Stracener, J 2017, 'Measures of Effectiveness through Transfer Characteristics of Black Boxes', *The Journal of Reliability, Maintainability, and Supportability in Systems Engineering*, Winter 2018, pp. 5–12.

Greenberg, S 2010, 'When the Editor Disappears, Does Editing Disappear?', *Convergence: The International Journal of Research into New Media Technologies*, vol. 16, pp. 7–21.

Hammersley, M 2006, 'Ethnography: Problems and Prospects', *Ethnography and Education*, vol. 1, pp. 3–14.

Kahan, M & Klausner, M 1997, 'Standardization and Innovation in Corporate Contracting (or "The Economics of Boilerplate")', *Virginia Law Review*, vol. 83, pp. 713–770.

Kimel, D 2007, 'The Choice of Paradigm for Theory of Contract: Reflections on the Relational Model', *Oxford Journal of Legal Studies*, vol. 27, pp. 233–255.

Kong, FL 2014, 'Fifty Shades of Bookselling', *Anne Summers Reports*, vol. 7, viewed 27 May 2020, <http://www.legacy.annesummers.com.au>

Kretschmer, M, Azqueta Galvadon, A, Miettinen, J & Singh, S 2019, 'UK Authors' Earnings and Contracts 2018: A Survey of 50,000 writers', *CREATe*, University of Glasgow (independent research commissioned by the Authors' Licensing and Collecting Society).

Leib, EJ 2009, 'Contracts and Friendships', *Emory Law Journal*, vol. 59, pp. 649–726.

Levin, J & McDowell, B 1983, 'The Balance Theory of Contracts: Seeking Justice in Voluntary Obligations', *McGill Law Journal*, vol. 29, pp. 24–87.

Li, J 2010, 'Choosing the Right Battles: How Independent Bookshops in Sydney, Australia Compete with Chains and Online Retailers', *Australian Geographer*, vol. 41, pp. 247–262.

Macneil, IR 1978, 'Contracts: Adjustment of Long-term Economic Relations Under Classical, Neoclassical, and Relational Contract Law', *Northwestern University Law Review*, vol. 72, pp. 854–902.

Macneil, IR 1985, 'Relational Contract: What We Do and Do Not Know', *Wisconsin Law Review*, vol. 4, pp. 483–526.

Magner, B 2012, 'Behind the Bookscan Bestseller Lists: Technology and Cultural Anxieties in Early Twenty-First-Century Australia', *Script and Print*, vol. 36, pp. 243–258.

Maskin, E & Tirole, T 1999, 'Unforeseen Contingencies and Incomplete Contracts', *The Review of Economic Studies* (Special Issue: Contracts), vol. 66, pp. 83–114.

Matulionyte, R 2019, 'Empowering Authors Via Fairer Copyright Contract Law', *UNSW Law Journal*, vol. 42, pp. 681–718.

Mitchell, C 2009, 'Contracts and Contract Law: Challenging the Distinction Between the "Real" and "Paper" Deal', *Oxford Journal of Legal Studies*, vol. 29, pp. 675–704.

Mouzas, S & Blois, K 2008, 'Relational Contract Theory: Confirmations and Contradictions', *Lancaster University Management School*, pp. 1–18.

Mouzas, S & Furmston, M 2008, 'From Contract to Umbrella Agreement', *Cambridge Law Journal*, vol. 67, pp. 37–50.

Pace, S 2012, 'Writing the Self into Research: Using Grounded Theory Analytic Strategies in Autoethnography' in McLoughlin, N & Lee Brien, D (eds.), *Creativity: Cognitive, Social and Cultural Perspectives*, TEXT Special Issue, No. 13, pp. 1–15.

Rhodes, M 1961, 'An Analysis of Creativity', *The Phi Delta Kappan*, vol. 42, pp. 305–310.

Suchman, M 2003, 'The Contract as Social Artifact', *Law Society Review*, vol. 37, pp. 91–142.

Throsby, D & Petetskaya, K 2017, *Making Art Work: An Economic Study of Professional Artists in Australia*, Department of Economics, Macquarie University, Sydney.

Throsby, D, Zwar, J & Longden, T 2015, *Book Authors and Their Changing Circumstances*, Macquarie University, Sydney.

Throsby, D, Zwar, J & Morgan, C 2017, *Australian Book Readers: Survey Method and Results*, Macquarie University, Sydney.

Wilkins, K 2014, 'Writing Resilience in the Digital Age', *New Writing*, vol. 11, pp. 67–76.

Zapata López, F 2002, 'The Right of Reproduction, Publishing Contracts and Technological Protection Measures in the Digital Environment', *Copyright Bulletin*, vol. 36, pp. 2–23.

Zwar, J 2013, 'What Were We Buying? Non-fiction and Narrative Non-Fiction Sales Patterns in Australia in the 2000s', *Journal of the Association for the Study of Australian Literature*, vol. 12, pp. 1–27.

Other

Adsett, A 2011, 'What to Look for in a Publishing Contract', viewed August 2018, <http://www.alexadsett.com.au>.

Arts Law, 'Arts Law Info Sheet: Moral Rights', viewed August 2018, <http://www.artslaw.com.au>.

Australian Society of Authors 2020, 'Trade Publishing' contract template, viewed June 2019, <https://www.asauthors.org/products/contract-templates/template-trade-publishing-agreement>.

Australian Society of Authors, 'ASA Survey Results – Advances and Royalties', viewed February 2021, <www.asauthors.org/news/asa-survey-results-advances-royalties>.

Authors Guild 2018, 'US Published Book Author Income Survey', viewed 1 December 2021, <www.authorsguild.org/industry-advocacy/authors-guild-survey-shows-drastic-42-percent-decline-in-authors-earnings-in-last-decade/>.

Baker, DJ 2015, 'Self-publishing Matters: Don't Let Anyone Tell You Otherwise', *The Conversation*, 13 March, viewed September 2019, <https://theconversation.com/self-publishing-matters-dont-let-anyone-tell-you-otherwise-37986>.

Crosby, P, Zwar, J, Lawson, A & Shin, SY 2021, *Success Story–International Rights Sales of Australian-Authored Books: Main Report*, Macquarie University, Sydney, accessed December 2021 <https://research-management.mq.edu.au/ws/portalfiles/portal/177288594/177088842_Main_report.pdf>.

Guibault, L & Hugenholtz, PB 2002, 'Study on the Conditions Applicable to Contracts Relating to Intellectual Property in the European Union', Europese Commissie. https://pure.uva.nl/ws/files/3563234/24667_final_report2002.pdf.

Hans, VP & Mott, N 2000, 'How Jurors Construct Schemas of Legal Contracts', Paper Presented at the 2000 Annual Meeting of the Law and Society Association, Integrated Computer Services Pty Ltd v Digital Equipment Corporation (Australia) Pty Ltd.

Levey, N 2016, 'Post-Press Literature: Self-published Authors in the Literary Field', *Post45*, 2 March, viewed September 2020, <https://post45.org/2016/02/post-press-literature-self-published-authors-in-the-literary-field-3/>.

Lim, K 2011, 'What Really Went Wrong for Borders and Angus & Robertson', *The Conversation*, 24 March, viewed May 2019, <https://theconversation.com/what-really-went-wrong-for-borders-and-angus-and-robertson-341>.

Macaulay, S 2003, 'The Real and the Paper Deal: Empirical Pictures of Relationships, Complexity and the Urge for Transparent Simple Rules', in Campbell, D, Collins, H, and Wightman, J (eds), *Implicit Dimensions of Contract: Discrete, Relational and Network Contracts*, Hart Publishing, Oxford, pp. 51–102.

Martin, GRR 1979, 'Guest of Honor Speech Delivered at Coastcon II, Biloxi, Mississippi', 10 March, viewed October 2019, <https://georgerrmartin.com/about-george/speeches/editors-the-writers-natural-enemy/>.

Millar, C 2021, 'Why Publishing Workers Are Leaving the Industry', *Kill Your Darlings*, 6 September, viewed September 2021, <www.killyourdarlings.com.au/article/why-publishing-workers-are-leaving-the-industry/>.

Oldham, K & Farquharson, S 2018, 'For Love or Money: Employment in the Australian Publishing Industry 2018', *Books + Publishing*, 21 November, viewed September 2019, <www.booksandpublishing.com.au/articles/2008/11/21/118475/for-love-or-money-analysing-the-employment-survey/>.

Peschel, S 2019, 'Strategies to Help Bookstores Survive Reader Atrophy', *DW*, viewed 2 December 2021, < www.dw.com/en/strategies-to-help-bookstores-survive-reader-atrophy/a-47775287>.

PwC Australia 2011, *Cover to Cover: A Market Analysis of the Australian Book Industry*, Department of Innovation, Industry, Science and Research, Canberra, viewed October 2019, <www.innovation.gov.au/Industry/BooksandPrinting/BookIndustryStrategyGroup/Documents/PwCCovertoCover.pdf>.

The Australian Copyright Act 1968 (Cth) (Copyright Act).

The Berne Convention for the Protection of Artistic and Literary Works.

Throsby, D et al. 2015, *Book Authors and Their Changing Circumstances: Survey Method and Results*, Macquarie Economics Research Papers, viewed 15 July 2018, <www.mq.edu.au/__data/assets/pdf_file/0004/705865/BookAuthors_WorkingPaper_2015.pdf>.

Throsby, D et al. 2017, *Australian Book Readers: Survey Method and Results*, Macquarie Economics Research Papers, viewed 15 July 2018, <www.australiacouncil.gov.au/workspace/uploads/files/australian-book-readers-24-05-592762e0c3ade.pdf>.

Wood, C 2014, 'I Have Had My Vision', *Sydney Review of Books*, viewed 1 September 2021, <https://sydneyreviewofbooks.com/essay/editing-writing-charlotte-wood/>.

Writers' Union of Canada 2015, 'Devaluing Creators, Endangering Creativity – Doing More and Making Less: Writers' Incomes Today', viewed 1 December 2021, <www.writersunion.ca/sites/all/files/DevaluingCreatorsEndangeringCreativity_0.pdf#overlay-context=news/canadian-writers-working-harder-while-earning-less>.

ACKNOWLEDGEMENTS

I acknowledge and pay my respects to the traditional owners of the land on which this book was written and researched, the Wurundjeri Woi Wurrung and Bunurong peoples of the Kulin Nation, and to their Elders past and present.

Thanks to Taylor Eggleton of Origami Graphics for the figures and Max McMaster for the index, which were made possible through the generous financial support from the School of Culture and Communication at the University of Melbourne.

Thank you to Brigid Magner, Sybil Nolan and Rose Michael for their feedback and assistance in putting this research together. I am so thankful for your expertise and support. To Jessica Wilkinson, Julienne Van Loon, Tracey O'Shaughnessy, Ronnie Scott, Bonny Cassidy and Zoe Dzunko – your collective excellent advice was appreciated, and I hope I have integrated it into this book.

Thank you to Writers Victoria, Romance Writers Victoria and the Australian Society of Authors for helping me to contact and gather the many authors who contributed to my survey. Special thanks to Olivia Lanchester for providing the most recent ASA contract to include in this study, and thanks to the generous publishers who also allowed me to view their boilerplate contracts. To the authors, publishers, editors and literary agents who participated in this research – I know how busy you all are, so to agree to carve out some time for me is extremely generous of you.

Julie Watts OAM gave me my very first job in publishing. Who knew I would love it so much and then want to study it! Thank you for your encouragement and guidance in my first years as an editor.

To all my fellow publishing people (you know who you are), I have enjoyed every minute working with you. Nobody else puts in such long hours, yet you do it with humour and passion. You are truly inspiring.

Thanks to Mum, Dad, Mitch and Jess, who are my biggest supporters. To my children – I love you very much. And lastly, I thank Dan. I couldn't have done this without you.

GLOSSARY

acquisitions	The process of acquiring new titles for the publishing list
addendum	An addition or amendment to a contract
advance	A sum of money given to an author upon delivery of the final manuscript (usually 50 per cent of the return of the first print-run)
AI sheet	Advance Information sheet, which outlines the specifications of the book and the rights and selling points
ANZ rights	Australia/New Zealand rights
ASA	Australian Society of Authors
audible	Audiobook company
audiobook	A book published in an audio format (as a recorded reading of the work)
author platform	An author's popularity in the social sphere, which can assist their publication
backlist	Titles that keep reprinting
BCYA	Books for Children and Young Adults
BD	Business Development
bidding scenario	An auction to secure a contract for particular title
binding	How the pages of a book are gathered and secured
boilerplate	A standard contract template with formulaic clauses
Bologna Book Fair	A book fair for children's titles that takes place in Bologna, Italy
Bookscan	A database that records the sales of titles with an identifying retail number
bulk stock	A large order of books
CAL	The Copyright Council collection agency, which collects payments on behalf of authors
cannibalise	When an edition of a title is competing against another edition of the same title
chains	Bookstores such as QBD, Dymocks and Collins

collection agency	A collection agency that collects royalties on behalf of authors (outside of their publishing contract)
commissioning editor	An editor who has the authority to commission new works
Commonwealth rights	Rights assigned to the Commonwealth territories
copyedit	The second stage in the editing process after the structural edit
costing	An estimation of a titles revenue based on recommended retail price and print-run
DDS	Discount department store
delivery	Delivery of a final manuscript to the publishing house
developmental edit	The first stage of the editing process
dump bin	A large order of a title, usually discounted
EBA	Enterprise Bargaining Agreement
ebook	A book in a digital format
ELR	Educational Lending Right, which is a government program that pays authors for the use of their titles for educational purposes
extent	The length of a book according to the number of pages
format (A, B, B+, C and Z)	The dimensions of the book
Frankfurt Book Fair	An book fair for adult titles that takes place in Frankfurt, Germany
freelance	To work on a project outside of the publishing house
frontlist	A title in its first print-run
global rights	All territorial rights across the world
hardback	A book with a hard cover
high-discount clause	A contract clause that specifies a certain royalty for a high-discount sale
hybrid	An author who self-publishes as well as being published by a publishing company
in-house	Inside the publishing house
independents	Independent bookstores (such as Readings)
indies	As above
IP	Intellectual property
ISBN	A unique identifying number for books for sale
jacket	The soft paper cover on a hardback book
kindle	An e-reader that allows access to digital reading material
layout	The design of the pages of a book within its format
legalling	The act of checking a manuscript for anything that might result in litigation
line edit	Copyediting
list-building	The act of acquiring titles
literary gatekeeper	A name given to someone who makes the decisions about what is acquired for the publishing list

margin	The percentage of how many titles are sold at a particular price
midlist	Books in their first print-run – especially books that aren't expected to make a large financial return
MS	Manuscript
net receipts	The total financial return for a title sold at any price (discounted or at recommended retail price)
Nielsen Book	The company that creates Bookscan
OP	Out of print
option clause	A contract clause that requests an author to give their publisher the right of first refusal for the author's next title
page proofs	The first print out of pages in the book's text design
paperback	A book with a soft cover
paratext/paratextual	The key signifiers of a book in terms of its cover, format and text design
permissions	The act of seeking permission to use copyrighted material
PLR	Public Lending Right, which is a government program that pays authors for the use of their titles for educational purposes
POD	Print on Demand
PPB	Print, paper and bind – a production term used to describe how the book is put together in terms of the way in which it is printed, the paper used and the binding
price point	The price decided for a book
print-run	The number of copies printed for each instalment of the book
proofread	The third stage in the editing process
publishable	When a work shows promise according to a publisher
publishing list	A curated collection of texts within a publishing house
refresher advance	A sum of money offered to the author after the initial advance
reprint	When a book sells out of its first print-run and is printed again
reversion	When the publisher's rights go back to the author
riser	A royalty increase when a book goes to reprint
rising royalty	As above
royalty	A percentage of the book's projected return paid to the author
RRP	Recommended retail price
self-publish	To publish without the assistance of a publishing house
sell-in	The act of spruiking the publishing house's list to potential book buyers
slush pile	The unsolicited manuscripts that come into the publishing house
specs	The specifications of a book – the dimensions, paper stock and any cover finishes
structural edit	Same as for developmental editing. The first stage in the editing process
subsequent edition	Reprinting a book but in a different format or with a different cover
subsidiary rights	Rights not covered by territory rights (such as ebook, audio, translation and film and TV)

term of copyright	The length of time to which copyright has been assigned
track changes	A computer Word tool used to show the changes an editor makes to a manuscript
typesetting	The act of setting the words in the manuscript into the design for the book's pages
umbrella term	A standard contract clause
unsolicited manuscript	A manuscript that was not requested but sent to the publishing house anyway
workflow	The process involved in getting a book from manuscript to print
YA	Young Adult

INDEX

For Product Safety Concerns and Information please contact our EU representative GPSR@taylorandfrancis.com
Taylor & Francis Verlag GmbH, Kaufingerstraße 24, 80331 München, Germany

www.ingramcontent.com/pod-product-compliance
Ingram Content Group UK Ltd.
Pitfield, Milton Keynes, MK11 3LW, UK
UKHW050233200926
475702UK00020B/3001
* 9 7 8 1 0 3 2 3 7 3 5 2 2 *